THE OPEN FIELDS

Oxford University Press, Amen House, London E.C.4

GLASGOW NEW YORK TORONTO MELBOURNE WELLINGTON
BOMBAY CALCUTTA MADRAS KARACHI CAPE TOWN IBADAN

Geoffrey Cumberlege, Publisher to the University

FIRST EDITION   1938
SECOND EDITION 1954

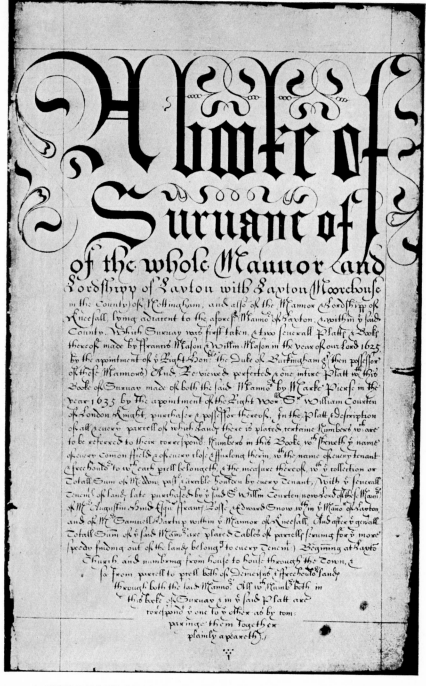

1. TITLE-PAGE OF THE *BOOKE OF SURVAYE OF THE MANOR OF LAXTON* 1635

THE
OPEN FIELDS

BY

C. S. AND C. S. ORWIN

SECOND EDITION

OXFORD
AT THE CLARENDON PRESS
1954

In the Dark and Middle Ages,
If we trust to History's pages,
You might search the landscape round,
Not a hedge was to be found.
Instead of little tidy squares,
Mine, and his, and yours, and theirs,
My field, his field, your field, their field,
All formed one enormous bare field.
How they knew without a hedge
   How far any land extended,
Which was middle, which was edge,
   Where the whole caboodle ended,
History, that tells so much
About the French wars and the Dutch,
Never says a word to show.
I should also like to know
In a land of hedge divested
Where on earth hedge-sparrows nested,
   And what did hedgehogs do about it?
Hedge for them means home and name;
   What was their life like without it?
Were they simply—what a shame!—
Hogs until their hedges came?
History, that talks so much
   Of wars and dates and lists of kings,
   And stuffy constitutional things,
Growth of Parliament and such,
Always somehow seems to miss
Interesting points like this.

R. H. CHARLES

(*Reprinted by permission of the Proprietors of 'Punch'*)

PRINTED IN GREAT BRITAIN
AT THE UNIVERSITY PRESS, OXFORD
BY CHARLES BATEY, PRINTER TO THE UNIVERSITY

PREFACE TO THE SECOND EDITION

IN this revision of the text of THE OPEN FIELDS, cuts have been made where it was felt that essential material would not be sacrificed, to secure economy in production. On the other hand, fresh matter has been inserted, arising out of further research by various historians and the constructive criticism of readers. The opportunity, too, has been taken to correct a few errors.

The details of the descent of the Manor and Sub-manor are now omitted, together with the tables compiled from *Inquisitiones post mortem*. The transcript of the Laxton Terrier, 1635, has not been reproduced; a few pages of it in facsimile are retained, and anyone wishing to work upon Mark Pierce's map and terrier can have access, probably, to library copies of our first edition, or to the originals in the Bodleian Library.

The main part of the material incorporated embodies a further discussion of the occurrence of dividing balks between the strips in the open fields; it includes, also, some amplification of the chapter on the extent of the open fields, which has led to the withdrawal of the map by which this was illustrated; and there is a brief account in the last chapter of the sale of the manor and open fields of Laxton by the sixth Earl Manvers to the Minister of Agriculture in 1952, and of the arrangements made for their preservation and administration.

Further, shortly before going to press, we received a valuable report on the excavation of an Iron Age hill-fort and a very fine series of terrace lynchets associated with it, in Berkshire, which goes a long way to confirm our contention that the accepted theories of the construction of the latter are, on agricultural grounds, no longer tenable; this evidence we have incorporated in the Appendix.

In these revisions we have been helped by information and advice from Professor R. F. Treharne, of the University College of Wales, Aberystwyth; Professor J. D. Chambers and Miss Audrey Beauchamp, of the University of Nottingham; Dr. A. L. Poole, President of St. John's College, Mr. W. G. Hoskins, Reader in Economic History, and Mr. A. B. Rodger, Balliol College, of the University of Oxford; Mrs. Vera Chapman and Miss Dorothy Sylvester, of the University of Manchester; Mr. A. E. P. Collins, of the Northern Ireland Archaeological Survey; Mr. H. Sharpe France, County Archivist of Lancashire; Mr. L. J. Smith, Secretary of the Agricultural Land Commission and Mr.

J. R. Rundle, the Commission's Local Agent in Nottingham-shire; Mr. M. D. Nightingale; and our old friends Mr. W. E. Tate, Miss Margaret Hennings, and Mr. James Price. To each and all of these we offer our warmest thanks.

C. S. O.

C. S. O.

BLEWBURY, BERKSHIRE

October 1953

PREFACE TO THE FIRST EDITION

THIS study of the Open Fields needs some explanation, if not, indeed, some apology, for we are not historians; but long consideration of the processes by which the practice of husbandry has been evolved has left us with the conviction that much still remains to be explained. This does not refer so much to the days of prehistory, upon which light is slowly being thrown by archaeological research, as to a system of land distribution and use which may be seen, in all its essentials, in practice today.

It may be remarked that while the progress of inclosure and its economic and social consequences have received full attention from students of history in recent years, very little has been published upon the Open Fields themselves since the work of the classical historians of half a century ago. They approached the subject on its constitutional side, and their conclusions upon the division of the land and the methods of its occupation were based upon their consideration of man as a political animal, and his relations to his fellow men, rather than upon man as a hungry animal, combining with his neighbours to wring a living from the land. The first part of this book, then, is an attempt to reconsider the problem of the Open Fields as an agricultural one, to determine how far the system may be regarded, in fact, as the natural consequence of the practice of the art of tillage. The explanation generally accepted of strip farming and intermixed holdings, namely, the desire to secure to all cultivators equality of soil and situation, is discussed, and an alternative is suggested, based upon the needs of practical farming and the physical features and properties of the land. Nor is this all, for an examination of the system at work shows that the conventional exposition of three-field farming is descriptive in a strictly academic rather than in a technical sense, and that much can be added to it to explain the mode of life of the people of whom William Langland has given us a glimpse at their work in the Open Fields.

As to the second part of this book, we were stimulated to attempt to supplement the information available in recognized authorities by a study of the only Open Fields still surviving in England in economic integrity, those at Laxton, in the county of Nottingham. Records of the place beginning with the Domesday Survey are available in a quantity and a variety which is rare. Since the year 1640, it has been in the possession of one family, that of Pierrepont, in whose muniment room at Thoresby Park

a magnificent collection of maps, deeds, and documents has accumulated. These begin with a map and terrier, made in 1635,
which are reproduced here. Now strip maps are not uncommon
and there are many estate terriers, but it is rare, if not unique, to
find a combination of both at such an early date, made by the same
hand and of such surpassing workmanship, detail, and accuracy
as that which the artist and craftsman, Mark Pierce, has left of
the manor of Laxton. To study them in conjunction is to realize
how inadequate for historical research is a map without its accompanying terrier, and that is the justification for the reproduction
of them here. The use which we have made of them to illustrate
our story leaves much still to be done, but the material will now
be available to others.

    A hundred years later than Mark Pierce's survey, sketch-maps
were made to record certain inclosures and reclamations at Laxton.
A hundred years later, again, the Tithe Map and Award is available, and today, after another hundred years, the maps of the
Ordnance Survey and the estate records disclose the present position. There is a set of Court Rolls, Suit Rolls, and Juries' Presentments beginning in 1651 and continuing to the present day, very
nearly complete, which throw a strong light upon the practice and
control of farming and administration in the Open Fields through
nearly 300 years. Preserved in the parish are some runs of accounts
of the Constables, of the Overseers of the Poor, of the Overseers
of the Highways, and of the Churchwardens, in the eighteenth
and early nineteenth centuries. Finally, the late Rev. C. B. Collinson, M.A., vicar of the parish from 1898 to 1916, has left an
exhaustive manuscript collection, in three large quarto volumes,
of references to Laxton men and matters in the Public Records,
national and local, Diocesan Registries, Thoresby Deeds, and
other sources. In the collection of this material Mr. Collinson had
the collaboration of the late Mr. William Stevenson and of his
son, the late Mr. W. H. Stevenson, M.A., Fellow of St. John's
College, Oxford. He left, also, a typed transcript of the Parish
Registers, and without his thorough and painstaking work, which
he calls 'Materials for the History of Laxton', the chapter in this
book on the Descent of the Manor could not have been written.

    The short chapter on the extent of the Open Fields in England,
and the map which accompanies it, are based upon material supplied by Miss M. Hennings, M.A., compiled from original
sources during a search extending over two years for evidence in
grants, charters, Feet of Fines, Inquisitions *post mortem* as well as
Inclosure awards, Chancery Certificates, &c., of open-field tenure.

    In conclusion, it is a pleasure to record our gratitude and in-
debtedness to the many who have helped us in our work, by direct

information, by references and access to sources, by constructive criticism, and in other ways. Particularly would we thank Earl Manvers and his agent, Mr. Hubert D. Argles, for all the facilities given to us so freely for access to the contents of the muniment room at Thoresby Park; and the Steward of his Manor of Laxton, Colonel H. Tallents, D.S.O., for the use of the later Court Rolls and Suit Rolls; Lady Elinor Denison and her agents, Messrs. Beevor and Weetman, for information about Laxton Moorhouse; Lord Savile and his agent, Mr. John Baker, for information on the Rufford connexion with Laxton; the Rev. W. J. N. Thurston, Vicar of Laxton, who has sought out and assembled many parochial records dispersed in private hands; the late Mr. J. Cartledge, Master of Laxton School; Mr. John Rose, Chairman of the Parish Council; Mr. William Merrills, Mr. James Price, Mr. John Clarke, Mr. John Dewick, late Bailiff of the Manor, and other of our friends amongst the Laxton farmers who have made clear to us many points that were obscure in the practice of open-field farming.

We owe a very great debt to Professor V. H. Galbraith, who read the whole of the manuscript and who helped us with criticism, suggestions, and encouragement at every stage. Other Oxford friends for whose help we are grateful are Professor G. N. Clark, Professor J. A. Scott Watson, Mr. K. N. Bell, Mr. R. A. B. Mynors, Mr. A. L. Poole, and Mr. G. Turner.

Further, we wish to thank Dr. G. Herbert Fowler, and Professor J. Tait, whose practical interest in our work has helped us much; Professor J. D. Chambers, and Mr. W. E. Tate, historians of Nottinghamshire. Finally, to Sir Daniel Hall, K.C.B., we owe more than we can say for the stimulus and help which we have derived from discussions with him of the problems of early agriculture and the Open Fields, extending over many years.

For some of the illustrations we are indebted to Major George Allen (pp. 16 and 192), Dr. N. Cunliffe (p. 20), Mr. Seton Gordon (p. 30*a*), Mr. Montague Fordham (p. 165*a*), Miss Helen Orwin (p. 31), Miss M. Cranfield (p. 30*b*), The Proprietors of the *Farmer and Stockbreeder* (p. 12), Gaumont-British Instructional, Ltd., for pictures from their film *A Mediaeval Village* (p. 135*b*), Aerofilms, Ltd. (p. 46*b*), and to the Director-General of the Ordnance Survey, Southampton, for permission to use some of its maps in the construction of those appearing here. The reproductions of the Laxton map of 1635 are taken from a faithful copy made by Miss Helen Orwin.

C. S. O.
C. S. O.

AGRICULTURAL ECONOMICS RESEARCH INSTITUTE
OXFORD
May 1938

CONTENTS

LIST OF ILLUSTRATIONS

PLATES

MAPS

At end

PART I

The Open Fields of England

INTRODUCTION

Few people, probably, are aware that here and there in England today examples still survive of the system of farming which was practised over so much of the country for the greater part of two thousand years—and who can say for how much longer?—known as the Open-Field system. But every schoolboy has been instructed in it. He has seen the diagrammatic representation of the medieval manor with its nucleated village, its church, and its manor-house; its demesne land, or, as it might be called today, its home farm, from which the household of the lord of the manor was supplied; its three great arable fields, scattered throughout which the freemen and the tenants of the manor alike held the small strips which went to make up the ploughland portion of their farms; its meadow land by the stream, where the village farmers made their hay, and its waste, or common, upon which they turned their sheep and cattle. And as the manor was an economic unit the picture is usually completed by indicating a watermill on the stream, or a windmill on the highest spot, where there was no water-power, at which the corn was ground into flour. Every schoolboy, too, has some knowledge, academic rather than technical, of the practice of agriculture within the pattern manor: how all the ploughland was divided into three fields, approximately equal, in one of which wheat or other autumn-sown corn was grown, in another barley or other spring-sown crop, while the third was rested in fallow; how this system of cultivation rotated, the autumn-sown field becoming, next year, the spring-sown field and then the fallow field; how the division of each farmer's land into a multiplicity of small strips, distributed evenly over the Open Fields, was made to give each one his due proportion of the good and of the less good soil, of the near and of the more remote parts of the fields; how the cornfields after harvest and the meadows after mowing were thrown open to all farmers alike to graze their stock for a season.

Such a picture and such an explanation of it may serve the schoolboy well enough who reads history as but one subject amongst many in a general education, a subject, moreover, in teaching which it has long been customary to emphasize the political and the constitutional rather than the economic and the social sides. But in the student of history it can do little more than rouse a curiosity which he will not easily satisfy. Many maps of the old open-field parishes, made in their later days, when the system had evolved to its farthest limits, have survived, and to look at one of them is to realize at once how much remains to be explained. How was the farming rotation, two corn crops and then a fallow, evolved, and why? Why did every freeholder or tenant conform to it, instead of following each of them his own inclinations? Why, in any particular manor of which records and maps still remain, was the three-field system practised, in fact, sometimes in one or two and often in four, five, or more fields? Why were the little strips assembled in blocks, roughly parallelograms, containing some of them a few and some of them many of these strips, and the blocks themselves arranged at every sort of angle to each other like a patchwork quilt, instead of planning the strips to follow one another uniformly across the fields? Why did the farmers suffer the inconvenience of moving from strip to strip all over the manor instead of occupying compact holdings and equalizing differences in the quality of the land, or in its accessibility, by adjustments in the respective sizes of the holdings or in the rents assigned to them? Lastly, how were these great fields laid out and allotted in this multitudinous muddle of little unfenced bits? In number they are to be counted in thousands; in size they conform to no uniform standards of measurement. There is nothing to explain their seeming haphazard agglomeration and changing direction as they appear in the old maps. To get from a village homestead to its tenant's remoter strips without trampling across the crops on the intervening strips looks more difficult than to find the exit from a maze—and yet there was easy access both for men and horses, by roads, by paths, by balks, and by headlands, to every strip in the manor. Given a block of two or three thousand acres of land today, lying irregularly round a village, there is no farmer in the kingdom, and very few land agents or surveyors, who could divide it into fields, furlongs, and strips as was done as a matter of course by the farmers of nearly 2,000 years ago.

The answers to these questions and to others which arise in the study of the Open Fields are not to be found in the works of the historians from whom so much of our knowledge of them is derived. For the most part they have approached their problem from the legal and the constitutional or from the ethnic side, with the consequence that the significance of farming practice and the extent to which the control and the direction of social institutions were determined by the technical processes of agriculture have been insufficiently appreciated. It is the purpose of this study to consider the evolution of the Open Fields from the standpoint that the fundamental problem confronting primitive communities was less the legal status and constitution of their members than the urgent task of wringing a bare subsistence from the land in the face of all the difficulties imposed by their rudimentary technical knowledge and by Nature herself; to suggest that the social organization was the consequence rather than the cause of the system of land tenure and cultivation.

It has generally been accepted by historians that the open-field farming system was introduced into Britain by Germanic settlers. Of the evolution of the practice itself in northern Europe, written evidence is almost entirely wanting and such as there is is difficult to interpret. Stubbs has pointed out that the emergence of the German tribes from the nomad state had begun in Caesar's time, and it was complete 150 years later when Tacitus wrote, anyhow for that part of northern Europe which he described. If their system of husbandry was the open-field system, its recorded history begins, therefore, about A.D. 100.

But the record of Tacitus is very slight, and the passage in which he deals with the occupation of land is obscure. In the translation of Church and Brodribb it reads:

Land proportioned to the number of inhabitants was occupied by the whole community in turn, and afterward divided among them according to rank. A wide expanse of plains makes the partition easy. They till fresh fields every year, and they have still more land than enough; with the richness and extent of their soil, they do not laboriously exert themselves in planting orchards, inclosing meadows, and watering gardens. Corn is the only produce required from the earth; . . .[1]

Stubbs, however, notes that there are alternative readings, of which there are numerous interpretations, and he concludes that what Tacitus meant was that the land was occupied by communities according to the number of their cultivators, and that allotments, changed annually, were assigned to the several freemen according to their estimation or social importance.[2]

Here, at all events, is a picture of a system of farming by a settled community. According to Stubbs, the social and political organization of the German tribes from which the invaders of

[1] Church, A. J., and Brodribb, W. J., *The Agricola and Germany of Tacitus*, p. 106 (ed. 1926).
[2] Stubbs, W., *Constitutional History of England*, p. 19 and fn. (4th ed., 1883).

Britain derived in the fifth and sixth centuries was the Mark system, and this he has described as follows:

> . ˙. The general name of the *mark* is given to the territory which is held by the community, the absolute ownership of which resides in the community itself, or in the tribe or nation of which the community forms a part. The mark has been formed by a primitive settlement of a family or kindred in one of the great plains or forests of the ancient world; and it is accordingly, like any other clearing, surrounded by a thick border of wood or waste, which supplies the place or increases the strength of a more effective natural boundary. In the centre of the clearing the primitive village is placed: each of the mark-men has there his homestead, his house, courtyard, and farm-buildings. This possession, the exponent as we may call it of his character as a fully qualified freeman, entitles him to a share in the land of the community. He has a right to the enjoyment of the woods, the pastures, the meadow, and the arable land of the mark; but the right is of the nature of usufruct or possession only, his only title to absolute ownership being merged in the general title of the tribe which he of course shares. The woods and pastures being undivided, each mark-man has the right of using them, and can turn into them a number of swine and cattle: under primitive conditions this share is one of absolute equality; when that has ceased to be the rule, it is regulated by strict proportion. The use of the meadow-land is also definitely apportioned. It lies open from hay harvest to the following spring, and during this time is treated as a portion of the common pasture, out of the area of which it is in fact annually selected. When the grass begins to grow the cattle are driven out, and the meadow is fenced round and divided into as many equal shares as there are mark-families in the village: each man has his own hay-time and houses his own crop: that done, the fences are thrown down, and the meadow becomes again common pasture: another field in another part of the mark being chosen for the next year. For the arable land the same regulative measures are taken, although the task is somewhat more complex: for the supply of arable cannot be supposed to have been inexhaustible, nor would the mark-men be likely to spend their strength in bringing into tillage a larger area than they could permanently keep in cultivation. Hence the arable surface must be regarded as constant, subject to the alternation of crops. In the infancy of agriculture the alternation would be simply that of corn and fallow, and for this two divisions or common fields would suffice. But as tillage developed, as the land was fitter for winter or spring sowing, or as the use of other seed besides wheat was introduced, the community would have three, four, five, or even six such areas on which the proper rotation of crops and fallow might be observed. In each of these areas the mark-man had his equal or proportionate share; and this share of the arable completed his occupation or possession.
>
> This system of husbandry prevailed at different times over the whole of Germany, and is in complete harmony with the idea of a nationality constituted on a basis of personal rather than territorial relations. . . .[1]

Later he says that by the opening of Anglo-Saxon history in this country the redistribution of the arable land year by year, under

[1] Op. cit., pp. 53–55.

which 'the freeman can but set his foot on the soil and say "this
is mine this year, next year it will be another's, and that which is
another's now will be mine then" ', had given place to a permanent allocation of particular strips to particular individuals.[1]

It is apparent at once that this is a description of the Mark
system in being, not of the Mark system in origin. There is no
difficulty in picturing a family or a group of families settled on
land in dwellings of some kind, with the necessary appurtenances.
The existence of 'the woods' and 'the pastures' again presents no
difficulty, for these were nothing more than the land surrounding
the settlement in the state to which Nature had brought it at the
time. But what was 'the arable land of the mark' in which each
member of the community had his share? How did the 'meadowland' differ from the natural pasture? How was it 'definitely
apportioned', and how were 'the same regulative measures' taken
for the arable land? Stubbs's description supplies no answer to the
question: How did the early farmers till the soil, and by what
process did they allot it amongst themselves in the complicated
system which he describes?

However, this theory of the Mark is no longer accepted, and
we turn to Seebohm for a fuller description of the Open Fields.
His conclusion that they were an evolution of the Roman Vill
rather than of Stubbs's hypothetical German Mark need not be
examined here. He is at pains to show that the normal strip, the
smallest division of the Open Field, is a statute acre—'The strips
are in fact roughly cut "acres" of the proper shape for ploughing'
—although he notes that in many places they are half-acres.

Next, it will be seen that the strips on the map lie side by side in groups,
forming larger divisions of the field. These larger divisions are called 'shotts'
or 'furlongs'.... This grouping of the strips in furlongs or shotts is a further
invariable feature of the English open field system.[2]

Seebohm goes back to nothing earlier or more primitive than
the three-field system, of which he writes as if it were practised
everywhere in three fields. But he goes much farther than Stubbs
in providing a clue to the origin of the system of holding land in
scattered strips in large fields, when he describes the system of
co-aration. On the hypothesis that in early times few cultivators
possessed a full ox-team and that the land was ploughed by composite teams of oxen in different ownerships, he suggests that
strips were allotted in rotation, as ploughed, to the individual
owners. Thus, if a team consisted of eight oxen, each contributed
by a different owner, each owner would have one of every eight

[1] Op. cit., p. 80.
[2] Seebohm, F., *The English Village Community*, pp. 2–4 (1883).

strips ploughed by the team, a strip being one day's work. Or if one partner contributed two oxen his share would be two strips, and so on.

This, and this alone, would give the requisite elasticity to the system, so as to allow, if necessary, of the admission of new-comers into the village community, and new virgates into the village fields. So long as the limits of the land were not reached, a fresh tenant would rob no one by adding his oxen to the village plough teams, and receiving in regular turn the strips allotted in the ploughing to his oxen. In the working of the system, the strips of a new holding would be intermixed with the others by a perfectly natural process.[1]

That Seebohm had many misconceptions of the structure of the Open Fields, and that he committed himself to many misstatements about them, will be shown later. But in these sentences he has supplied the only explanation offered by any of the historians for the origin of the system, although he does not elaborate it fully and it is quite certain that he did not realize all its implications in determining at once the whole layout of the fields, their division into furlongs, and the sizes and the directions of the strips. No other writer, however, has come so near to that which seems to be the probable explanation of these things, while several have made statements about them which are demonstrably wrong.

Maitland, who challenged Stubbs's view of the Mark system, has stated also that one purpose of his work was to dispute Seebohm's conclusions—that is to say, about the Roman origin of the English manorial system.[2] In his description of the Open Fields and in his explanation of them he says:

And whence, we must ask, comes that system of intermixed 'strip-holding' that we find in our English fields? Who laid out those fields? The obvious answer is that they were laid out by men who would sacrifice economy and efficiency at the shrine of equality. Each manse is to have the same number of strips; the strips of one manse must be neither better nor worse than those of its neighbour, and therefore must be scattered abroad over the whole territory of the village.[3]

And again:

Great pains had been taken to make the division equitable; each householder was to have strips equal in number and in value, and to secure equivalence each was to have a strip in every part of the arable territory.[4]

Here, as in Stubbs, there is the idea of a community of farmers gathering together from somewhere, taking possession of an area of uncultivated land, clearing it, marking it out in great fields,

---

[1] Op. cit., pp. 113–14. See also pp. 120–1.
[2] Maitland, F. W., *Domesday Book and Beyond*, p. 354, also Preface, p. vi (1897).
[3] Op. cit., p. 337.   [4] Op. cit., p. 346.

and assessing the productive value of every part of them; next proceeding deliberately to divide them into furlongs and these into a multitude of tiny strips, which, last of all, they then allocated in rotation to the individuals of the community. 'When they were dividing the field', he says, 'men attempted to map out shotts in which approximately equal areas could be constructed';[1] and in a footnote, questioning Seebohm, he says, 'a distribution of acres when the ploughing is done is just what we do not see in England'.[2]

Incidentally, Maitland confirms Stubbs's conclusion that by the time the German land system reached England it had lost all traces of communal cultivation, and that individual occupation of the strips was the practice.

Vinogradoff follows the earlier writers in his description of a community of Teutonic invaders laying out the land of their choice in fields, furlongs, and strips sufficient for their number, and then allotting them by turns:

The possessions are intermixed; allotments are made, not in patches set apart for the use of the different householders, but in strips assigned to everyone in each of the shotts or fields occupied for tillage by the community. . . . One thing seems clear: although this system was not by any means the best for furthering the progress of cultivation, it was particularly adapted to the requirements of a community of shareholders who were closely joined together in the performance of their work, the assertion of their rights, the performance of their duties and the payment of their dues. On the supposition that the basis of social arrangements was to be a repartition of rights and duties according to the shares with which people were endowed in the tenure of land, the complicated open fields, intermixed strips and graduated holdings of the *tuns* would suggest themselves naturally; and in this cumbrous form the different obligations of economic and political life would, as it were, strike root into the soil.[3]

It is a supposition, surely, that may be questioned. Is it not more likely that the business of keeping alive was the first and most serious consideration, and that the land system was evolved solely out of this necessity? So far from its being 'not by any means the best for furthering the progress of cultivation', it will be suggested, presently, that it was the natural one in all the circumstances, and it was dictated by the need to live. Unless the harvest could be got in due season, the community would starve, and under a primitive agricultural technique this must have been the dominant consideration in the use of the land, all other considerations, such as the political organization of the people and the social status of individuals, being subordinated to it.

[1] Op. cit., p. 383.   [2] Op. cit., p. 346, fn.
[3] Vinogradoff, P., *The Growth of the Manor*, p. 176 (1905).

The English Open Fields threw down a challenge to an American historian, Dr. Howard Levi Gray, and his important contribution to our knowledge of them was published in 1915.[1] He makes no attempt to discover their origins, or, if discovery be impossible, to offer any explanation of their evolution, accepting the fact that the English, throughout a large part of their country, practised their farming in common, in Open Fields. He is concerned, rather, to prove that there was not one field system common to all districts, but that it varied from district to district. Thus, he finds a Midland system, a Kentish system, an East Anglian system, and a system of the lower Thames basin. His conjectures and conclusions are considered later.[2]

Dr. G. Herbert Fowler has offered the following comment upon the theory commonly put forward in explanation of the Open Fields, namely, that the system of allotting land in scattered strips rather than in compact blocks arose out of the desire to secure equality for all parties:

It has been surmised that the Saxon system of holding land in scattered strips was the outcome of an attempt to assign a fair share of good land and bad land alike to every settler, on a supposed principle of Equality. This may have influenced the allotment to some extent, but I am not aware of any direct evidence in support; and when one considers the handful of men who first settled in each township, and the abundance of land available, the theory seems to be unnecessary. If one may hazard a mere guess at the reason for land being held in separate strips rather than in compact blocks, it will be safer to look rather in the direction of practical utility than political theory. Co-operation in agriculture and especially co-operative ploughing were essential, when heavy land needed a team of eight oxen; economy of time and labour demanded that the field be ploughed continuously selion by selion from one end to the other, not first a strip here and then a strip there. If men had held their land each in a compact block, all the others must in that case wait till the first holding was completely ploughed, and meanwhile stand the chance of a break in the weather; but if men held in strips, acre by acre, each man could get to work on an acre as soon as it was ploughed, and the weather risks were fairly distributed.[3]

This is confirmation of Seebohm's suggestion, which is, in effect, that the allocation of strips was the outcome of practical utility rather than of political theory.

E. Lipson examined Seebohm's explanation of the origin of the system of intermixed holdings, based on the practice of co-aration with the eight-ox plough, and rejected it. He follows Maitland and Vinogradoff in thinking that the early cultivators scattered their holdings over the manor in a multitude of little strips from a desire to have an equal distribution of the favourable and of the unfavourable land.

This explanation [Seebohm's] of the English system of scattered owner-ship seems to be untenable. It may be admitted that the scale of graduated holdings appears to correspond to the different parts of the plough-team; and the size of the strip was undoubtedly the measure of a day's ploughing. But there is no evidence that in England the ploughing was followed by any distribution of strips. Moreover, we find the system in Central Russia where only a single horse goes to the plough. In England again, while the heavy plough drawn by eight oxen was usual on the lord's demesne, yet the villagers themselves for their own holdings commonly employed the small four-oxen plough. It is clear also that if the principle underlying the allotment was based upon shares in the plough-team, then the owner of a hide, a hundred and twenty acres which corresponded to a full team, would have been independent of his neighbours' assistance and in possession of a compact and separate holding, instead of a scattered tenement as was actually the case. The virgater, on the other hand, with his two oxen would have been grouped with three other villagers, in a like position to his own, in the sequence of the strips. It is more probable, therefore, that the system of strip-holding originated in the desire to secure equality.[1]

But Seebohm's explanation is in no way dependent on the practice of co-aration by composite plough-teams. When the ploughing season began, there would be the lord's team, the teams of the owners of hides, and the composite teams of the owners of virgates and bovates, all of them at work. If they went to work daily, side by side, the result would be an automatic alternation of strips between the plough-owners, those contributing to the composite teams having proportionately fewer strips than the owners of whole teams. There is nothing in Seebohm's account of the cus-tom of distribution of strips by co-aration which is inconsistent with this explanation, nor is it upset by Lipson's introduction of the hide-owner and his team.

A French writer, the late Marc Bloch, has described the Open Fields as they manifested themselves in France, but he is con-cerned more particularly with the fields in being, and he is content to remark that, in its origins, the system has its roots in prehistory.

Lorsque s'ouvrit la période que nous appelons moyen âge, lorsque, lente-ment, commencèrent à se constituer un État et un groupement national que l'on peut qualifier de français, l'agriculture était déjà, sur notre sol, chose millénaire. Les documents archéologiques l'attestent sans ambages: d'in-nombrables villages, dans la France d'aujourd'hui, ont pour ancêtres directs des établissements de cultivateurs néolithiques; leurs champs furent moisson-nés avec des outils de pierre bien avant que jamais faucille de métal ne tranchât l'épi. Cette préhistoire rurale, en elle-même, est hors du sujet que

[1] Lipson, E., *The Economic History of England*, i, 'The Middle Ages', pp. 64–65 (1929).

je traite ici; mais elle le domine. Si nous sommes si souvent embarrassés pour expliquer, dans leurs natures diverses, les principaux régimes agraires pratiqués sur nos terroirs, c'est que leurs racines plongent trop loin dans le passé; de la structure profonde des sociétés qui leur donnèrent naissance, presque tout nous échappe.[1]

Later, however, he describes two clearly defined open-field systems, the one resembling that met with in England, in which strips, generally long and narrow, are grouped in furlongs, in large fields; the other in which small rectangular plots take the place of the long narrow strips. Under either system, individual occupation is in scattered parcels, and the individual occupiers conform to the same general cropping system.

Bloch attributes this striking difference between the two systems to the use of different types of plough. The long strips, he says, resulted from the use of a plough furnished with wheels in front, *la charrue*. It was too long to be turned quickly, so the ploughman was encouraged to draw a long furrow, and the longer the furrow the narrower would be the acre strip, so called, which represented his day's work. The rectangular plots, on the other hand, were made, he suggests, by a short plough without wheels, *l'araire*. This implement, ploughing less deeply and turning more easily on a narrower headland, facilitated work in rectangular plots, in which advantage could be taken of their greater width to secure better cultivation by cross-ploughing.[2]

R. G. Collingwood has applied Bloch's theory of differential ploughs to explain the systems of little square enclosed fields, which air photography has revealed during the last few years in many parts of the southern counties, and the large Open Fields divided into strips. He describes how there were two agricultural systems existing side by side in Britain during the Roman occupation. There were the villas and the villages, and the difference between them was in the layout of their arable land.

The villas cultivated large open fields, the villages small enclosed ones. The undivided arable land of the villa points to undivided ownership or tenancy; the small fields of a village suggest that its arable land was divided into parcels held by individual villagers. . . .

It also suggests a difference in agricultural technique. All over the Roman world, the ordinary type of plough was the light wheelless plough which the Romans called *aratrum*; but here and there they found the Celtic peoples using the heavy wheeled plough, invented, as Pliny says, by the Gauls, which the Gauls called *caruca*. The essence of the invention was that by supporting it on wheels the cultivator could use a much heavier implement with a much higher penetrating power. Even on light soils this gave the *caruca* an advantage, for it could do at one operation as much work as the

[1] Bloch, Marc, *Les Caractères originaux de l'histoire rurale française*, p. 1 (1931).
[2] Op. cit., pp. 51–57.

aratrum, by cross-ploughing, could do in two; but also the *caruca* could be used on heavier soils where the *aratrum* could not be used at all. To utilize its penetrating power to the full, the wheeled plough was fitted with a coulter or vertical knife in front of the share, to cut the soil in preparation for turning a sod, and a share designed to lift the sod sideways so that the mould-board could turn it clean over, whereas the *aratrum* was normally provided with nothing more than a share that grubbed the soil like a pig's snout, and mould-boards that would heap the disturbed soil into a ridge.

Of these two types of plough, the *aratrum* would be the more suitable for the small fields of village-arable, which are seldom more than an acre or two in extent, and whose peasant cultivators must have used plant of a cheap and simple kind. The open fields of a villa, on the contrary, would suit the more powerful and expensive *caruca*, especially in view of the fact that villas are sometimes situated on heavy soils where the *aratrum* would be useless. In fact, it has lately been pointed out that in France both kinds of plough have survived into modern times, together with two types of field-system: the *araire* being co-extensive with systems of plots resembling the 'Celtic fields' of Britain, the *charrue* with open fields divided into strips.[1]

In other words, both Collingwood and Bloch associate strip farming with the introduction of a wheeled plough, the *caruca* or *charrue*, the former suggesting that it cultivated more deeply than the wheelless plough, and the latter that its greater length made a long furrow necessary. Collingwood suggests, further, that the wheeled plough was brought into Britain by the Belgae during the first century B.C.

There are two serious difficulties in the way of his theory. First, what evidence is there for the introduction of a wheeled plough so early as this? The word *caruca* did not mean, originally, a plough; it was a carriage of some kind, used by the wealthier classes, nor does the name appear to have been applied by any of the classical authors, or for long centuries after them, to the plough. Bloch, following Servius, Virgil's commentator, regards Virgil's plough as wheeled, but Gow has pointed out that this is most improbable.[2] The elder Pliny, writing in the first century A.D., speaks of the addition of wheels to the plough as a novelty invented by the Rhaeti, who called the implement *plaumoratum*.[3] The device, he says, was a recent one, and obviously it had not been adopted by the Romans in his day. Nor do wheels appear as parts of any of the ploughs portrayed on their coins, vases, reliefs, &c. In short, there seems to be no evidence which would place the introduction of the wheeled plough into Britain at a time before the Roman occupation.

[1] Collingwood, R. G., and Myres, J. N. L., *Roman Britain and the English Settlements* (Oxford History of England), ch. xiii, pp. 210, 211 (1936).
[2] Gow, A. S. F., 'The Ancient Plough', *Journal of Hellenic Studies*, vol. xxxiv (1914), p. 274.   [3] *Nat. Hist.* xviii. 48.

However, the date of the addition of wheels to the plough is not of much importance for the present purpose, and it is the function ascribed to them by Collingwood which raises the second difficulty. He suggests that the plough supported on a fore-carriage has greater penetrating power than the wheelless plough, but this is not borne out in practice. While the majority of horse-drawn ploughs in use in Britain today have wheels, the wheelless plough, also, is quite a common object of the countryside in many arable farming districts. The advantage of the wheeled plough is not that it can undertake heavier work, but that it enables the ploughman more readily to control the depth of his ploughing. The wheels are adjustable, upwards and downwards, and when set they fix the height of the beam, and the plough will cut a furrow of the desired depth without any further effort on the part of the ploughman, who may be seen, sometimes, walking beside his horses. Ploughing without wheels, on the other hand, calls for constant attention, because, in the absence of the fore-carriage, he himself has to steady the plough and control the depth of its work by throwing his weight upon the stilts or handles.

Certainly the primitive scratch-plough, which may have been used in the cultivation of the little square fields disclosed by air photography in association with British villages,[1] would have been an inefficient implement for the cultivation of the long strips of the Open Fields. For them, however, any plough of a more developed type, equipped with coulter and mould-board, would have been suitable, quite apart from the provision of wheels.[2] Plate II shows a wheelless plough or swing-plough, drawn by four horses, at work in the Weald of Kent. No work could be heavier, nor could any other type of horse-drawn plough penetrate deeper.

This short summary of the more important references to the Open Fields and their origins may be concluded with the mention of a report by the Research Committee of the Congress of Archaeological Societies upon some characteristic features of the Open Fields. The chief sources of evidence drawn upon by the Committee are stated to have been

the size and shape of fields, the character of ridges and lynchets in present day grassland, the study of old village, tithe and estate maps and of early books on the agricultural practice of separate counties or districts; in some parts, these have been supplemented by photographs from the air.[3]

[1] See p. 16, *post*.
[2] For a full account of how the mould-board plough works, see p. 32, *post*.
[3] Congress of Archaeological Societies, *Report on Lynchets and Grass Ridges*, pp. 32–35 (1932).

PLATE 2

THE SWING (WHEELLESS) PLOUGH

From this evidence, the Committee concluded:

The agricultural system which the Anglian and Saxon invaders seem to have brought from their homelands had produced by the end of the 18th century a fairly uniform lay-out of the parish or of the manor over the greater part of Middle England. For the purpose of our study, the important feature of this lay-out was the presence of three vast unhedged 'Open Fields' of arable land, often of some hundreds of acres; in these each man ploughed his land in strips or selions, not lying together but scattered over the Open Fields and often far apart from each other. With the growth of population, more land was gradually taken into cultivation from the Waste or Common and added to the Open Fields, in haphazard fashion as needed. Consequently, the later sub-divisions of the Open Fields (generally called Furlongs) are of all shapes and sizes, and the irregularity of their component Furlongs seem to distinguish the Anglo-Saxon agriculture of Middle England from other systems in this country.

The statement that the important feature of the system was the presence of 'three vast unhedged "Open Fields" ' must not be taken literally. In many places the three-field system in practice is a name applying only to the farming rotation, which was followed sometimes in one great field, as in many parishes in the chalk country, and sometimes in four or more, as topographical conditions dictated. Nor must the suggestion that the furlongs were laid out 'in haphazard fashion' be taken to imply a purely arbitrary arrangement of them, either in size or in direction. It will be shown presently that these considerations were dictated by the contour of the land, the strips being laid out always to secure natural drainage by taking advantage of the fall of the land.

The report proceeds to suggest that the distinctions in the sizes of different strips which may be noted will be explained by assigning them to different dates, races, and cultures:

Over nearly the whole of the kingdoms of Anglian Mercia and Saxon Wessex are found in certain grasslands to-day conspicuous arched ridges; these are generally characterised by being

   long, up to a furlong of 220 yards;
   high, from 1 to 3 feet between ridge crest and furrow;
   broad, generally from rood width (16½ ft.) to half-acre width (33 ft.) but
      often not all of equal breadth;
   curved slightly, often in the form of a reversed long S.

These represent the old strips or selions of the Open Fields. . . . In some parts of England may be seen ridges less clearly marked, which differ from the Anglo-Saxon type in being either shorter, lower, narrower, or straighter, or all of these; they have not yet been referred to any particular dates, races, or cultures, and apparently have not been recorded at all from Middle England.

It may be doubted whether the Committee has given full consideration to the formation of strips in relation to farming practice, to surface geology, and to topography. In a flat country the strips may have been long; on a light, porous soil they may have been broad; in a clay country they may have been high. But in an undulating country, where the contour was continually changing, they must have been short, and in a clay country they must have been narrow, to provide water-furrows at frequent intervals. While it is not suggested here that differences of race and culture had no influence on the farming system, it must be pointed out that there is very little in the characteristic features of the Open Fields which cannot be explained, simply and naturally, by the common sense of farming practice.[1]

This completes our brief summary of the theories propounded by the principal authorities of the past sixty years to explain the origins of the open-field farming system.

[1] In another paragraph in their report, the Committee associate themselves with Seebohm's explanation of the terrace lynchets found in many parts of England and with particular frequency on the escarpments of the chalk, namely, that they 'are an adaptation of the selion (strip) to the steep hillside. On the theory usually accepted, they were formed by ploughing always in one direction, turning the sod downhill to an unploughed balk, the plough returning idle.' The theory of an Anglo-Saxon origin for the lynchet terraces, which associates them with the Open Fields and the work of the plough, has been seriously challenged, and the whole question of their formation needs much more systematic examination before any generalizations about them can be justified. When this has been made, there are good grounds for believing that it will not disclose any connexion between them and the Open Fields. (See Appendix, p. 175.)

I. THE TAMING OF THE WILD

No one can tell when the cultivation of crops in Britain first began, but the country in which our forefathers lived was in most places entirely unfitted, in its natural state, for the practice of any sort of agriculture. Much of it must have been covered with dense woodland or scrub forest, extending from north to south and from east to west, out of which rose the mountain-ranges and high moorlands, too steep or too exposed for the growth of timber, and the higher downlands of the chalk formation. In certain parts, too, on the poor, dry sand and gravel soils which were unfit for the growth of natural woodland before the introduction by man of coniferous trees, there must have been great stretches of heathery wastes. In other parts, again, the river valleys and estuaries, there were extensive areas of marshland and water. But with these exceptions, and they were considerable, it is fair to assume that in the beginning all the land of England now occupied for agricultural purposes was woodland of varying degrees of density. Today, whenever a field is left untilled by the plough and unstocked by cattle or sheep, Nature asserts herself at once, and a process of reversion sets in forthwith which clothes the land, first with weeds and wild grasses, then with brambles and thorns, and finally with scrub. This is not conjecture. The process, in all its stages, can be seen in many places today. So it may be stated, as a jumping-off point, that with the exception of the mountain pastures, of the downland grass and arable lands, and of the moorlands and marshes, the whole of the farm lands of England have been reclaimed, at an infinite expenditure of manual labour, from natural woodland.

Of the attempts at land-reclamation for the practice of agriculture before the coming of the Romans there is, of course, no documentary record, and little enough for the next thousand years, but it is possible to speculate upon the practices of the early inhabitants from evidence which the land itself supplies. In many parts of the country, and particularly on the chalk downs of the southern counties, remains of prehistoric cultivation may still be seen. Village settlements can be identified, field systems traced, and evidence of human activity of many kinds—camps, terraced lynchets rising one above the other, dikes, dewponds, earthworks, tumuli, and flint-mines—abounds. Air photography is adding much to that which is visible to the eye, and in districts so remote from one another as Northumberland and the south-coast counties it is bringing to light an agricultural organization the extent of which was previously quite unsuspected.[1]

It discloses a field system of small rectangles, many of them only an acre or two in extent, enclosed by well-defined boundaries, consisting, it is suggested, of stones removed from the surface of the land. How these fields were cultivated, when, and by whom, we do not know. It is said that their farmers were a hill people, that they occupied mainly the downlands and table-lands, making little or no attempt to reclaim the woodlands or swamps which covered so much of the country. There is evidence for this in some of the air photographs, which have disclosed nothing resembling this system in the valleys and plains. Moreover, it is natural that a rather primitive people, equipped probably with very simple tools, would cultivate those districts where the labour was lightest and the difficulty of removing heavy timber and superfluous water was least.

But while it is mainly on the bare uplands that evidence of early cultivation still remains, these were not the only lands to be occupied by our farming forebears. At some period unknown— it may have been contemporary with downland farming, it may have preceded it or succeeded it, or both—men began to make clearances in the woodlands of the valleys and plains for the practice of their primitive agriculture, while the surrounding unreclaimed forest gave them pannage for their pigs and rough grazing for their other live stock. Here again, no record exists of the beginning of the work, nor is there ocular evidence of how it proceeded, such as that which is provided by the marks left by man in the downlands and in hill country. But the early recorded history of some of the forest districts makes a reconstruction of the process possible. In Andredswald, the great forest which covered the Weald of Kent and Sussex, men had settled at one time or another in the denes or dens, which were hollows and valleys in the woods, attracted to them, probably, by the proximity of water and of shelter, and by the ease of communication along the rivers and streams. From these centres began the attack by man upon Nature, and little by little, as the population grew, the woodland began to give place to pasture and to cultivated land, the process continuing until none of it was left except in places associated usually with the wetter or the more intractable soils. The place-names which survive today on the great Wealden formation, the 'dens' (Tenterden), 'deans' (West Dean), and 'hursts' (Midhurst), are indicative of these settlements in woods which have long since been cleared. In the Midlands, the great clearance which has

[1] See Crawford, O. G. S., and Keiller, A., *Wessex from the Air* (1928); also Crawford, O. G. S., *Air Survey and Archaeology* (1928).

PLATE 3

PREHISTORIC SQUARE FIELDS, BURDEROP DOWN, WILTS.

been made of Wychwood Forest is indicated by names such as Milton-under-Wychwood, a village now six or seven miles from the nearest point of the still existing woodland, and by the various 'assarts', clearings in a wood, which are met with here, as also in Sherwood Forest and elsewhere, far outside the present forest boundaries.[1]

That which happened in Kent, Surrey, and Sussex, in Oxfordshire and Nottinghamshire must have been going on equally in all the lowlands of England. Begun in prehistoric times, the task was hardly finished in the days of our grandfathers, but the face of the country now shows how complete the achievement has been. Where today are the great forests of Knaresborough, Charnwood, Sherwood, Wyre, Arden, and Rockingham, in the Midlands; Cranborne Chase, Savernake, and Bere, in the south; the forests which once covered large parts of Sussex, Kent, and Essex, and many others? All are gone, except for some attenuated areas to which some of these names still attach, and a few larger tracts on infertile soils unattractive to the husbandman, such as Cannock in the Midlands, the beechwoods on the thin chalk of the Chilterns, the Royal Forest of Windsor on the barren Bagshot Beds, the New Forest, and the Forest of Dean.

For a long time the uplands and the forests must have sufficed to occupy the energies of the early farmers, but the potential fertility of the marshlands bordering the coast was well known to the ancients, and successful attempts were made, at very early dates, to embank some of the alluvial deposits occurring at certain places adjoining river estuaries. The great alluvial flats on the Kent and Sussex border, between Hythe and Rye, represent the washings from the Weald brought down by the river Rother and accumulated on the coast through the centuries. Romney Marsh is the best known of them, and it was the earliest to be reclaimed from the sea, the construction of the sea-wall from Hythe, by Dymchurch, to New Romney, which protects it from the south, and of the bank from New Romney to Appledore, which guards it from the west, being attributed sometimes to the Romans. In more recent times the work was continued westward so far as Rye, successive Archbishops of Canterbury being active in the inclosure of the marshes in this area, to which their names are still attached. Other examples of the reclamation of the coastal mud flats for farming are found at many points on the east coast, where the mud brought down by Yorkshire Ouse and Trent is deposited,

---

[1] It must be remembered that the term 'forest' is used here in its meaning of an uncultivated tract of trees, underwood, and grass, rather than in the sense of heavily timbered woodland.

and where the more sluggish rivers of the Fens, similarly, are slowly silting up the Wash. At many points along this coast the agricultural land of today has been made, literally, by the men of past generations, who erected sea-walls round the mud flats whenever the deposit of warp had reached a depth which placed it only a little below the high-water mark. The Roman Bank along the Lincolnshire coast, near Skegness, may have been one of these, and today any one approaching the shores of the Wash, at certain points, passes over a succession of banks running parallel with the coast, which mark what were, at various earlier times, the bounds of sea and land. This process of adding new acres to England can be seen today, for still the rivers are bringing down the fertile mud, and still sea-walls are being built to reclaim it as fast as it reaches a height suitable for inclosure. It can only be a matter of time before the whole of the shallow salt-water basin which is called the Wash is silted up; indeed it would not be an impossible task to embank it now, with a sea-wall running between the Norfolk and the Lincolnshire coasts, and so to make almost a new county, just as the Dutchmen have done by embanking and draining the Zuider Zee.

But the salt marshes were not the only ones to which men turned their attention in their endeavours to wrest land from its natural state and to turn it to productive uses. The freshwater marshes, great areas of low-lying land, water-logged and sodden, early challenged attention. In the time of Henry VII Archbishop Morton, then Bishop of Ely, cut a great drain, which still bears his name and which still is serviceable, from Peterborough to Wisbech. But the greatest task was not undertaken before the time of the Stuart kings, when the Fens of Ely, of Cambridgeshire and the adjoining counties, of south Lincolnshire and the Isle of Axholme, were taken in hand for reclamation by arterial drainage. Dutchmen, with an engineering science in advance of our own, taught us how to control the flow of tidal waters and how to secure an artificial discharge from drainage dikes and ditches against the force of gravity. A hundred years later the great expanse of marshes stretching from the foot of Mendip on a front nearly twenty miles wide, south-west past the Isles of Avalon and Athelney, to Taunton, of which the Pawlett Hams are today the most fertile and Sedgemoor the best known, were dealt with in the same way. The problem of the reclamation of the salt marshes was, in the main, the exclusion of the sea; that of the inland marshes was the discharge of fresh water from areas having no natural outlets for it.

In considering the agelong conflict of man with Nature to exploit the potential resources of the land for the production of food, nothing is so impressive as the reclamation of the Fens and marshes. Downland man, with his primitive tools, may have had no easy task, but it lay clear before him and its limits were of his own setting. The woodlanders were faced with heavy labour in effecting their clearances, but the problem itself was a simple one. It is difficult, however, today, to appreciate the immensity of the task which confronted the drainers of the Fens, and the skill and courage with which they applied themselves to it. The land stretched before them in great flats for many miles; it was practically untraversed by roads; visibility was obstructed in every direction by tall reed-beds; they had few of the modern instruments for the construction of accurate maps, or for the accurate levelling upon which so much of their success would depend. Steam-power, which would have immensely simplified the work, was still 200 years ahead of them, and the new rivers which they made here and there, the main drains which they cut everywhere, and the multitudinous drainage ditches feeding them, all had to be excavated by manual labour. Everywhere they encountered the hostility of the marshmen, who could see nothing in the work but the destruction of their fishing and wild-fowling. This was not the reclamation of land, piecemeal, by those who were to till it, but the co-operative undertaking of a company of adventurers, great landlords, who imported a Dutch engineer and his workmen to perform a stupendous task, in the face of the opposition of the local inhabitants, which, under Charles I, the Commonwealth, and Charles II, added nearly three-quarters of a million fertile acres to the farmlands of England.

The lighter and poorer heath lands and moors which covered large areas, more particularly in the midland and eastern counties, were the next type of land to be broken in to productive use in this country. Whereas the woodlands, the marshes, and the Fens were all of them potentially fertile, the former needing only clearance of timber and scrub, and the latter embankment and drainage, much of the heath land was inherently unprofitable under the farming systems which persisted in most parts of England right into the eighteenth century. But the increase and spread of knowledge from that time onwards, the introduction of new crops and of methods of husbandry calculated to improve the soil, brought many of these areas within the range of profitable tillage. Until then, they had been looked upon as being below the margin of cultivation, just as tracts such as the brecklands of Norfolk and the Yorkshire moors are still regarded today.

With the breaking-in of regions such as that which Coke of Norfolk reclaimed, and others similar in Norfolk and Suffolk, and with the inclosure of Lincoln Heath, the Lincolnshire and

Yorkshire Wolds, Exmoor Forest, and many others, during the eighteenth and early nineteenth centuries, the making of the land of England may be said to have been finished, in the sense that these works mark the end of the attempt to win land from the wild, on a large scale, for the purposes of husbandry of one kind or another. Other areas still remain in the primitive state, whether woodland, moorland, or marsh, and by experiment and research the way may be found, one day, to turn them to more productive uses. Here and there, and on a small scale, the reclamation of marsh and moor is still going on, but until the margin between costs and returns in farming shows signs of a considerable and permanent widening it is unlikely that the country will witness any parallel, say in the Norfolk Broads, the Yorkshire Moors, on Dartmoor, or on the Welsh mountain-sides, to works such as the drainage of the Bedford Level, the reclamation of Lincoln Heath, or the inclosure of Exmoor Forest. The pressing need for land and more land, on which to produce food and more food, to satisfy the ever-growing industrial population of England, which continued to stimulate the pioneers of agricultural progress right up to the middle of the nineteenth century, became less and less from that time onward, as improvements in transport made food from the New Worlds available to the nation.

In leaving this impressionist picture of the reclamation of the land for farming, coloured as it is, in its earliest years, largely by conjecture, the point cannot be too heavily emphasized that the farm lands of England today are the work, literally, of men's hands, that they represent the subjugation of Nature by man, as the result of an immense and continuous struggle carried on through the centuries, often with inadequate weapons and at a cost which it is impossible to measure. The struggle, once begun, has been and must always be continuous, for land in a state suitable for the practice of agriculture is something entirely artificial, and Nature, never finally subjugated, is ever awaiting the opportunity to shake herself free, to throw off the costume of civilization in which man has clothed her, so that she may resume, once again, her first covering of woodland, water, and wild grass.

PLATE 4

OLD PLOUGHLANDS IN OXFORDSHIRE REVERTING TO SCRUB

II. BEFORE THE NORMAN CONQUEST

In the last chapter the steps by which the face of the country was changed from the natural to the artificial, for the purposes of husbandry, have been outlined briefly. It would be possible to speculate with some plausibility upon the progress of farming from its earliest beginnings in this island, by reference to the practices of nomad and primitive races still existing in Africa, Australia, and elsewhere. But for the present purpose it will suffice to begin with the first people to practise anything worthy of the name of husbandry in Britain. Archaeologists tell us that the tillers of the little square fields were Celtic invaders from the continent of Europe, and their descendants, and that it was they who inhabited most of Britain at the dawn of the Christian era. Exploration of their villages and burial-sites has thrown some light upon their culture, and it seems fairly clear that they were by no means primitive savages, but that their knowledge of agriculture was considerable. Julius Caesar has recorded, of his first expedition to Britain in 55 B.C., that his soldiers were able to cut corn, and of his second that he made the Britons give him corn. Strabo, too, about 24 B.C., writes that the Britons exported corn, and Tacitus, writing of the year A.D. 79, remarked upon the fertility of the soil of Britain, which would yield abundantly all ordinary produce.[1] It is true that Caesar says, also, that most of the people of the Midland parts did not sow corn but lived on milk and meat.[2] It does not appear that he had been to see, but much of the Midlands must have been under forest in his day and occupied by a people mainly pastoral.

In the southern part of the country, at all events, farming had reached a high standard before the Roman invasion. Excavation of the villages of Cranborne Chase has yielded quantities of agricultural implements, underground granaries have been found, and it is known that Britain exported considerable quantities of wheat.[3]

The coming of the Romans added to the extent and quality of the farming in those parts over which their influence extended. Calgacus, the Caledonian chief, complained that the Romans wore down the very hands and bodies of his people by the toil of clearing forests and morasses,[4] though whether this was in the

<hr />

[1] *Agricola*, ch. xii.   [2] *De Bello Gallico*, v. 14.
[3] Collingwood, R. G., *Roman Britain*, ch. iii.   [4] Tacitus, *Agricola*, ch. xxxi.

construction of roads and camps or for the purposes of husbandry does not appear. But an examination of the finds made on the excavation of places such as Silchester shows that many of the tools and implements which were then in use may be seen on any farm today, their form and make inherited almost without change from the farmers of nearly 2,000 years ago: ploughshares and coulters, picks, spades and shovels, reaping-hooks and scythes, sledge-hammers and anvils, harness—in fact, nearly everything in common use today, except machinery.

Thus equipped for dealing with the soil, their tillage must have been of a high order. Indeed, except for their lack of fertilizers and of some new crops and improved varieties of old ones which agricultural science has provided in modern times, their methods cannot have differed very much from those of many small farmers today. Mechanical power applied to farming processes may have increased the efficiency of labour, but it has done little to improve the efficiency of cultivation. It is possible, even, that the ox-teams and the great wooden ploughs of medieval days produced a better tilth under some soil conditions than the modern tractor with its multiple iron plough, and the parts of the Romano-British plough which have survived suggest a good deal more than a primitive implement which only scratched the soil.

Remains of domestic animals of all kinds, horses, cattle, sheep, pigs, fowls, dogs, have been found in British villages. In Agricola's engagements with the Britons, cavalry in large numbers are said to have been used on both sides, besides chariots on the British side.

The pre-Roman Britons are often said to have been a people of the hills, and certainly most of the evidence of their activities comes from the plateaux, downlands, and hills. Most of the village sites and the little square fields known today are in such districts, as also are those which air photography is bringing almost daily to light. While it is conceivable that these sites, being the more open, were naturally selected for first cultivation, they were early abandoned, and centuries of continuous cultivation by farmers of a later civilization may have destroyed the evidence of an equally early occupation of the valleys and plains.

It cannot be asserted too strongly that our knowledge of the square-field people and their farming practice is very slight. Historical evidence there is none, for there is nothing to show that the two or three mentions of English agriculture in the classical authors have reference to them, and the evidence of the land itself is becoming available only slowly, as scientific technique for its study is developed. Much more is needed to justify the theories that are sometimes offered, or, indeed, to make possible any tolerable explanation. And, whatever may be known of tribal organization or of political institutions in Britain before and during the Roman occupation, and this is very little, nothing at all is known of the ownership of the land or of its distribution amongst the people. Did it belong to the village, and was it culti-vated in common for the general good? Or did men even in those days enjoy some private rights of property in the soil which they tilled? Or were such rights the privilege of a few who com-manded the service of communities living in a state of serfdom? To look at that which remains of some of the activities of these early people, the immense banks and dikes with which they en-circled their camps, the terraced lynchets which they made along the escarpments of the hills in so many parts of England, these and similar works suggest a control of labour hardly to be asso-ciated with a free people. Nothing, however, is certain; indeed, by the time of which we can speak with any precision, the economic and technical organization of the land had advanced so far that in some important features it has remained unchanged until today.

In most parts of Britain the farming systems in practice nowadays have evolved from that which is thought to have been introduced by settlers from northern Europe commonly called the Saxons. Archaeologists and historians tell us that the shores of Britain had long attracted tribesmen from the continent of Europe, pushing northward and westward across the English Channel and the North Sea. The people who inhabited most of the country at the time of Julius Caesar's coming are supposed to have descended from such invaders, and to them have been ascribed the little square fields. But over a great part of Europe there were people who practised a system of husbandry based upon a method of land-division entirely different, which is known today as the Saxon system. When it was that the 'Saxons' first began to settle in Britain, driving back the 'Celtic' people as they, before, are supposed to have driven back a still earlier race, we do not know, and for the present purpose the date is mainly of academic inter-est. This page of prehistory is being interpreted only word by word and very slowly. At present we can say no more than that the division of the land for agriculture in Britain today seems to derive from two widely different systems, the little square fields of the Celtic system, so called, and the big, open fields of the so-called Saxon system. For descriptive purposes, these labels may serve, but the implication that they date or locate the systems to which they have been applied is hardly warranted. The suggestion that the 'Celtic' system prevailed from some date in prehistory up to some time about that of the Roman occupation, and that it was then gradually superseded by the 'Saxon' system, is no more than a generalization. At the same time, it is possible that the square-field husbandry antedates that of the big, open fields, and there, for the present, the question must be left.

Coming to historical times, the first recorded date for the arrival of the Saxons is A.D. 287, when raids upon the coast led the Roman governor to fortify it from the Solent to the Wash, and to appoint, as warden, a Count of the Saxon Shore. There is evidence that during the Roman occupation incursions by these invaders were frequent, culminating in the great raid of A.D. 367, after which the penetration of the country went on more and more rapidly, until Romanized Britain was entirely submerged.

For the next two centuries or more there is practically no recorded history of Britain, but it seems that by invasion and settlement the Angles, Saxons, and Jutes came to dominate almost the whole of the country, except the south-western extremity and that which is now the Principality of Wales. Centres of Romano-British civilization were blotted out, and the Britons were so completely submerged as to lose all their political and social institutions.

How the conversion of agriculture proceeded so that the little square fields were entirely superseded, when this began, or when it was finished, we do not know. Nor can we say when the big attack upon the unoccupied parts of the valleys and the plains began, or how they were opened up and colonized. When the curtain rings up, after the long period of obscurity following the end of the Roman occupation, a social and agricultural system already highly developed is disclosed.

Assuming the accuracy of the theory that farming began upon the plateaux and hills, there had now been a great extension of agriculture into the valleys and plains. Much more than this, it can be said that the English people of Saxon times had advanced so far in their methods of land-reclamation and farming practice that today a thousand parishes bear witness to their skill in land-utilization. The layout of the land in townships for occupation by communities of men, which culminated in the setting of parish bounds, was effected long before the Norman Conquest, and over most of rural England it so remains. A study of the map in any region of hill and valley shows how parish boundaries were defined by farming considerations. Taking extreme examples so as to demonstrate the point more clearly, it may be shown how the need for shelter, for water, for grazing-land and land for tillage, in the proportions necessary to sustain the community, deter-mined the size and shape of the allocation of land which came, ultimately, to form the parish.

Two examples will suffice. The county of Lincoln exhibits an

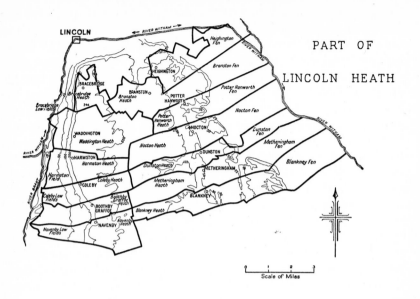

PART OF

LINCOLN HEATH

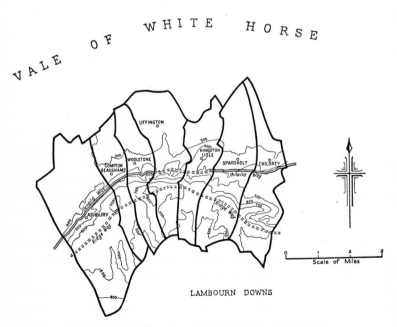

VALE OF WHITE HORSE

LAMBOURN DOWNS

LINCOLNSHIRE AND BERKSHIRE PARISHES

interesting geological feature in the long, narrow ridge of the oolites which runs, like a backbone, due north from Stamford to Lincoln and so on to the Humber, which is known as 'the Heath' south of Lincoln, and as 'the Cliff' north of the city. Like most of the high lands of England, it exhibits a steep escarpment on the west, while on the east it runs off in a more gentle slope to the low country. At Lincoln it is cut through by the river Witham, running up from the south on the western side and thence back in a south-easterly direction, cutting off a tract of country between itself and the foot of the Heath on each side. On the eastern side most of the land between the river and the foot of the Heath is fen; at one time it was waterlogged and possibly under water in winter, but even before it was drained it must have afforded valuable pasturage in the summer-time. Through all this country the parishes, representing the land of the old village communities, run in long, narrow strips from the river to the top of the Heath. Starting from Heighington, near Lincoln, and going south, there are no fewer than nine villages in the first ten miles. The villages are placed near the 100-ft. contour at the foot of the Heath, and their ploughlands were round about them. They had shelter and water; on the Heath above them, running up to the 200-ft. contour, they had a dry range for their stock; and in the fen beneath, lying below the 25-ft. contour, they had meadow land for hay and summer grazing. These parishes, little more than a mile in width, run, some of them, for ten miles from the river to the top of the Heath, and they were perfectly laid out for their purpose, that of giving sustenance, the year round, to their village communities.

On the western side of the Heath the distribution of the land is identical. The Witham, running at the western foot of the Heath, northward to Lincoln, again incloses a tract of low-lying land, and the narrow parishes just described on the eastern side abut on others on the top of the Heath which run down the western escarpment across the lowlands to the river. On the eight miles of road going south from Bracebridge, near Lincoln, there are six of them with their heath land and their low fields, though on the western side the steepness of the escarpment and the nearness of the river give parishes which, though still little more than a mile in width, are not so long as those on the eastern side.

Although, as will presently be shown, the land of the village was divided amongst the inhabitants in Saxon times in a way which had no resemblance to the compact farms of today, then, as now, the layout of the parish was reflected in the farmers' holdings, for each of them had his share of dry land on the Heath, of the good, tillable land at the foot of the Heath, and of the wet grassland by the river.

To come southward for the second example, there is a string of parishes in Berkshire, going west from Wantage along the Icknield Way to the Wiltshire border, laid out exactly in the same way as are these Lincolnshire ones. The ancient roadway follows the foot of the chalk downs along the 400-ft. contour. North of it the land falls sharply into the Vale of the White Horse, most of it lying between the 300-ft. and 200-ft. contours; on the south, the downs rise to another ancient track, the Ridgeway, reaching an elevation of over 800 ft., in some places, in a mile or so.

Here again there are eight villages in ten miles, lying on or just below the Icknield Way, each with its long strip of grassland running down, northward, into the wet land of the Vale, its strip of light ploughland in the middle, and its downland grazing longer still, climbing southward up the chalk.

These examples illustrate, rather obviously, the wisdom and the good sense of those who first partitioned the land amongst the village communities, and many like them are to be found under similar topographical conditions. The point is that the principles which actuated these early cultivators in the organization of their townships and farms were economic and technical, and they were everywhere observed, in all the farming districts of England, even though often less obviously. Nearly everywhere the village lands consisted of arable lands on the better parts, grasslands, for mowing, along the streams or wetter parts, and commons and woodlands, for grazing, on the poorer parts. Although the growth of population in a thousand years has led to a great extension of the cultivated area, necessitating the grubbing of great areas of woodland and the ploughing of many commons and wastes to provide the extra food which the country needed, nothing has happened during that time to suggest how the planning of the countryside for agriculture, as it was done long years before the Norman Conquest, could have been bettered.

This claim may sound fantastic, and there are no maps and few records, beyond the boundaries of the old parishes themselves, to substantiate it. But a number of deeds or transcripts of them have survived by which a Saxon king granted an estate in land to a vassal, in which the limits of the land granted are defined by reference to prominent features in the landscape—roads, brooks, stones, trees, cultivation-marks, and so on.[1] In places, these landmarks can still be identified, and an exceptional example is provided by a charter of Edward the Elder, son of Alfred the Great, to his vassal Tata, confirming a grant of land at Hardwell, by

---

[1] In a later century, one such was 'so far as the beech tree wherefrom the thief hung' ('. . . usque ad fagum ubi latro pependit'): *Cart. Mon. S. Petri Gloucestriae*, i, p. 205 (Rolls Series; A.D. 1121).

Compton Beauchamp, in Berkshire, dated A.D. 903, a translation of which runs as follows:

Bounds of Hordwell

On Swinbroc first, thence up from Swinbroc on to rush-slade, from this rush-slade's corner foreagainst Hordwell-way, thence along this way until it comes to the Ickenild way, then from these ways upon the old wood-way, then from that wood-way by east Tellesburgh to a corner, then from that corner to a goreacre, thence along its furrow to the head of a headland, and which headland goes into the land, then right on to the stone on ridgeway, then on west to a gore along the furrow to its head, then adown to fernhills slade, thence on a furrow in the acre nearer the lince, then on that lince at fernhills slade southward from that lince to its head, forward then on a furrow to a stonerow, then right on to the ridge-way, thence thereon to a goreacre at its head, the goreacre being within that land, thence along a furrow till it comes to a corner, thence from that corner forward on a furrow till it comes to a headland, which headland is within the land, then on the Ickenild way by Tellesburg west, thence north over the Ickenild way to Sican-well, thence over a furlong right on to an elder-bed at Hedgehill's brook corner, along this brook till it comes to two goreacres, which goreacres are within that land, thence on a headland to its head, then right onto Red-cliffe on Swinbroc, then along this brook on that rush-slade.[1]

Nearly all the features named in this thousand-year-old grant for an identification of the area are still to be seen. The estate extends to some 380 acres, and it lies in one of those parishes figured in the map on page 25 which run from the Vale of the White Horse southward to the top of the chalk downs. A glance at the map of Hardwell itself shows how its layout conforms to that of the parish in which it lies—a strip of land nearly 2½ miles from north to south, and nowhere more than 500 yards in width. The rush-slade on Swinbrook has gone, destroyed, no doubt, by later land-drainage, but Hardwell Way, the old road to the farm, cut deep by the usage of centuries at its southern end, still leads on to the Icknield Way, and the old wood-way can be traced in a double hedge going up the hill on the east side of Tellesburg, a great earthwork known to-day as Hardwell Camp. From this point, some of the cultivation-marks—gore acres,[2] furrows, and headlands—have to be conjectured, but a boundary fence of later times carries their line on to the Ridgeway. The stone on the Ridgeway has gone, but the boundaries of the land can be traced farther south to Fernhills Slade, now Pinsgoose Covert, and so back by the stonerow to the Ridgeway, and thence by a series of gore acres and corners, past the west side of Tellesburg, to the Icknield Way again. The Sican Well has not been identified, but

---

[1] *Chron. Monast. Abingd.* i. 56–59.

[2] Gore acres are triangular pieces of ploughland arising in corners where the ploughed area is not rectangular. See p. 35.

Hedgehill's corner and its elder-bed are there, followed by the
gore acres and headland, no longer under the plough, leading
back to Swinbrook and the starting-point.

Hardwell Farm today forms part of the Craven Estate, and
except at one point, where one of the fields has been extended to
a road made within the last 150 years, its boundaries now are the
same as when Edward the Elder confirmed his grant to his vassal
Tata, in 903, and how long before that no one can tell. Much

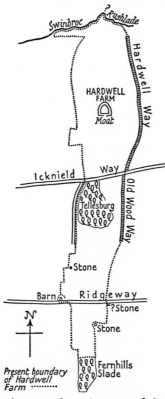

has happened since then to alter the use of the land in England in
many places. Woodland and waste have been taken into cultivation; great open fields have been partitioned; land which was
ploughed for centuries to produce bread food before the importa-
tion of grain began, is now grassland for the practice of dairying;
on the other hand, the drainage of the Fens has made it possible
to turn much wet grazing into fertile arable land. Everywhere,
the country has been cut up by the construction of roads. But
Hardwell stands today as a proof of the high pitch to which the
Saxon farmers had brought their farming skill, for, after a
thousand years, no better way than theirs has been found for the
planning of this bit of England for the practice of husbandry.

III. THE OPEN FIELDS

THE Royal Charter by which Hardwell was granted suggests, very definitely, the existence of a highly developed
agriculture in pre-Norman times. There is mention of
headlands, furrows, gore acres, all of them terms connected with arable cultivation of no primitive kind. Indeed, it is
certain that the practice of crop-production had been carried to
a far higher pitch than that of live-stock farming. Not for nothing
has bread been called the staff of life, and whereas the live stock
of Saxon times, and for many centuries after, got what living they
could on the natural grasses of the waste lands and open woodlands, grain crops were grown at an early date with much care
and no little skill. Thus, it may be said that farming in these days
centred in the plough, and to understand the evolution of the
farming system and the social life of the community which lived
by it, some knowledge of the plough and of its work is necessary.

To secure conditions favourable to the growth of a crop, some
stirring of the soil is needed, to produce a loose surface in which
the seed can be deposited and buried, safe from the attack of
birds, protected from the heat of the sun, and in contact with the
subsoil moisture. It may be conjectured that the first implement
devised for this surface cultivation was something fashioned from
a branch or a stag's antler, which was used as is the modern hoe;
the tiller struck it into the ground and pulled it through the soil
towards himself. At a very early date, however, the advantage of
something which man could thrust or draw through the soil was
realized. Even today, tools such as the breast-plough and the
caschrom are still in use in remote parts of the British Isles, heavy
wooden beams attached at an obtuse angle to a stout block of
wood, iron-shod and pointed, which is thrust through the soil,
stirring it to the depth of a few inches.

The first plough made to be pulled instead of pushed resembled
the caschrom with the addition of a beam attached to its upper
arm. The point was drawn through the soil by power, human or
four-legged, attached to this beam, while the ploughman held the
end of the upper arm and used the leverage which it gave him to
keep the point at the required depth in the ground.[1] Next an iron
point, the ploughshare, was added to the lower arm, and this
simple structure was superseded, sooner or later, by an implement
the same in principle, but built of timbers put together so as to
give maximum mechanical advantage to the draught of the ox-

---

[1] Gow distinguishes four types in the evolution of the plough.

PLATE 5

a. THE CASCHROM (SKYE, 1936)

b. ROMANO-BRITISH PLOUGH FROM PIERCEBRIDGE (BRITISH MUSEUM)

PLATE 6

a. ANGLO-SAXON PLOUGH (HARLEIAN MS.)

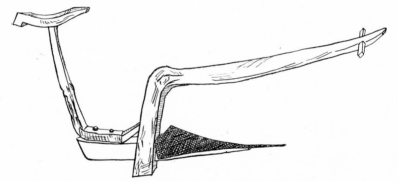

b. ARAB PLOUGH (TWENTIETH CENTURY)

team attached to the beam, and to the ploughman's control at the handle, or tail, attached to its other end. Such an implement may be seen in use today amongst the tribesmen of Palestine and else-where, and, with modifications to suit local taste or needs, it is the plough of the husbandmen of Castile and of other districts of Spain.[1] If the bronze model of a ploughman with an ox-team, found at the Romano-British settlement at Piercebridge, county Durham, is evidence, this type of plough, the scratch-plough, *aratrum*, was in common use in this country at the date of the Roman occupation. It did nothing more than break the surface of the soil, producing a few inches of fine mould, and upon this the seed-corn was broadcast.

At an early date, however, an important advance was made in the efficiency of the implement, by the addition of a mould-board on one side, or sometimes on either side. It had the effect of throwing the soil broken up by the ploughshare into a series of ridges and furrows. Varro, and after him Pliny, mention ploughs thus equipped, which were used, they say, to bury the seed-corn.[2] Palladius, writing in the fourth century A.D., describes a type of *aratrum* equipped with 'ears', which was used on flat land to throw the land into ridges with intervening furrows, into which the water could drain.[3]

The next addition to the primitive plough was the coulter. It is obvious that an implement equipped with share and mould-board would move with difficulty through ground overgrown with weeds and grass. And so the coulter was devised, which was a knife, as its name implies, fixed in the beam and descending into the ground just above the share. Its purpose was to cut the turf and any rubbish above it, so as to give a free passage to the share which followed. 'My coulter shall carve through and cleanse out the furrows,' wrote William Langland some 600 years ago.[4]

The addition of the mould-board, which antedated, probably, the use of the coulter, although both are mentioned by Pliny, marked a great advance in the technique of cultivation, and the implement thus compounded gives us the common plough as we know it to-day. It was known in Britain during the Roman occupation, and its use became general in the centuries that followed, as the penetration of the country by Germanic invaders proceeded. If the plough-beam was supported, sometimes, at its fore-end on a pair of wheels, these were merely an aid to the

[1] *The Castilian Plough: a Preliminary Study.* Robert and Barbara Aitken. Anales de Museo del Pueblo Español (Madrid, 1935).
[2] Varro, *Res Rusticae*, i. 29, § 2; Pliny, *Natural History*, xviii, § 180.
[3] Palladius, *De Agricultura*, i. 42.
[4] *Piers the Plowman*, vi. 106.

ploughman in regulating the depth of his furrow; they involved no principle of construction or action.[1] The suggestion offered here is that it was the evolution of the mould-board, not the attachment of the wheels, which led to the ploughing of the long furrow, to strip farming, and to the Open Fields.

The classical authors described the mould-board as an ear, and Gow's illustration of it taken from a relief on the pedestal of a statue of Demeter shows it as a short, fin-like attachment, projecting outwards behind the ploughshare.[2] It caught the soil stirred by the share and threw it into a ridge on one side, or into ridges on either side if there were two of them. Thus, it would bury corn previously scattered on the surface, or it would make a slight furrow into which the seed would fall if broadcast after ploughing. As it evolved, its length increased, and in the form of a wooden board, a few inches in depth, fixed on edge behind the ploughshare, it ran backwards and outwards for 2 or 3 feet, at a slight angle to the line of the plough.

In action, the plough then worked as follows. First came the coulter, making a vertical cut in the soil to the depth to which it was desired to plough, say 3 or 4 inches. Immediately behind the coulter came the ploughshare, a flat half-arrowhead, which made a horizontal cut below the ground of its own width, say 6 inches. Immediately behind the share followed the mould-board, which, being set at a slight angle to the direction of the plough, turned over the slice cut by the coulter and the share and laid it alongside, to the right, parallel to the direction of the plough. In principle, the plough is the same today. Indeed, except that generally it is now made entirely of iron, instead of mainly of wood, it is almost the same in detail.

Now, the mould-board is attached on the right-hand side, and the furrow-slice is turned over to the right side as the plough is drawn through the ground. It follows that if the plough were to return down the field the second furrow-slice would be piled against the first, the two forming a ridge with a strip of unploughed ground underneath it. The third journey would turn a slice away from the second, while the fourth would throw another towards the third, forming a second ridge. To plough across a field in this way would produce nothing more than a series of ridges, each overlying a strip of unploughed ground and separated from each other by a furrow of the width of two slices.

Clearly, such work would be useless, and so, instead of ploughing backwards and forwards right across the field, the work is done in sections. The field is marked off into parallel widths,

---

[1] See p. 11, *ante*.   [2] Gow, op. cit., p. 253.

PLATE 7

Mould-board   Share Coulter

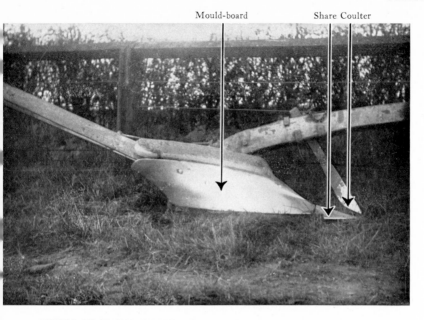

a. SWING PLOUGH, SHOWING COULTER AND MOULD-BOARD

b. THE PLOUGH IN ACTION

PLATE 8

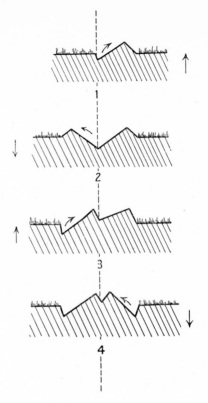

1

2

3

4

a. DIAGRAM OF PLOUGHING A RIDGE

b. THE RIDGE COMPLETED

called 'lands',[1] of 22 yards or less, and the ploughman then ploughs a ridge down the middle of the first land.

The ridge is made thus: The ploughman ploughs a straight furrow the full length of the land, laying a furrow-slice to the right (Fig. 1), and returning in the same track, he deepens it and lays a second furrow-slice away from the first one, on the other side (Fig. 2). This is called 'Opening a top'. Then the ploughman turns his team again and goes down along the outer edge of the second furrow-slice, just turned, throwing it inward again (Fig. 3), and then he comes back once more along the edge of the first one, throwing it, too, inward against the other, thus closing the top and forming the ridge (Fig. 4).

After that he ploughs round and round his ridge, turning all the furrow-slices on one side of it one way, and all those on the other side the other way, towards his ridge, until he has ploughed the 11 yards on either side. He then ploughs a ridge in the middle of the next 'land', and when he has ploughed his 11 yards on either side of that, he goes on to the third, and so on, until the field is finished.

From this description and the accompanying illustrations, it will be clear that every furrow-slice is turned over towards the ridge in the middle of the 'land'. It follows that where two 'lands' join, the last furrow-slices of each are turned away one from another, and this produces the 'furrow' which is such an obvious line of demarcation between the 'lands' in any ploughed field. The plough has dug out two furrow-slices and laid them in opposite directions.

Now, if the ploughman should repeat this work, year after year, marking out the field in the same 'lands' every time, this ploughing-out of the furrows and piling-up of the slices against the ridges will lift the soil from the outsides towards the middle of the 'land', and it produces, ultimately, the effect of a regular rise and fall over the field across the direction of the ploughing, to which is given the name of 'ridge and furrow'. It should be noted, however, that ploughing with the fixed-mouldboard plough does not necessarily produce this effect. By setting out the ridges for this year's ploughing on the site of last year's furrows, the soil which was ploughed up last year can be ploughed back again, and the contour of the field remains as Nature made it.

But it was customary to keep the land in high ridges. The removal of excessive moisture from the soil is an important point in arable farming, and water ran readily from the rounded ridges into the furrows. If, at the same time, the 'lands' were laid out up

---

[1] Also 'ridges' or 'rigs' in some places, 'stitches' or 'stetches' in others, and 'selions' in others still.

and down the natural slopes of the field, it was an easy matter to arrange that the furrows should discharge this water into an adjacent ditch. The need for 'high-backed lands', as they are called, was greatest in heavy soils, in which percolation was slow, and this explains the appearance of ridge and furrow on tens of thousands of acres of grassland today, in any district of clay soils, all of which were under the plough in the days when England was self-sufficing in food.[1]

Thus far, we have seen how the use of the fixed-mouldboard plough divided the arable fields into a succession of 'lands'. It has been said that the width of these 'lands' was commonly 22 yards, but there was no rule about it, though very few were wider, and this limit was set merely by convenience. As the number of the furrow-slices laid up against the ridge increased, the oxen or horses of the plough-team had to walk a little farther each time that they turned at the end of the 'land' before starting back again, and when it was necessary to walk 22 yards, it was more economical of time and energy to set out another 'land' and start again. The bottom limit of width was set by the nature of the soil and of the situation. On heavy, flat land, where drainage was difficult, 'lands' might be no more than 3 yards wide, as on such soils they still are, in many parts of Suffolk and Essex, for example, to provide more frequent furrows in which the water could collect; and 'lands' were narrow for the same reason, often, on steep hill-sides, on which springs of water were apt to break out.

'Lands' were not always laid out and ploughed straight. Commonly enough, grassland today shows ridge-and-furrow of a perfect reversed 'S' shape, and here and there, 'lands' laid out in this form, no one can say how long ago, are still being ploughed on the curve. The reason for this layout is uncertain. It has been suggested that the object was to reduce the effective fall, and thus to prevent water running off the land in times of heavy rainfall so fast as to carry the soil with it; but 'S' lands are found in fields almost flat. It is suggested, also, that the bullock-team of eight oxen, yoked in pairs, would need an immense headland on which to turn at the end of a straight furrow, but by approaching it at an obtuse angle a narrower headland would suffice. This explanation, perhaps, is the more plausible.

Two other features of the practice of ploughing must be mentioned. It is obvious that the 'lands' cannot be ploughed right up to the boundary of the field if that boundary be a fence or a stream. The plough-team and plough must have room to turn at either

---

[1] In arable land today, where they might be expected, high-backed lands are less common. The introduction of under-draining with pipes has removed the need for deep furrows, while the use of machinery calls for a more level surface.

PLATE 9

'S' LANDS, APPLETON, BERKS.

end, and in fact they need some 15 or 20 feet. This margin at top and bottom is called, not inappropriately, the 'headland', in most parts of the country. In east Kent it is still called the 'foraker' (fore-acre), and the same term, *Voracker*, was in use in medieval Germany;[1] in Latin terriers it was *forera*. The headland itself was ploughed lengthways across the lands' ends when the rest of the field was finished.

Again, not all fields are rectangles, and where the two side boundaries are not parallel the outside lands on the far side will make a rough triangle, known as a 'gore', running into their headlands at an acute angle.

For reasons which will appear presently the arable fields under the open-field system were, for the most part, very large, running into hundreds of acres. The importance of using the slope of the ground to secure drainage has been mentioned as a controlling factor in the layout of the 'lands', and as these great fields were rarely, if ever, flat, or of the same contour throughout, it followed that the direction of the 'lands' in the field had to be varied from spot to spot. A layout might begin on a slope north and south, which tended, as 'land' followed 'land', to turn east and west. And so, at a given point, greater advantage could be taken of the slope by breaking off and starting a new layout of 'lands' going east and west, at right angles to the first set, until some new tendency in the slope of the field called for another change in the orientation of the 'lands'. Even where the fall was uniform, a break had to be made, now and again, in a long run of 'lands', for convenience of access. Further, there was a limit to the length of furrow which the team could plough before needing the relief which it got in stopping and turning on the headland, and this, too, had its effect upon the grouping of the 'lands'.

And so the big Open Field was composed not of parallel 'lands' stretching from one side to the other, but of many compact blocks of 'lands' of no uniform size but each block of such number and lying in such direction as the circumstances of the field might dictate. To these blocks of 'lands' the name 'furlong' is given, or, in some places, 'shott', or 'flatt', and the big field, ploughed ready for sowing, presented the effect of a patchwork quilt, each patch representing a furlong and its component 'lands'. (See Maps II, III, IV.)

Much has been written of the length of the furlong—the 'furrow-long'. We are told that it was 220 yards. We are told, also, that the width of each 'land' within the furlong was 22 yards and thus was derived the statute acre, which constituted a day's ploughing for one team.[2] In practice such conditions were rarely

---

[1] Seebohm, F., *The English Village Community*, pp. 5 and 381.   [2] See p. 101, *post*.

found. The configuration of the big fields, the consistency of the soil within them, and the provision of access to the different parts of them often made it impossible, in practice, to divide them into the theoretically orthodox 'lands', one acre in extent, 220 yards long and 22 yards wide; and even when horses displaced the slower-moving oxen and light iron ploughs took the place of the heavier wooden ones, it was not often possible to plough so much as an acre in a day.[1] The most constant dimension, probably, in any particular district was the width, dictated by the need for drainage, but in length 'lands' were anything, and not infrequently they exceeded the 'furrow-long' of 220 yards.

Here and there a furlong had to be fitted into an awkward piece of ground between two others, and the lands might be less than a quarter of the textbook length. These short 'lands' were often called 'butts', and all over the fields, where furlong joined furlong, or where the boundaries were reached, 'gores', or 'gore acres' as they were sometimes called, were frequent.

It is now easy to understand the delineation of King Edward the Elder's grant of land, in 903, to his vassal Tata.[2] As we walk its bounds we see the 'lands' running up- and downhill, where the furrows come up to the boundary; we see the end of the furlong where we strike a headland, and we see the boundary turning inward or outward where we find a gore. We realize, too, how ancient are the origins of the practice of husbandry today, under which these features of farming still are found, or, alternatively, how far advanced in it were the English people, already, in those days before the Conquest. Let us try, now, to discover the system of land-tenure under which their practice was applied.

The origin of the system is lost in the days of prehistory, and any attempt to describe it can be based only upon conjecture and upon the interpretation of its earliest manifestations in recorded times. It must be remembered that communal systems of cultivation were not peculiar to Britain and to neighbouring European countries from which Britain was colonized. Farming in Open Fields under conditions resembling our own was general all over the plains of Europe and central Asia and it persists today over large areas in some countries. Here we are concerned with its origins and evolution in Britain and more than one theory has been advanced to explain the 'Saxon' system of land-tenure, all of them ably supported by their authors. It is not proposed to

[1] Records extending over many years kept at the Agricultural Economics Research Institute, Oxford, show that a day's ploughing varies between ⅔ acre and ¾ acre.
[2] See p. 27, *ante*.

PLATE 10

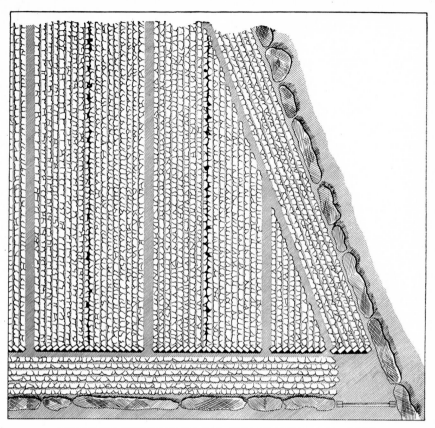

DIAGRAM SHOWING LANDS, HEADLANDS, AND GORE

examine them here, but those who are interested can consult the originals.[1] There are grounds for believing that the system was introduced into England, at various times before recorded history, by invaders or colonists from northern Europe. From the evidence of their settlements they were a valley people, that is to say they inhabited sites in the plains and valleys, even though their cultivation extended up the hill-sides and downs. Whether or no they had a tribal organization or what their social system was cannot be stated. It must suffice that they established themselves, ultimately, in village communities, each one occupying the land which would give it fuel and water, meadow land, plough-land, and grazing sufficient to produce the sustenance that it needed.

For in the earliest times, and for long after, the village communities were working to feed themselves and their families. Notwithstanding a little sale and barter, the idea of commercial farming in the modern sense was quite unknown. Each little human settlement was almost entirely self-contained, growing and fashioning nearly everything which it required to satisfy its needs; and what was true of the community as a whole was true, in the main, of each of its members. It follows, of course, that there was no division of the village community into several categories, social and economic, such as have been evolved since, as, for example, husbandmen and tradesmen, large farmers and small-holders, milk-producers and market-gardeners, stockbreeders and graziers. Each member was farming to produce sustenance for his family and nothing more, and for this the needs of all were the same. And so it follows that there was no demand for land beyond that which the village community must occupy to supply itself, for in the absence of opportunity for the sale of surplus produce there was no inducement to any member of it to occupy more than that which would satisfy his own needs.

From that which has been said here already about the natural state of the country, it is evident that the first people to abandon the nomad life and to form permanent settlements had to reclaim the land, from which their living was to be derived, from a condition of forest and scrub. The steps by which this was done are matters only for speculation. Whether the first settlers were a pastoral people living mainly on the produce of their live stock (like the Masai of East Africa today), who gradually increased their knowledge of crops and tillage until corn-growing came to equal stock-raising in its importance in their economy, or whether they were immigrants who had already a well-developed tradition of plough husbandry, we do not know. There is the authority of

[1] See Introduction.

Tacitus for the statement that the Germanic tribesmen of whom he wrote had emerged from the nomadic state by the end of the first century of the Christian era. There was land and to spare around each community, and he tells us that they cultivated fresh fields every year.[1] This was no more nor less than the practice, manifested somewhat extravagantly, of resting the cultivated land with a fallow. Continuous cropping of the soil removes its fertility faster than the processes of Nature can replace it. The growth and decay of weeds, grass, and other herbage, the disintegration of the subsoil, and other processes, mechanical, chemical, and biological, accumulate plant-food slowly in the land, and right up to the present time it is the practice of farmers to leave the land un-cropped for a season from time to time, or to crop it with some-thing and in such a way as to increase rather than to reduce its fertility. If so much may be inferred from the brief record of Tacitus, his Germanic tribes followed a course well known in parts of Britain even in recent times, by which a piece of land was selected and cultivated for corn for a season, and it was then abandoned to recuperate while another piece was laid under tribute during the next year, and so on, presumably, until the circuit of available land was complete, and the area first broken had to be cultivated again. This system was followed under the name of 'run-rig' in Scotland, and probably in parts of the north of England.

What were the implements with which the soil was tilled? The plough itself was well known, but whether the Germans of whom Tacitus wrote were equipped with the mouldboard plough, or with the more primitive scratch-plough, we do not know, nor how they divided the land among themselves according to the number of their cultivators. Stubbs's explanation that each free-man of the Mark was entitled to a share in the land of the com-munity, and that the land was definitely apportioned,[2] explains nothing, and Maitland's statement that it was allotted in alternate strips to each man in rotation, with the deliberate intention of securing equality even at the sacrifice of economy and efficiency, seems unlikely, to say the least of it, in that or in any other age. Nor does his explanation gain anything from its restatement by later writers.[3] Seebohm and Fowler have suggested a more natural basis in the idea of co-aration and practical utility, and it is in these directions, probably, rather than in political theory, that the explanation of the origin of strip farming in Open Fields must be sought.

It is not difficult to surmise how the continuous cultivation of the land of the communities was evolved, or how its bounds were

---

[1] See p. 3, *ante.*   [2] See p. 3, *ante.*   [3] See pp. 5-7, *ante.*

fixed. When the tribes were small and the land available for each was unlimited, the reasons for the practice of breaking fresh ground yearly, so as to take the maximum advantage of stored-up fertility, are obvious. But there would be limits to this practice as the communities grew, imposed partly by the practical necessity of finding land within a reasonable distance of the settlement, and partly by the competition of neighbouring communities for the land. And so a time would come when the land must be put under tribute more often, until, ultimately, a point was reached at which no more than half of it could be rested in fallow. In this way, probably, that which is known as the 'two-field' farming system was evolved, under which one half of the ploughland of the community was cropped and the other half was fallowed, in alternate years.

Now, as to the distribution of the land amongst the tribesmen, for which an adequate explanation has still to be offered: the suggestion made here is that the system of allocation by a multitude of small scattered strips was dictated by the common life of the community and by the manifestation of it in its daily work upon the land. In this the plough played a predominant part. It is the purpose of this study to show that the practice of farming in great Open Fields under a common system, rather than in compact inclosures in individual occupation, was natural and inevitable in primitive communities farming only to produce their own subsistence, and that it was evolved along with the mould-board plough, with which, and with the work that it does, every one can acquaint himself by observation in the fields today. Indeed, the Open Fields could only have attained their final form in association with the mouldboard plough.

We have seen that the effect of tillage by the mouldboard plough is to throw the field into a succession of ridges and furrows called 'lands'; that the direction of these 'lands' is determined by the slopes of the different parts of the field; that their length is decided partly by the same factor of contour and partly, also, by the need of the plough-team for periodical halts; that their width is controlled partly by the need for recurrent drainage furrows and partly by the desire to save time in turning the plough on the headland. We have seen, too, that in the absence of opportunity for commercial farming the amount of land cleared for ploughing around the settlement would be no more than that which was needed to supply enough corn, in a normal season, for the number of families of which it was composed. How was this land allotted amongst the people of the village?

In the first place, it must be remembered that in those early days, whenever they were, and indeed for long centuries after, life was a pretty grim business. The task of keeping body and soul together was hazardous, quite apart from the possibility of mis-adventures with hostile neighbours or wild beasts. Men had to support themselves and their families by the work of their hands, and in earliest days much of their time was occupied in rendering services in lieu of rent. Unequipped as they were with anything beyond the simplest aids to manual labour, the extent of land which they were able to handle gave them no more than a bare subsistence in a normal season and very short commons in a bad one. It follows that every minute of their own time was needed for productive work, and their farming system had to dispense with much that in an age of large-scale operations conducted with the aid of machinery and mechanical power is regarded as indis-pensable. For instance, the subdivision of the reclaimed land into fields grouped together to form separate farms was never con-templated by them before the period in which modern history begins. To make and maintain hedges and gates would have meant so much time taken from the cultivation of the land or the tending of live stock; to group fields thus created into farms would have given some members of the village community the advantage of holdings near their homes while entailing upon others the disadvantage of having to walk varying distances to reach theirs. In those days such handicaps could not be compen-sated. To secure protection, shelter, and water the people herded together in the village; there were no homesteads built on or near the remoter parts of the cleared area. With the development in modern times of commercial farming, inequalities in convenience or in productivity between the compact holdings which came to be created could be, and they were, adjusted by differences in rent. No such equalization was possible in the days when farmers were self-sufficient.

And so we get the origin of the Open Fields. They were the clearings in the natural woods and waste made by communities of tillage farmers and occupied by them in large areas, as cleared, without any attempt at subdivision by a process of inclosure. But how was the land in these fields allotted between man and man? We know what was done, but we can only conjecture how and why it was done, and the most probable explanation is to be found *in the action of the plough*. When every one was farming for subsis-tence, every one would follow, naturally enough, the same farming system. The land first cleared for cultivation would be that imme-diately adjacent to the settlement, and upon this the men of the community would go to work, setting out a day's ploughing for each team, side by side. By the end of the working-day each

would have ploughed one or more 'lands', according to the nature
of the soil and the length of the 'lands'. Next day the village
husbandmen would move on, to set out and then to plough the
section of the field next beyond the first day's work, and thus they
would proceed throughout the ploughing season. So, at the finish,
every man would have land ready for sowing which consisted not
of a compact field or group of fields but of a number of narrow
strips, each consisting of one or more 'lands' making up a day's
plough-work, and each of them divided from the next by those
of his neighbours.

An allocation of the Open Field in this way was the natural
consequence of a self-sufficient community following the same
farming system for the same purpose, and cultivating the soil with
the plough. Incidentally, also, it was the fairest, for it gave to each
member an equal share of the near and of the remoter land, and
of the good and of the less good parts of the field if it were not
uniform in every part.

Taking this description of the creation of open-field farming
as a diagram rather than as a picture of that which must have
happened, it is, moreover, a common-sense explanation. Seebohm
quotes, as an analogy, the evidence of ancient Welsh laws before
the tenth century for the practice of communal cultivation with
teams of eight oxen.[1] The first 'land' ploughed, he says, was for
the ploughman, the second for the owner of the plough, the third
for the owner of the sod ox, the fourth for the owner of the sward
ox, the fifth for the driver of the team, and so on for the owners
of the other oxen. The process repeated would give each parti-
cipant in the communal team and its work a farm holding scattered in strips over all the cultivated land of the community, and
the diffusion would be proportionate to the number of teams in
the village.

There is ample evidence, both in Domesday and in other
records, for the practice of co-aration, that is to say of cultivation
with communal teams. For example:

Each free tenant, who has a whole plough or some part of a plough, ought
to come with his plough or with his part, if he has not a whole plough, to
one ploughing boon-work at the sowing in Lent, and each one that has a
plough ought to plough an acre at each boon-work, and he who has less than
a whole plough shall plough according to what animals he shall have joined
to the plough.[2]

In practice, however, the same result of scattered holdings would
be achieved, whether the community were working with pair-ox
teams individually owned, or with two-, four-, or eight-ox teams

[1] Seebohm, F., op. cit., p. 120.
[2] *Battle Abbey Custumals* (Camden Society), p. 148, Extent of 5 Edw. II.

provided collectively, and whether the tenants were working for the lord, as above, or for themselves.

Such a system of distribution of the land would provide without difficulty or inequity for the growth of the community. As the numbers of the husbandmen increased, the area of the Open Field would be extended, as we know it was, by reclamation from the waste, and the new-comers would get their shares in the distribution of the land by the addition of their ploughs or of their beasts to the common task. In the Domesday Survey there is constant reference to the number of ploughs in the parishes. 'There is land for six ploughs' is the entry for the parish of Laxton, co. Notts., meaning, of course, cultivated land. At an earlier date it might have read 'for four ploughs'; at a later, 'for eight ploughs'. It is easy to visualize the growth of the cultivated area and the automatic allocation of land in scattered strips, as the community grew and plough was added to plough. This process suggests, of course, that in the early days of tillage people did not acquire rights over particular strips. In a stabilized community, 'lands' might be occupied in the same order year after year, but the extension of the Open Fields to accommodate a growing population would vary the allocation on the admission of each new-comer. At some time or other, however, individual occupation of particular strips was secured, though how we do not know, but it was often before the limits of the extension of the Open Field had been reached. It will appear, presently, that new furlongs were sometimes taken in from the waste, in which some of the earlier-defined holdings had no strips, and a time came when encroachments on the waste were made in the form of inclosures, occupied in severalty, instead of in furlongs added to the Open Field.[1]

We have now reached the point at which it can be said that the ploughland portion of the early farmer's holding consisted of strips representing one day's work and made up of one or more 'lands', scattered amongst those of his neighbours in the furlongs which composed the Open Field of his village. In the earliest days it is probable that the strips he occupied were not the same ones year after year. Later, however, perhaps when the fields had reached the limit of expansion, perhaps before, he acquired continuous occupation of the same strips. The extent of the ploughland holding of each ordinary villager must have been more or less the same, being so much as would give him, at once, occupation and subsistence. By the time that records begin, however, a good deal of inequality appears, and this will be dealt with later.

Before going on to the next stage in this description of open-

[1] See p. 104, *post.*

field farming, the task must be faced of challenging some widely accepted statements about it. Most of them derive from Seebohm, to whom students of agricultural history owe so much.

In the first place, he seems to confuse the *strips* with the *lands*, and he assumes that the typical strip was an acre or a half-acre 'land':

> These strips are in fact roughly cut acres of the proper shape for ploughing. For the furlong is the 'furrow-long', i.e. the length of the drive of the plough before it is turned. The word 'rood' corresponds with as many furrows in the ploughing as are contained in the breadth of one rod. And four of these roods lying side by side made the acre strip in the open fields. . . . There are 'long' strips and 'short' strips. But taking them generally, and comparing them with the statute acre, it will be seen at once that the normal strip was identical with it.[1]

In fact, as has been pointed out already, the size of the 'land' depended entirely upon the nature of the soil; on light soils it was fully 22 yards wide, but on heavy soils it might not exceed 3 yards, in order to provide more frequent drainage furrows. On flat land it might run the full 'furrow-long' of 220 yards and more; on land sharply contoured or in awkward corners it might not extend to one-quarter of that length. These facts are illustrated in a later chapter;[2] suffice it here to point out that there was not necessarily a connexion between the 'land', the strip, and the acre. Nor was the day's work, that is the strip, of however many 'lands' it might be composed, necessarily one acre or half an acre. Commonly it was less, as records show, nor is this surprising, for even in these days, with horses stepping faster than oxen and iron ploughs of lighter draught than the old wooden ones, to plough an acre is a long day's work.[3] Records show that, in fact, both the strips and the 'lands' composing them were of many shapes and sizes, and the 'acre', as the term is used in manorial records, was the measure of a day's work rather than of the strip.

In the second place, Seebohm says that the strips were divided one from another by balks of unploughed turf:

> These strips, common to open fields all over England, were separated from each other not by hedges, but by green balks of unploughed turf. . . . In many places the open fields were formerly divided into half acre strips. A turf balk separated every two roods in the ploughing.[4]

In support of this statement he quotes the ancient Welsh laws mentioned above, in which it is said that there were *two furrows* between each strip, and he interprets this as 'an unploughed balk

---

[1] Seebohm, op. cit., p. 2.   [2] See p. 101, *post*.
[3] See p. 36, fn.   [4] Op. cit., pp. 2–3.

of turf two furrows wide'.[1] He finds further evidence in *Piers the Plowman*:

> Now is perkyn and his pilgrymes to the plowe faren:
> To erie his halue acre holpyn hym manye,
> Dikeres and delueres digged up the balkes.[2]

And lastly he refers to a terrier of the West Field of Cambridge, in which he says that the names of the owners and occupiers of all the strips are given, the strips being divided by balks.[3]

Seebohm's statement that the strips in the Open Fields were divided by balks has been adopted without question by most later writers, and it is generally accepted.[4] But it should be noted that Dr. Fowler, who has made a particular study of the Open Fields of Bedfordshire, records that he has never found any indications of unploughed balks in that county.[5]

There can be little doubt that Seebohm's inference from this evidence is not justified. When a field is ploughed in 'lands', the junction of any two is marked by furrow-slices turned away from each other towards their respective ridges, leaving the space, two furrows wide, to which the old Welsh law refers. What Perkyn's friends were doing when they 'digged up the balkes' is explained later.[6] It is clear that his balks were not boundary marks between strips, for as such they would have been jealously preserved in their integrity and certainly not dug up.

As to the Cambridge terrier, it is very difficult to follow Seebohm's conclusions. He says that 'the balks were disappearing, and the strips, though still remembered as strips, were becoming merged in larger portions, so that they lie together, *sine balca*'. A recent examination of this manuscript[7] revealed, in fact, that balks are seldom mentioned, and then only as important boundaries. There is no indication that they divide strips, and the phrase *sine balca* could not be found. The following are typical references to balks contained in this document:

Selion lying next the balk which divides the field of Cambridge from the field of Girton. . . .

9 selions next the field of Girton, a certain wide balk intervening. . . .

15 selions of land of Bartholomew Burghash, the weie [way] balk intervening. . . .

---

[1] Seebohm, op. cit., p. 119.   [2] *Vision of Piers the Plowman*, passus vi, ll. 107–9.
[3] Op. cit., p. 19.
[4] See, for example, Vinogradoff, P., 'Feudalism', *Cambridge Mediaeval History*, vol. iii, p. 474, in which he says that the arable strips 'were marked off by narrow lines of turf called balks'; and Lipson, E., *The Economic History of England*, vol. i, p. 62, 'a multitude of strips, divided by narrow pieces of unploughed turf, termed *balks*'; and many other writers upon the Open Fields.
[5] *Quarto Memoirs of the Bedfordshire Record Society*, vol. ii, pt. i, p. 9 (1928).
[6] See p. 99, *post*.   [7] Cambridge University Library, Add. MS. 2601.

These references, and all the others in which balks are mentioned, are evidently to parish boundaries or to common ways.
Indeed, there could be no conceivable reason for so clumsy and
extravagant a means of strip demarcation. The process of land-
reclamation for tillage must have been very laborious, and a loss
of cultivable soil representing, in heavy land, so much as 12 per
cent. of the total area of the field would be serious, and, more than
this, the balk would be a nursery of weeds. In the open-field
parish of Elmstone Hardwicke, in Gloucestershire, there was no
trace of dividing balks, but one of the reasons for the inclosure
which was effected so recently as 1914 was that some of the
farmers had abandoned the cultivation of their strips, and the
encroachment of the weeds from these was hindering other
farmers in the cultivation of those adjacent.

Next, a common complaint in the proceedings in the manorial
courts is that against the man who encroached upon his neighbour's strip, which could not have happened if there were an
intervening balk. In this connexion it is interesting to quote Bloch
on the Open Fields of France:

> De parcelle à parcelle toujours, souvent de groupe de parcelles à groupe
> de parcelles, point d'autre limite que tout au plus quelques bornes, enfoncées
> dans le sol, parfois un sillon laissé inculte, plus souvent encore une ligne
> purement idéale. Tentation bien dangereuse offerte à ceux que la langue
> paysanne appelait du nom pittoresque de 'mangeurs de raies'! Un soc de
> charrue promené, plusieurs années durant, un peu au-delà de la démarcation
> légitime, et voilà un champ agrandi de plusieurs sillons (ou 'raies'), c'est-à-
> dire d'une quantité de terre qui, pour peu, comme c'est généralement le cas,
> que la pièce soit longue, représente un gain fort appréciable. On cite telle
> parcelle qui s'accrût ainsi, en une soixantaine d'années, de plus du tiers de
> sa contenance primitive. Ce 'vol', 'le plus subtil et le plus difficile à prouver
> qu'il puisse y avoir', dénoncé par les prédicateurs du moyen âge comme par
> les magistrats de l'Ancien Régime, était — est peut-être encore — un des
> signes sociaux caractéristiques de ces 'rases campagnes'. . . .[1]

At Averham Hall, near Newark, Nottinghamshire, built in the
Open Fields in the seventeenth century, there hangs a great picture of the house and its surroundings, painted in the year 1720,
the foreground of which is a tillage field. It is thrown up in 'lands',
with nothing but wide furrows between each. And nearly 200
years earlier the compilers of the Book of Common Prayer thought
it desirable to repeat the condemnation by the Law of Moses of
those who removed their neighbour's landmarks.[2] Clearly such
were not balks.

Again, the grasslands of England, marked as they are with the

---

[1] Bloch, op. cit., p. 38.   [2] Deut. xxvii. 17.

ridge and furrow of former arable cultivation, may be searched
from one end of the country to the other without showing so much
as a trace of these so-called balks between the lands. And finally,
in the few Open Fields which have survived in arable cultivation
to recent or to the present times—Elmstone Hardwicke, Eakring,
Laxton, and the parishes of the Isle of Axholme—there is no trace
of anything that even resembles a turf balk dividing one man's
strip from his neighbours'.

At Westcote, between Burford and Stow-on-the-Wold, a parish
on the Oxfordshire–Gloucestershire border, the arable land has
never been inclosed, though farming in common has long since
disappeared. Much of it is divided by grass balks, but most of
the parcels are large, having the appearance of small fields rather
than of strips, and they suggest that there has been a good deal
of consolidation at some time, the balks taking the place of hedges
as boundary marks.

Some writers have been misled by the practice, once pursued
on some of the heaviest clay-land in England which has long since
gone out of cultivation, of leaving a wide strip between each of
the narrow 'lands' unploughed to facilitate more efficient drainage, regarding this as evidence for dividing-balks.[1] Examples of
these 'green furrows', as they are called, may be found on the lias
clay south of Stratford-on-Avon, but they were not divisions
between different tenancies. This land was so wet and imper-
vious that it could only be tilled at all by ploughing it up in
little high and narrow 'lands', with a wide space between each
into which the water could drain and where, in flat parts, it
could lie.

A possible explanation of the idea that an unploughed turf balk
divided each strip from the next may be found in a practice, enjoined upon the tenants of certain manors, governing the cultivation of the fallow field. Constant ploughing of the 'lands' towards
a central ridge produces their characteristic 'high-backed' appearance. But it was undesirable, for obvious reasons, to go on piling
up soil on the ridge indefinitely, and so the opportunity was taken
in the year in which the field lay fallow to reverse the process. For
the first two ploughings the lands would be set out so that the new
ridges were over the old furrows, and the new furrows were on the
tops of the ridges. Ridges and furrows had changed places. At
the third or final ploughing, however, which preceded the wheat
sowing, the original order of the ridges and furrows was re-
established. Now, this casting-down process, which is still the
practice at Laxton today, would fill up and obliterate the dividing
furrow between two neighbours, and when the final ploughing

[1] See Venn, J. A., *Foundations of Agricultural Economics*, p. 32.

PLATE 11

a. THE FURROW

Aerofilms, Ltd.

b. LANDS AND GREEN FURROWS AT CRIMSCOTE, WARWICKSHIRE

was done there might well be a mistake, honest or dishonest, as to its exact position. It was ordained, therefore, in the by-laws of some manors, that when ploughing the fallow field every man should leave unploughed two furrow-widths along the outsides of his strips, until the final ploughing. For example, in the by-laws of the manor of Cardington

It is also Ordered and Agreed that all Persons in this Manor that have Lands in the Common Fields shall lay down Sweard Balks between Every Man's Land and set down three good Stamps [i.e. Stumps] in every Baulke the Baulke to be a full Foot one Person lay down one half and the other halfe To begin this Fallow and then the next Breach and then the last Field the next Fallow on Paine of Forefeiting to the Lord of this Manor by every Person refusing Five Shillings.[1]

Dr. G. Herbert Fowler, to whom we are indebted for this reference, expands it thus:

... To begin [at] this Fallow [Field 3], and then the next Breach [Field 2] and then the last Field [which will then be] the next Fallow [Field 1].

The marking by stumps, he adds, will then identify the boundary between any two neighbours at the end of each fallow, which otherwise might then be difficult to find, and they would plough by the stumps, turning the sod each on to his own 'land'.

There is an entry somewhat similar in the Court Rolls of the manor of Tackley for the year 1631.[2] These unploughed balks were found only every third year, when the field was fallow, and then only during the time of the spring and summer cultivations. After the final ploughing, when the field was once more ready for sowing, the balks had gone and only a broad furrow marked the boundary between neighbour and neighbour.

Clearly, an unploughed balk between each 'land' or even between each strip could have served no useful purpose, while it would have reduced very materially the area available for cultivation. Certainly there were balks in the Open Fields, but they were relatively few and their purpose was not, mainly, the division of holdings. In considering a great field of several hundred acres, divided into furlongs running in all directions and these sub-divided into strips composed of 'lands' in scattered occupation, the problem of access to individual strips presents itself at once. How could Farmer A approach his strips without crossing those of his neighbours? Many strips abutted on the parish roads, but many more did not, and access to these was got in various ways. In

---

[1] *Bedfordshire County Muniments*, Anc. Deed 333, pp. 16–17, Cardington Court Roll 1766.
[2] *Transactions of the North Oxfordshire Archaeological Society*, 1911, p. 69.

many of the big fields, tracts of land occurred, low-lying and often beside a stream (known in some districts as 'sikes'[1]), which were unsuitable for ploughing. Upon them furlongs abutted without headlands, and they were utilized for purposes of access. The headlands of the furlongs, too, were sometimes common ways, upon which the occupiers of abutting strips could turn their teams, and in some places they were called balks. But they ran across the strip-ends, not between the strips, and they were cultivated and sown, not left in turf.[2] Where none of these means of access offered, a 'common balk' was often left, this being neither more nor less than a grass path.

The cumulative evidence against Seebohm's theory of balks of unploughed turf left, as boundary marks, between every strip in the Open Fields, seems conclusive. Since the first issue of this book, however, this conclusion has been challenged, and it is said that in some districts such balks were general, and that they may still be found. While it is not questioned that in the great farming districts of the Midlands and elsewhere the strip boundaries were big open furrows made in the course of ploughing, it is now claimed that there were other districts, the chalk formations of the southern and eastern counties, for example, in which this function was served by unploughed grass balks. In fact, it is suggested by some recent writers that it is a question of geology. Whereas it was necessary, they say, to gather the surface of heavy land into high ridges divided by deep furrows if it is to be drained, the need for conservation of moisture on the light lands, on the other hand, caused farmers in the Open Fields to keep the surface flat, leaving balks to take the place of furrows as strip boundaries. The argument seems based, to some extent, upon a misunderstanding of the operation of ploughing. Except where a one-way plough is in use, an implement very local, all ploughing produces a ridge-and-furrow formation. This is not to say, however, that the lands cannot be kept flat, if desired, even though ploughed round a ridge and finished with a furrow. The surface is kept flat by alternately 'gathering' and 'splitting', that is to say by throwing up the furrow slices round a ridge at one ploughing and casting them down again at another.

It must be remembered that many of the terms used in farming carry more than one meaning, and that this may lead to the misinterpretation of descriptions and documents. Thus 'lands', 'ridge-and-furrow', 'balks', are terms each of which may denote more than one thing, and it is very important to be clear as to the sense in which the words are being used when reading or writing of the

[1] See p. 58, post.   [2] See p. 99, post.

Open Fields. 'Land' may be land in general, or arable land in particular, the whole common field; or it may be a small part of this area, a small piece of ploughland with a ridge in the middle and bounded by open furrows, sometimes called a 'stitch'.[1] This is *not* synonymous with the strip or parcel, representing one man's holding intermixed with others in the Open Fields, and much misunderstanding occurs when the two are confused. Strips were made up of one, two, or more lands, according to the length of the furlong in which they occurred and the lie of the land generally. At Laxton there are strips of less than a quarter of an acre containing two lands, where the furlong is very short, while there are also strips of half an acre consisting of one land only, where the furlong is long. It is all a matter of technical convenience when laying out the field for cultivation, and it affords a good example of the flexibility of the open-field system and its adaptability to differences of soil, climate, and topography. Similarly, 'ridge-and-furrow' means to a farmer no more than any piece of ploughing for which the field is laid out in lands. To the uninitiated observer of the countryside, it means the high-backed, rolling surface often manifest in grasslands in the heavy soils of the Midlands and elsewhere, today, which is taken sometimes as evidence of old Open Fields.[2] Kerridge quotes *The Book of Husbandry* (1598) for a description of three kinds of ploughing: 'eyther they be great Lands as with high ridges and deepe furrowes . . . or els flatte and plaine, without ridge or furrow . . . or els in little Lands, no land containing aboue two or three furrowes.' From this he argues that all light, dry soils were ploughed by the second method, working from one side of the field to the other without laying it out in lands at all. Thus, he suggests that 'without water furrows a grass balk was needed as a dividing line between land and land [*sic*]. Such grass balks obtained throughout the open fields of chalk Wiltshire and in all chalk countries generally. . . . Flat fields with balks were just as common as fields in ridge and furrow.'[3]

Unfortunately historians are not all of them ploughmen. To Kerridge, a furrow seems necessarily a water-furrow, but in point of fact the dividing furrow only functions as such on heavy land calling for surface drainage. In a flat, dry soil both plough ridges and boundary furrows are formed, but having no draining purpose to serve the disadvantages of gathering into high-backed lands by continuous ploughing round the same ridge are obviated

[1] See p. 33, fn. *ante*.
[2] Of course it may be, but it has been proved conclusively by Dr. J. D. Chambers and Mr. Eric Kerridge that high-backed lands, being laid up for drainage purposes, occur also on land which is known never to have been in Open Field.
[3] Kerridge, E., *Economic History Review*, Second Series, vol. iv, no. 1, 1951, p. 19.

by regular splitting as described above. Three pre-inclosure authorities quoted by Kerridge—Worlidge,[1] Bailey and Culley,[2] and Arthur Young[3]—for evidence of ploughing light land on the flat, make definite reference to ridge-and-furrow.

There seems little, therefore, to support the theory that the farmer's cultivation strips scattered throughout the Open Fields were divided from those of his neighbour by grass balks in dry, light-land districts. While it is conceded that there is ample evidence for division by the open furrows of normal ridge-and-furrow ploughing, as practised all over the country, the case for dividing grass balks is a generalization from one, or perhaps two, examples in the west of England, where conditions are exceptional and possibly unique, which further investigation may show to have no general application. In a short article by Lt.-Col. E. Drew, reference is made to the remains of grass balks visible in what were at one time open fields in the Isle of Portland, from which he draws the conclusion that strips throughout the limestone and chalk country were 'widely and perhaps always separated one from another by such balks'.[4] Conditions of life and industry on Portland are unique; the underlying Portland Stone, sometimes so much as 30,000 tons to the acre, gives an abnormal value to the agricultural land, through the mineral rights conferred, so that any generalizations in determining the boundaries of ownership, where farming had ceased to be the first consideration, seems hardly warranted, pending further investigation.

Braunton Great Field in north Devon, extending to some 350 acres, is held in strips of intermixed ownership, most of which are divided by unploughed grass balks known locally as 'landsherds'. There has been a considerable amount of consolidation. In the original edition of this book the authors followed Gray in suggesting that the Great Field was a reclamation from the marshes of the river estuary and of relatively recent origin. Evidence for the existence of cultivated strips within it has now been found so far back as the early fourteenth century by H. P. R. Finberg, whose work has done much to correct and augment that which has been written upon the extent of open field in Devon.[5]

[1] Worlidge, *Systema Agriculturae*, 1681, p. 36. 'Where the land is dry, they do not lay up their Ridges, as in other places (i.e. they do not gather them into high-backed lands. C.S.O.).

[2] Bailey and Culley, *General View of the Agriculture of the County of Northumberland*, 1805, p. 67. 'The ridges are quite flat, and alternately gathered and split.'

[3] Arthur Young, *General View of the Agriculture of Suffolk*, 1813, p. 47. 'In Suffolk the form of laying arable lands upon dry soils is on the flat, with finishing furrows, alternate gathering and splitting.'

[4] *Antiquity*, no. 86, June 1948, p. 79. See also ibid., No. 91, Sept. 1949, p. 140. Robert Douch, 'Customs and Traditions of the Isle of Portland'.

[5] See *Antiquity*, No. 92, Dec. 1942, 'The Open Field in Devonshire'. See also *Devonshire Studies*, W. G. Hoskins and H. P. R. Finberg. Jonathan Cape. 1952.

There can be little doubt that the Great Field was reclaimed at some unrecorded period from the river estuary as it silted up. As to the balks or landsherds by which it is divided, in a large measure, into separate ownerships, all references to these seem to be historically quite modern, and much more evidence would be needed to establish the contention that arable strips in the common field were thus divided.

Indeed, it may be said of all the cases put forward recently in proof of the existence of unploughed turf balks as boundary marks between arable strips in common fields, that they are open to this criticism. Present-day examples of these balks can undoubtedly be found, here and there, but they will continue to lack the position, now often claimed for them, as essential elements in the open-field layout until it can be shown that they derive from medieval days. There seems to be a complete lack of evidence for them, however, either documentary, pictorial, or literary, going back to the Middle Ages, anywhere in this country, or, indeed, from anywhere in Europe. Unless such can be produced, it is fair to say that the weight of the evidence is clearly in favour of the double-furrow division made, inevitably, by the action of the plough. It was based on practical agricultural usage, reinforced by public opinion and the vigilance of the jury of the Manor Court on the occasions of their triennial visitations.[1]

This, then, it is suggested, is the synthesis of the Open Field and of the farms within it. First, there was the reclamation of the wild by the clearance of scrub and timber, after which, as husbandry developed, cultivation by the mouldboard plough produced the 'land'. The contour of the field and the texture of the soil determined the size of the 'land', and thus, also, the number of 'lands' making up the typical strip, the day's work or the customary acre. The contour of the field, too, determined the size and direction of the furlong, and the texture of the soil decided its width and so, also, the number of 'lands' within it. The size of the village community, that is, its number of ploughs, determined the extent of the clearing for cultivation in the Open Field.

Second, subsistence farming called for equal treatment for each member, so that farms approximated to each other in size. Subsistence farming entailed upon every one the same farming system, so that men went to work together on the same tasks at the same seasons. Of these, plough-time came first in the farming year, and as day's work followed day's work, so one man's 'lands' followed those of his neighbours as they all worked, side by side, through

[1] See p. 129, post.

the Open Field. This system accommodated itself to the growth of the community by means of further clearances in the waste to make room for new furlongs and the introduction of the new-comers and their plough-teams into each day's work.

Let us now consider the evolution of the system of farming practised by the community in the Open Fields thus created and distributed.

IV. THE FARMING SYSTEM

THERE are grounds for believing that in the earliest days of plough farming the land was treated on a system of alternate cropping and grazing. The removal of a corn crop reduces the fertility of the soil, while land in a condition of natural grass accumulates fertility. It is suggested, then, that in prehistoric times, when it may be supposed that little was known about the restoration of fertility by manuring, it was the practice of the primitive ploughman to cultivate and crop a given area, and then to let it go back to Nature for a period of recuperation, while he turned his attention to fresh ground.[1]

However this may be, it is certain that by the time at which our knowledge becomes more definite, farmers had realized the advantage of resting the soil. We find that the village community had cleared and occupied more land for ploughing than it needed for the production of the year's bread food, and that this land was farmed in a regular rotation, part of it being under crop while the rest of it was left fallow, in alternate years. This rotation of alternate corn and fallow is the origin of all the farming systems in the country today, and it is known as 'the two-field system'.

Under this system, the farmers' holdings consisting of so many strips, each of which represented a days' work with the plough, were divided approximately equally between the two portions of the ploughland of the community, and every man had half his land in crop and half in fallow. By the time that any written evidence exists, it is clear that one part of the cropped land was customarily sown with autumn corn, wheat, winter beans, or rye, and the other part with spring corn, barley, oats, spring beans, or peas, and this practice may have been an essential part of the two-field system from its earliest days, when the village community first began to have permanent occupation of any particular area instead of moving constantly to fresh land. For only in this way could its labour be regularly employed and fully rewarded, autumn cultivation and sowing being followed by winter cultivation and spring sowing, after which the way was clear for the busy summer time of haymaking and harvest.

But such an arrangement suggests the obvious advantage of a 'three-field system' under which the land for autumn corn occupied one section, that for spring corn another, while the fallow

---

[1] See p. 38, *ante.*

made the third. Indeed, in practice, this is what the two-field system itself must have been, for the village farmers would have worked steadily across one-half of the year's corn-land for the autumn-sown crop, and, that finished, they would have gone on to the other half and cultivated that for spring corn. It would be only a short step from this arrangement to one by which the land was divided into three more equal parts, on each of which winter corn, spring corn, and fallow rotated. As Gray has pointed out, the difference between the two-field and the three-field systems is not one of principle but of proportion, and he may be right when he suggests that

> What determined the adoption of the one or the other form of tillage was agricultural convenience, and this in turn depended largely upon the locality and the nature of the soil. . . . Under two-field arrangements there was left fallow one-half of the arable, under three-field arrangements one-third. The cultivated portion, whether one-half or two-thirds, was sown in the same manner; it was divided between winter and spring grains.[1]

Both systems were in common use in the thirteenth century, when Walter of Henley wrote:

> If your lands are divided in three, one part for winter seed, the other part for spring seed, and the third part fallow. . . . And if your lands are divided in two, as in many places, the one half sown with winter seed and spring seed, the other half fallow. . . .[2]

Gray's investigations show that in no part of the country given up to open-field farming was either one or the other system found alone. Always both were to be found, though he concludes that in some districts either the one or the other seems to have predominated.[3] But there is nothing in his facts to conflict with the idea that the three-field was an evolution of the two-field system, proceeding variously, and carried to different stages of completeness, in different places. On this supposition, a two-field system of alternate corn and fallow was the first step in the evolution of farming from its most primitive forms, and it developed, naturally, wherever open-field farming was practised, into something more productive. On all agricultural grounds it is quite unnecessary to associate it with particular districts, for it is difficult to conceive how better the primitive agricultural improver could have gone to work than by a change to the more intensive system. It is difficult to believe, too, that there was any part of England in which the evolution of open-field farming stopped short at the two-field system, for, as knowledge of crops and tillage increased, nothing

---

[1] Gray, H. L., *English Field Systems*, p. 71 (1915).
[2] *Walter of Henley's 'Husbandry'*, ed. Lamond, E., p. 7 (1890).
[3] Op. cit., p. 70 and Appendix II.

is more natural than that the two-field should have developed
everywhere into the three-field system, though not everywhere
at the same rate and with the same completeness.

For it is clear that the two-field system of farming was expensive of land, only one-half of it being applied to productive use in
each year. When the village communities were small, and land
was plentiful, this might not matter, but as population increased,
and the need for greater food-production grew, the wisdom of a
more economical use of the land must have suggested itself, if
such could be devised. Sometimes a new field may have been
taken in from the waste. Gray mentions evidence in many places
of a third field in embryo. But at least the limits of one of the two
fields could be reduced by the transfer of some furlongs to the
other, and this one, thus augmented, could be cultivated in halves
so as to make a three-field system with the other.

One-third of the cultivated land was now in fallow; one-third
was sown in the autumn with wheat, or perhaps rye, crops needing a long growing-season to give a full harvest; one-third was
sown in the spring with barley, oats, spring beans, or peas, crops
which come to harvest in a few months. As to the rotation of the
crops, the bare fallow, ready for sowing at any time, was followed
naturally by the autumn corn. This, sown and harrowed in, say
by the end of October, left the farmers and their teams free to get
to work upon the wheat stubbles in the second field and to plough
it whenever weather conditions in winter permitted. In the spring,
this land, pulverized by winter frosts and dried by March winds,
was sown in its turn.

Both winter and spring corn needed protection from possible
depredations from straying stock or from stock going to and from
the commons and other grazing-grounds of the village. So it was
the duty of every man to fence the ends of such of his strips as
abutted on any road or common way, by erecting wattle hurdles,
or stakes and brushwood, across them, each man's fence joining
those of his neighbours. In the presentments of the manorial
courts a common complaint was that a tenant had failed to fence
his lands' ends, and Gray has pointed out that so long ago as the
seventh century King Ine's laws provided compensation to those
whose crops or grass were damaged by straying cattle because
their neighbours had not hedged their share.[1]

When the winter corn and spring corn had been sown and the
lands' ends fenced, the village folk had not finished with the
arable land. The third field had borne two successive corn crops,
the barley, say, of the previous year having followed the wheat
of two years ago. Its fertility had been lowered, and weeds and

[1] Gray, op. cit., p. 61.

grass had multiplied. It needed a rest to restore its fertility, and cultivation to check unwanted herbage. So the third field, the old barley stubble, became the fallow field for the year. Livestock had been turned out to graze upon it after harvest and through the winter, and in the summer it was ploughed, whenever opportunity offered, to prepare it for autumn sowing in due season.

But corn-growing was not the whole of the farming system. Indeed, it is possible that primitive man, as he emerged from the hunting stage, was a livestock farmer before he began to till the soil.

Among the Saxons the pig was the most important source of meat-supply, just as it was recently in some parts of the country, in which two fat pigs killed and salted, one at the beginning of winter, the other just before the coming of spring, furnished the greater part of the family's meat. Cattle came next in importance, to supply milk for drinking, for butter-making, and particularly for cheese. So late as Cobbett's day, cheese was still being made for domestic consumption in most parts of England. On the farm, if not on the road, oxen were used for draught purposes. The heavy shoulders and light quarters of the cattle depicted in eighteenth-century illustrations, before the work of the early live-stock improvers had spread through the country, show how draught rather than beef-formation was the first function of the ox right up to within the last 150 years. Similarly, sheep were kept more for their wool than for their mutton, and in medieval times ewes were milked.

It must be understood that the problem of maintaining live-stock has always been how to provide a sufficiency of winter food. Today the farmer has at command all the members of the great *Brassica* family, turnips, swedes, cabbage, kale, as well as the mangold and its near relative the sugar-beet, to supply the succu-lence provided by grass at other seasons of the year; while grasses and clover sown in rotation on the ploughland and cut and made into hay have added immensely to winter stocks of dry food, which were limited, at one time, to hay made from natural grassland, supplemented by straw from the grain crops. But all these things are of very recent introduction in the history of agriculture, and even so late as the latter part of the seventeenth century the diarist Evelyn was at pains to discuss the comparative fodder values of the leaves of the common forest trees—articles of diet which no farmer today would dream of including in his cattle rations.[1]

[1] Evelyn, John, *Sylva*. See, for example, his remarks on the superiority of the leaves of the ash. A hundred years earlier, Master Fitzherbert advised farmers to do any topping and lopping of trees in winter, 'that thy beastes maye eate the brouse, and the mosse of the bowes, and also the yues [ivies]': *The Book of Husbandry*.

Speaking generally, all the livestock of the open-field farmers was maintained on the natural herbage of those parts of the parish which were not under the plough. These included the woodlands, the wastes, the 'sikes' or tracts of unploughed land in the Open Fields, and the meadow land by the streams and in the bottoms. The meadows, however, were created by reclamation from a state of woodland or swamp to give a hay crop, and they represent a later stage in the progress of farming than does the utilization of woodland and waste for grazing. People found that the grass grew best in the wetter or lower-lying places, and they proceeded to clean them up and to improve them for mowing.

At some date, too, and probably an early one, small crofts or inclosures of grassland were made behind the houses of the village farmers, in which to keep a cow, or other animals in daily use, and breeding-stock.

The main source of grazing, then, was the waste land of the parish, which must have been plentiful enough in the early years of the settlements. These lands were wastes mainly in the sense that they were over and above that which the community needed for ploughing, or were unfitted for it by reason of soil or situation. All those who occupied lands in the Open Fields had the right to graze stock upon the common wastes, probably without any restriction of numbers, in early times. Later, however, as the needs of the growing community caused the fields to encroach more and more upon the wastes, the grazing-rights, in many places, were stinted, and each man might turn out no more than a specified number of cattle, or their equivalent in horses or sheep. The wastes or commons were also the source of fuel, and the right to cut gorse or turf on them was valuable.[1]

Up to the thirteenth century, and later, possibly, in some places, the woodlands in autumn provided food for the pigs, which grew fat upon the beech-mast and acorns. 'Pannage for pigs' is a common entry in Saxon charters, the Domesday Survey, and elsewhere, when the agricultural resources of a place or property are described.

But there is no doubt that by medieval times, and how much earlier no man can say, the natural grazing-resources of many parishes were being taxed to the uttermost in the effort to maintain the head of livestock, and the village community had organized

---

[1] For example, upon the inclosure of the parish of Cumnor, Berks., the right of the inhabitants 'to cut and carry away furze on their backs but not otherwise' on about 12 acres of land adjoining the well-known Hurst was valued at £14. 6s. 10d. per annum, being 25s. per acre. The award provided that this sum should be paid, by the person to whom the land was allotted upon inclosure, to the overseers of the poor, as the representatives of the persons damnified by the withdrawal of the right. Today the money is paid to the vicar and churchwardens and expended upon coal.

a system by which they could use the Open Fields themselves as an adjunct to the commons. That they were potential food-sources was clear, and, provided that their use by livestock were regulated to interfere neither with the growing crops nor with the preparations for them, there was no reason why they should not be grazed.

It may be assumed that with their limited range of implements and the calls upon the time of self-sufficient farmers before the days of even simple machinery, cultivation was not very clean, and weeds abounded. Then, too, the reaping-hook left a long stubble, so that the fields after harvest carried a fair bite of one kind or another. Moreover, there were considerable tracts of unploughed land in every Open Field. The modern inclosures in fields of, say, from 15 to 50 acres were planned according to the lie of the land, to give the farmer a surface which he could till, and the steep banks and wet bottoms and awkward corners were excluded from them. But in Open Fields of, say, 400 to 600 acres, such spots, locally known as 'sikes', were bound to occur, and in some localities their size might even be considerable. In addition to the rough ground there were also the common ways, paths, and balks, partly grass-grown. At Laxton, Notts., the sikes and other un-ploughed ground amounted to about 5 per cent. of the area of the common fields.

It is clear, then, that the feeding-value of the arable fields at certain seasons must have been recognized at an early date in their history, and some system under which they could be stocked had been evolved before the time of written records. The practice, as it emerged, was very rigidly controlled. Stock might be turned upon the wheat stubble immediately after harvest, to pick up the fallen ears of corn and to graze upon the weeds and grasses in the stubble and upon the grass of the sikes. This could not be permitted for long, as the wheat stubble had to be ploughed before winter in preparation for the next year's spring corn. By the end of October the stock had been transferred to the spring-corn stubble, the field which would be fallowed next in the three-course rotation. Here the sheep, at all events, were allowed to remain throughout the winter, until, by springtime, men had finished all their sowing for that year's harvest and were ready to set about the tillage of the fallow field. By that time the grass upon the common wastes would have begun to grow, and the stock which the community had contrived to maintain through the winter could be moved on to them. For it must be remembered that, even with all the resources of the parish lands mobilized in this way, winter food-supplies were of the scantiest, and it was possible to maintain little more than the breeding-stock and the young stock needed to replenish flocks and herds. There was a general killing of other animals as the autumn drew on and fodder reserves dwindled, the carcasses being salted for the winter meat-supply.[1]

We have now seen how both the cultivated and the uncultivated portions of the parish were worked in a kind of rotation conforming to the seasons of the year, to maintain the livestock. There remains, however, the meadow land. It is probable that in very early times farmers were in the habit of cutting wild grasses in the summer season, before they became busy with their corn harvest, and storing the hay for winter feed. At some time a definite selection was made of the better parts of the unploughed land, such as low-lying places and stretches adjacent to the streams where the grass grew strong, and these were set aside for mowing under a system of communal control which was just as rigid as that exercised over the Open Fields, and very like it.

The mowing-land came to be allotted to the village farmers, so far as we know, by one of two methods. The first, and probably the more general, resembled the allocation of the open arable fields. Each farmer in the Open Fields had also a holding of mowing-grass, consisting of little strips alternating with those of his neighbours just as those of his ploughland alternated, but the strips of grassland were smaller still. We may suppose, too, that the method of allocation arose in the same way. There is some evidence that the strips were 1 rod in width and about 20 rods in length, thus measuring an eighth of an acre. The farmers of the village community went to work together. A strip was allotted to each, and as they finished the first lot they moved on to the next block. This method explains the scattered allocation of meadow grass as we know it existed, and it resembled the method by which it has been suggested that the ploughland allocation was made, in that it provided for the admission of new-comers quite simply,

---

[1] The winter was often a period of scarcity for man as well as for beast, and even more, perhaps, the spring-time following a scanty harvest in the previous year. Flour had to be diluted with bean-meal and bran, poultry was almost the only source of fresh meat, and even salt meat and bacon might be scarce. William Langland wrote of such days:

'I've no penny' quoth Piers, 'young pullets to buy,
Nor bacon nor geese, only two green cheeses,
Some curds and sour cream, and an oaten cake,
Two bean-loaves with bran, just baked for my children.
And I say, by my soul, I have no salt bacon,
Nor eggs, by my Christendom, collops to make;
Only onions and parsley, and cabbage-like plants; . . .

.   .   .   .

By such food must we live, until Lammas-time come,
I hope I may then have some harvest afield;
And I'll dight thee a dinner as dearly will please me.'

The Vision of Piers the Plowman, passus vi, ll. 282–93 (Skeat's Modern English version).

until all the available land was taken up and the strips were finally allocated to individuals. Strips of meadow grass were commonly called 'doles'.

The second method of allocation was by lot. The meadow land was divided with stones or posts into equal areas, which were allocated annually, amongst those entitled to the grass, by the drawing of lots.

Under either system the meadow lands became commonable after the hay crop had been gathered, and so the aftermath added its quota of grazing to the area available for the livestock of the community. A usual date for turning stock on to the aftermath of the meadow was Lammas (1 August), the Feast of the First Fruits; and the names Lammas Meads and Lammas Land which occur in many places today are evidence of the one-time existence of the old farming system.

To sum up: under the open-field system, at the time when we first begin to see it clearly, those parts of England covered by it consisted of communities living in what, today, are termed nu-cleated villages—places in which the population is concentrated at one spot—who farmed the land round them to provide their own subsistence, rather than to give them produce for sale.

Before their occupation of it the land had been woodland or scrub or wild grass, some parts of which, doubtless, had been cultivated to some extent by an earlier people, under farming systems more primitive than theirs. As occupied by them, it fell into three clearly defined categories. A large part—the greater part, ultimately, as the community grew—was kept under the plough to produce corn for man and straw for his beasts. Another part, much smaller, consisted still of the natural herbage, though cleared of trees and bushes, and this was mown yearly to give hay for winter feed for livestock. By the mere process of regular mowing, weeds were destroyed and the quality of the herbage improved. The third part comprised all that was left of the area under the control of the community, and it remained in its natural state of woodland or waste, except in so far as this was affected by grazing and by cutting timber and scrub for building and fuel.

The extent of the arable land, lying in great Open Fields, was determined, subject to the limitations imposed by the competition of adjacent communities, by the number of ploughs in the community, and it was allotted amongst its members in strips repre-senting a day's work with the plough, so that each man's strips alternated with those of his neighbours as day followed day. The strips were assembled in blocks, which varied in size and in direction with the contour of the land. The land was farmed in a rotation under which one-third was cropped with autumn-sown corn, one-third with spring-sown corn, while the other third was rested in fallow. At seasons of the year when any part of the Open Fields had no crop on it, the live stock of the community grazed together over it on the stubbles and on the balks and sikes—the odds and ends of grassland unfit for ploughing.

The meadow land was allotted amongst the community under a system the same as that which was applied in the allocation of the ploughlands, giving each man little scattered strips of grass to mow for hay. After the hay harvest, the meadows were grazed in common.

The waste lands, or commons, were not cultivated, nor were they mown. They served two purposes: first, to provide a permanent grazing-ground for the livestock; and, second, to allow of the expansion of the arable land as the community grew, the limit of expansion being set by the need to maintain a minimum of grazing-ground.

This, then, was the economy of the open-field land system as it developed in England. Remembering the equal need of all to extract their subsistence from the soil, its balance and fitness are at once apparent. Each of the village farmers had so much land as his own hands and implements could cultivate in the year. Each one followed the same system of husbandry. The method by which the holdings were distributed followed upon the simultaneous employment of every one upon the same task in the same season of the year, both in the arable fields and in the meadows. It resulted in holdings divided into strips of a day's work each, scattered evenly over the whole of the land, giving to every one, incidentally, but only incidentally, an equal share in the advantages and in the disadvantages of soils and situation.

Further, the farming system thus evolved spread the work evenly through the seasons. Autumn sowing on the fallow was followed by winter cultivation of the stubble and spring sowing, after which fallow cultivation and hay-making occupied the farmer until the corn harvest finished the farming year. The livestock fitted naturally into this system, the commons and the aftermath of the meadows providing their summer and autumn keep, which was supplemented after harvest by the stubbles and sikes of the Open Fields, while the hay and straw kept them through the winter, until, in springtime, the grass on the commons began to grow again.

The system of farming in Open Fields was common in England by the time that historical records of land-tenure begin; and from thence onward through the centuries, until their inclosure was virtually complete, say, a hundred years ago, its fundamental characteristics had undergone no change. The essence of the system was that it demanded the rigid adherence of every member of the village community. The right, jealously guarded, of common grazing on the stubbles made it impossible for anyone to grow a crop which would still be unharvested when his neighbours had gathered their corn. It was this rigidity in the system which killed it, ultimately, as knowledge of new crops and more productive methods developed, while at the same time the pace of change was that of the slowest.

V. THE EXTENT OF THE OPEN FIELDS

As a generalization, it may be said that most of the people of England were fed and clothed by the open-field farming system for many centuries. At the same time, there were large areas in much of which production was carried on in other ways. Even until times comparatively recent, woodlands and wastes accounted for much of the surface of the country, and here, as well as in the mountain districts, there is naturally little evidence of open-field farming.

For the purpose of this study, an attempt was made to secure more accurate definition of the extent of the Open Fields. At what date the increase in strip farming, by the addition of new furlongs, was stayed and additions to the farming area were made as closes, we do not know. Probably the Open Fields were complete before the end of the Middle Ages. At least it may be said that whereas no evidence has been found of the addition of new furlongs after that time, there is plenty for the creation of closes, not only by reclamation from woodland and waste, but also by the inclosure of parcels of strips. How long before record it had begun we shall never know, but there may have been places or districts or even counties in which inclosure was complete so long ago that the existence of Open Fields in them may have eluded the notice of investigators.

With such limitations in mind, a search was begun for documentary evidence of the existence of open-field farming, county by county, to determine, so far as possible, its extent and limits. Evidence would be, clearly, of two kinds. There would be direct evidence, such as that of Inclosure Acts and Awards and Chancery certificates, dealing specifically with common lands, and the indirect evidence to be extracted from oblique references in earlier documents relating to land, which might not make specific mention of Open Fields.

A start was made with the Inclosure Maps and Awards of the eighteenth and nineteenth centuries, discriminating, of course, between those applying to the Open Fields and those for inclosing grass commons and waste. In the midland and eastern counties the system largely survived up to that time, and these Acts and Awards were sufficient to establish its prevalence in Bedfordshire, Berkshire, Buckinghamshire, Cambridgeshire, Gloucestershire, Huntingdonshire, Leicestershire, Lincolnshire, Middlesex,

Norfolk, Northamptonshire, Nottinghamshire, Oxfordshire, Rutland, Warwickshire, Wiltshire, and the three Ridings of Yorkshire. The findings of the Inquisitions into Inclosures of 1517[1] provided additional evidence for Berkshire, Buckinghamshire, Leicestershire, Lincolnshire, Oxfordshire, Norfolk, Northamptonshire, Nottinghamshire, Warwickshire, and the North Riding of Yorkshire. Slater's list of 'Private Acts enclosing Common Fields'[2] proved useful as a starting-point, but it had to be supplemented by reference to the Journals of the House of Commons and to the Local, Personal, and Private Acts themselves. Unprinted Private Acts were not consulted, but information on the legislation of the eighteenth and nineteenth centuries for the inclosure of Open Fields may be regarded as practically, if not technically, complete.[3]

Use was made also of the following:

The Public Record Office List of Inclosure Awards.

The 1904 Return of all Inclosure Awards or Copies Deposited with Clerks of the Peace or County Councils.

The 1893 Return of Inclosure Awards Deposited with the Board of Agriculture.

The 1836 Return from the Inclosure and Other Private Acts in which Provisions are included for the Commutation of Tithe.

For counties from which open-field farming had largely disappeared by the eighteenth century, other evidence had to be sought. Manorial extents and surveys of all dates were consulted, but medieval evidence mainly was used, and grants of land, especially those contained in the collection of Ancient Deeds in the Public Record Office and in monastic cartularies, were fruitful sources. Feet of Fines of the twelfth and thirteenth centuries often gave clear evidence, and Inquisitions *post mortem* and wills were useful for some places. A considerable number of these sources are printed, and much has been derived from the publications of the county record and archaeological societies, but so many books and documents have been consulted that it is impossible to do more than indicate the kind of material used.

The evidence upon which reliance has been placed is that of the main features of open-field farming:

1. Large arable fields which run often into hundreds of acres.

2. Holdings scattered in small strips through the fields.

---

[1] See Leadam, I. S., *The Domesday of Inclosures*, 1517–18, and *Transactions of the Royal Historical Society*, New Series, vols. vi, vii, viii, and xiv.

[2] Slater, G., *The English Peasantry and the Enclosure of Common Fields* (1907), Appendix B.

[3] W. E. Tate's *County Handlists of Parliamentary Enclosure*, published since 1935 and still appearing, have added much to the extent of this information, while correcting at the same time some earlier errors and omissions.

3. Fields lying in fallow every second or third year.
4. Grazing-rights exercised in common in the arable fields.

These features can be deduced from early descriptions of land in places where Open Fields survived into modern times, and the suggestion is that an open-field system may be inferred in all places in which the same kind of evidence is to be found.

The examination of all this evidence confirms the general conclusion of historians that there was a great district, well defined, covering the counties already enumerated, in which there is no question that open-field farming prevailed. As we go westward and northward the system is still encountered, but evidence for it tends to thin out all the time. To a great extent this may be explained by the physical conformation of the land. The great Pennine ridge stretching north from Derbyshire, the mountains and lakes of Westmorland and Cumberland, and districts similar to these in central and north Wales, are not natural areas of arable farming and the livestock farming which predominated over them developed its own system. But even in these areas there is some evidence to show that where the lie of the land permitted, communal farming in open fields was practised. In Cumberland, Westmorland, and Cheshire[1] a few scattered instances have been found, and there were still Open Fields in four townships of *Monmouthshire*, on the Severn, in the eighteenth century, but elsewhere in the county none have been traced. In *Lancashire*, medieval descriptions of land show that holdings might be scattered, though not necessarily in small strips, and evidence of other open-field features is lacking. The examination of private documents and maps deposited in the County Record Office at Preston, however, suggests that open-field systems may have been more extensive than at present is appreciated. John Holt, writing in 1795, says: 'There are but few open or common fields at this time remaining.'[2]

In *Devon*, a county lacking any evidence of statutory inclosure of common fields, recent research and work still in progress show conclusively that farming in open fields was practised in various parts where the topography permitted, though inclosure began early and was more or less complete by the sixteenth century.[3]

---

[1] Valuable work is in progress in Cheshire on the pattern of rural settlement, which should throw light on early field systems. See Sylvester, Dorothy, 'Rural Settlement in Cheshire: Some Problems of Origin and Classification', *Transactions of the Historic Society of Lancashire and Cheshire*, vol. ci, 1949: also Chapman, Vera, 'Open Fields in West Cheshire' in the same series, 1953.

[2] Holt, John, *General View of the Agriculture of the County of Lancaster*, 1795. We are indebted to the County Archivist, Mr. H. Sharpe France, for this and for other interesting references on the subject, which suggest a profitable field of research.

[3] See Hoskins, W. G. and Finberg, H. P. R., *Devonshire Studies*, 1952. Also Finberg, H. P. R., 'The Open Field in Devonshire', *Antiquity*, no. 92, Dec. 1949.

Cornwall, like Devon, lacks the evidence of statutory inclosure, but here also recent research has demonstrated the existence of arable lands held 'in stitchmeal' in the sixteenth century, a reference presumably to open-field farming.[1]

Next comes a group of counties which seem to have been farmed on the open-field system, but which were inclosed in great part before the eighteenth century. Considerable medieval evidence shows that the cultivated land of *Durham* was open, and surveys of the sixteenth and seventeenth centuries confirm this. In the seventeenth century, however, inclosure was fairly widespread, and by the end of the eighteenth, only some six parishes had any Open Field.

In the Middle Ages the system prevailed all over *Northumberland*, except in the moorland areas. Inclosure must have begun early, and medieval documents both of Northumberland and of Durham allude to coal-mining often enough to suggest that this may have been a factor in the break-up of the system. There was much inclosure in the seventeenth and in the early part of the eighteenth centuries, but parliamentary inclosure appears to be limited to a few Acts and Awards. It is interesting to note that sometimes it affected only the surface, the Award specifying that ownership of minerals should remain as before.[2] This produced a difficult problem when coal leases came to be negotiated in later times, but it was resolved, of necessity, on the assumption that the Award applied also to the minerals.

In *Derbyshire*, Open Fields survived in nearly a hundred parishes until the eighteenth century, and medieval evidence confirms that the system originally must have been widespread in the county. There was much mountain, forest, and waste land, however.

Nearly seventy parishes in *Staffordshire* were inclosed in the eighteenth and nineteenth centuries, but evidence from medieval records and from the sixteenth and seventeenth centuries shows that open-field farming was the rule except in the north.

Shropshire was early inclosed, for only some dozen parishes were dealt with by Acts of Parliament. The evidence shows that in medieval times the county as a whole had Open Fields. The Inquisition into Inclosures of 1517 shows that inclosure was going on actively at that time.

Conditions in *Herefordshire* were similar, but the Inquisition of 1517 found less evidence of recent inclosure.

In *Worcestershire* the Open Fields were widespread, and in

---

[1] See Rowse, A. L., *Tudor Cornwall*, 1941.
[2] See, for example, Chancery Decrees and Orders, 1718 A, fol. 247 (Balliol College Lands), P.R.O.

nearly eighty parishes they persisted into the eighteenth century and later.

Somerset, too, except for Exmoor and the parishes on the Devon border, had open arable land in the Middle Ages, and some fifty or sixty parishes were affected by parliamentary inclosure. There must have been a steady if unrecorded inclosure movement in the sixteenth and seventeenth centuries, influenced probably by the commercial and maritime progress of the southwestern counties.

Dorset was much the same, and seems to have been affected, by the same external influences which made for the disappearance or modification of the old system, as was Somerset.

In *Hampshire*, outside the New Forest, the system was widespread. About eighty examples survived to be dealt with by Inclosure Acts.

Surrey and *Sussex* disclose a position of special interest. All the land outside the Weald, and in Sussex, too, outside the coastal marshes, was farmed in Open Field in medieval times. Between thirty and forty parishes in either county were affected by Inclosure Acts, several of the Surrey parishes thus surviving being now in the London area. The Weald, of course, has its own agricultural history, and no Open Fields can be traced within it. A map of Surrey and Sussex showing medieval open-field villages would coincide, approximately, with one showing those mentioned as being cultivated at the time of the Domesday Survey.

Hertfordshire was a county of Open Fields. Inclosure began early, and Sessions Rolls[1] of the seventeenth century supply evidence of the care with which unauthorized inclosure was checked. Even in the eighteenth century the evidence of the rolls is that there was much Open Field not affected by later Acts, so that inclosure must have been carried out by private agreements. Between sixty and seventy parishes were dealt with by Acts.

There is abundant medieval evidence of open-field farming throughout *Suffolk*, and it survived into the eighteenth century in nearly seventy parishes, most of them in the west.

There remain the counties of *Essex* and *Kent*, both of which are said to have been inclosed from time immemorial. In the sixteenth century John Hales referred to *Essex* as being one of those counties 'wheare most Inclosures be'.[2] The parishes, nearly thirty in number, which were affected by parliamentary inclosure, were most of them on the borders of Cambridgeshire and Hertfordshire. But Belchamp Otten, in the north, had Open Fields until 1840, Redham, adjoining east Suffolk, was not inclosed until

---

[1] *Hertfordshire County Records*, various volumes of Quarter Sessions Books and Rolls.
[2] *Discourse of the Commonwealth of this Realm of England*, p. 49, ed. Lamond.

1803, and Walthamstow, on the opposite side of the county, not until 1850. The Inquisition of 1517 found that there had been a few recent inclosures, and fifteenth-century deeds show traces of Open Fields. Medieval evidence suggests that they were numerous at that time in many parts, but descriptions of land, particularly in the Feet of Fines, seem to show that piecemeal inclosure was already destroying the system in many places in the thirteenth century. It must not be forgotten that considerable districts of Essex were woodland and marsh with little population.

Kent, too, was considered an inclosed county in the sixteenth century. Unlike Essex, however, there were no subsequent Acts for inclosing arable land in the county, and in 1794 John Boyes, reporting to the Board of Agriculture, was able to say that there were no common fields in Kent.[1] Yet earlier records seem to show traces in the north and east and recent research provides definite confirmation of this.[2] It must be remembered that the Wealden formation, extending almost right across the middle of the county, and the marshes along its southern coast, both of which were cultivated in severalty after they had been reclaimed and improved, would account for the absence of Open Fields in these parts. Moreover, certain peculiarities of Kentish history may explain their disappearance at an exceptionally early time in the north and east. These parts of Kent formed the main line of communication between London and the Continent, and the early appearance of money rents shows that a money economy developed early here. This must have had a disintegrating influence upon customary farming, and may have helped to destroy the orthodox manorial organization which crystallized the open-field system in most parts of England. But perhaps the most powerful influence in the early break-up of the old agricultural system may have been a provision of the law of gavelkind. This gave tenants the right to buy and sell holdings without licences from their lords, provided that rents and services were not prejudiced thereby. Such a power, joined to a comparatively wide distribution of ready money, may well have enabled the yeomen of Kent to consolidate their strip holdings long years before such a step towards inclosure had been taken elsewhere.

---

[1] *General View of the Agriculture of the County of Kent.*

[2] See Muhlfeld, H. E., *A Survey of the Manor of Wye*, Columbia University Press, 1933. Also Nightingale, M. D., *Some Evidence of Open Field Agriculture in Kent*, thesis presented for the degree of B.Litt. in the University of Oxford, 1952, at present unpublished.

PART II

The Open Fields of Laxton

VI. FROM DOMESDAY TO 1625

THE manor of Laxton, in Nottinghamshire, is presented as an example of the working of the open-field system, under which so much of England was occupied and cultivated until modern times.

The prevalence of the system and the forms in which it was manifest still provide matter for discussion. Study has been based, hitherto, largely upon racial differences amongst the people who resettled Britain, leaving still to be considered the extent to which variations in the topography, in the climate, and in the soil of different parts of the country influenced the system. It has been suggested above that these may prove to have been the dominant factors in the determination of local forms and practices, rather than political or constitutional considerations. During the ages in which commercial farming was unknown, and every one was engaged upon the task, often difficult enough, of wringing a living for himself and his family from the land, its use must surely have been regulated mainly by agricultural considerations. Even to-day, when racial origins are so largely merged, whatever local patriots may say, when the ease of travel and communication has made the knowledge of farming practices all over the country common stock, and when agricultural legislation has done so much to standardize them, every sort of difference in conditions of tenure and systems of farming is still to be found. Some of them are common to wide areas, others are more local, some are confined to particular estates, but underlying them all and common to them all are the principles of good husbandry. Everywhere, the explanation of all the many variations that occur is to be found in the needs of local agricultural practice; there is nothing anywhere to suggest that they have been determined by political or social considerations. The dates, for example, upon which tenancies begin and end vary between new Michaelmas and old May Day according to local convenience; the custom regulating the payment of compensation to the outgoing tenant, so far as this is not now prescribed by the Agricultural Holdings Acts, is determined by the county practice, largely traditional, or by that of the particular estate; and the liability of landlord and tenant for the repair and maintenance of the holding may vary from estate to estate. Nevertheless, two systems only of land tenure prevail today, the system of landlord-and-tenant and that of owner-occupation, and the only purpose of all these variations in the customs and agreements which control the relations of landlord and tenant and define the practice of farming is to secure the best use of the land. Everywhere the underlying principles are the same.

The suggestion of this study, then, is that in its fundamentals the open-field system was the same wherever it was found; that whether it was practised in two fields, or in three, or in more, whether the lord's demesne lay scattered or was held in severalty, whether the freemen were many or few, and whatever the infinite variety of services and customs—all of these represent differences in the local evolution of the same system or local variations necessitated in its practice, none of which affect, in any way, the principles upon which it was based. These principles were evolved by communities whose only means of life was the land, whose opportunities for barter and exchange were few. Speaking broadly, each of their members was engaged in the cultivation of the land, in the tending of livestock, and in the exploitation of the natural products of the woodlands and wastes, for the subsistence of himself and his family. In this respect the needs of everyone were equal, and it follows that the system of land tenure had to be one which gave equal opportunities to all. The common technique of the Open Fields, wherever they occurred and at whatever period, was the outcome of this common need, and the variations found in it at various times and in different places left the fundamental conception unaffected, through the centuries, until the time when subsistence farming began to give place to farming for a market. This conception was that the common stock of knowledge should be pooled in a system of land utilization calculated to give an equal livelihood to all. It involved the practice of a common farming rotation on the arable land—though not the same one in all places and at all times; the common use of stubbles and fallows for grazing—though not subject to the same control conditions everywhere and always; and the common enjoyment of grazing and other rights on the grass commons and wastes—though these might differ widely both in their nature and in their value as between one manor and another. On this interpretation of the evidence, the history of a particular manor and of its economic and social organization should have a general application to the study of the Open Fields.

The manor of Laxton,[1] in Nottinghamshire, has been chosen for

[1] Known in earlier times also as Laxington, Lexington, and Lessington.

two reasons. First, it is the only place in England where the open-field system of land tenure and farming is still practised in all its essentials; second, because of the wealth of materials existing for the study of its economic and social history.

Laxton is situated on the eastern edge of Sherwood Forest, about four miles west of the river Trent at Sutton-on-Trent, and the same distance east of Ollerton, while East Retford, to the north, and Newark, almost due south, are each of them ten miles distant from it. It lies on the ridge of high country which forms the western boundary of the Trent valley, midway between the Great North Road and the road which runs north from Nottingham, through Ollerton, to join it at Bawtry. Laxton and the adjacent villages are small agricultural communities connected by narrow and twisting roads, and the streams of traffic moving north and south on the two great thoroughfares on either side still leave this quiet backwater undisturbed. This isolation, and the complete preoccupation of the locality with agriculture, may explain, perhaps, the survival of the Laxton Open Fields. All of the parishes adjacent were late inclosed: Kneesall and Ompton, the earliest, about 1780, Egmanton and Kirton in 1821, Ossington in 1845, Boughton and Wellow in 1871, while Eakring, two miles south of Ompton, still retains some features of the open-field system.

Laxton parish lies between the 100-ft. and the 200-ft. contours, except for a small part on the northern border which rises to 220 ft. It is here that the village was placed and here that the family of de Caux built their Norman castle, on a site commanding the whole countryside for many miles; Lincoln Cathedral, twenty-four miles away to the north-east, is clearly visible from it. The West Field, the Common, and some of the old demesne lands lie at the same elevation as the village and castle and on either side of them. The Mill Field and the East Field fall gently southward to the 100-ft. contour and to the meadows along the stream which runs across the middle of the parish. On the far side of the beck the South Field rises towards the 200-ft. level again, at which the parish ends on this side in some big woodlands.

At the eastern end of the parish is the hamlet of Laxton Moorhouse. When Mark Pierce made his survey, in 1635, Moorhouse had a separate economic existence, although it formed part of the parish and manor of Laxton. It had its own open arable fields, its meadows and its commons, all occupied by its own freeholders and tenants, notwithstanding that they owed suit and service to the Laxton court. Earlier references suggest that they had always been organized thus, while, in more recent times, the economic separation of Laxton and Laxton Moorhouse was finally established by the parliamentary inclosure of the latter, in 1875.

The extent of the parish of Laxton, as recorded by Mark Pierce, was 3,853 acres, of which Moorhouse comprised 333 acres.

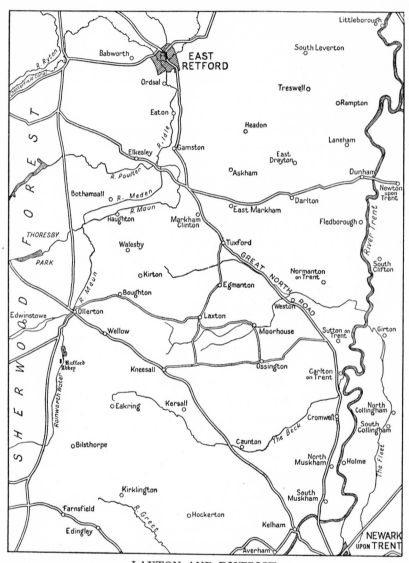

LAXTON AND DISTRICT

The descent of the manor of Laxton can be traced, without a break, from the Norman Conquest and before, down to the present day. William the Conqueror granted the lands of its Saxon owner, Tochi, to Geoffrey Alselin, and for 550 years it passed by inheritance, sometimes through heiresses, to the families of de Caux, de Birkin, de Everingham, de Etton, and Roos, the first sale occurring early in the seventeenth century. After that it changed hands twice, coming in 1640 into the possession of the Pierrepont family, whose descendants held it till 1952.

The lords of the manor and of the sub-manor provide examples of almost every type of English landlord through the centuries. There is Geoffrey Alselin, the great Norman baron; Robert de Caux, feudal magnate and builder of the castle; Robert and John de Lexington, great judges and administrators; their brother Henry, churchman and Bishop of Lincoln; the second Robert de Everingham and his son, Adam, barons whose fame was not so much national as local, being very prominent in the affairs of the county and representing it in Parliament; the third Adam de Everingham and Sir Thomas Rempston, soldiers who were constantly absent on active service at home and abroad; Thomas de Bekering, sheriff of the county; the Ettons and the Rooses, plain country squires; Augustine Hinde, Master Clothworker and Alderman of the City of London; George Villiers, Duke of Buckingham, courtier and statesman; Sir William Courten, the great merchant prince who had made a fortune in foreign trade; and so back once more, full cycle, to the Dukes of Kingston and the Earls Manvers, great territorial magnates. Under the lordship of each and all of them, the life of the people has gone on with little material change, in the village and in the Open Fields.

In the Domesday Survey Laxton and its people are described as follows:

The Land of Geoffrey Alselin

In Laxintune Tochi had 2 carucates of land [assessed] to the geld. [There is] land for 6 ploughs. There Walter, a man of Geoffrey Alselin's, has 1 plough and 22 villeins and 7 bordars having 5 ploughs and 5 serfs (servi) and 1 female serf (ancilla) and 40 acres of meadow. Wood[land] for pannage 1 league in length and half a league in breadth. In King Edward's time it was worth 9 pounds; now [it is worth] 6 pounds.[1]

This is the first reference found about Laxton, its people, and its farmlands. The adult male population is put at 35, and between them they had land for six ploughs, say about 700 acres if some 120 acres was the scope of a plough-team; they had 40 acres of land for mowing and a considerable extent of woodland for pannage. The rest of the manor must have been waste and scrub, used in later times and so, presumably, at the time of the Domesday Survey, for common grazing and to provide materials for fuel, fencing, and building.

There is no mention of a mill at this time, but one was standing

---

[1] *Domesday Book*, fol. 281.

in 1252, and the small community appears as a self-sufficing economic unit practising agriculture already by the three-field system, grazing their livestock on the stubbles and wastes, fattening their pigs on the fall of acorns and beechmast in the woods, grinding their corn at the manor windmill—in short, exploiting all the resources of nature with their primitive technique to get their living by the oldest art known to man.

The land tenure was the English manorial system, the holdings scattered in strips, each of one day's work, throughout the tillage lands. As the population recorded in Domesday increased, the area of the ploughlands was increased, also, by encroachments upon the waste.

The Domesday Survey mentions meadow land. This lay along the little stream running east and west through the middle of the manor, and here, as in the Open Fields, the farmers held the land in little scattered strips, or doles, each sufficient for a day's mowing when allowance is made for the other work of the farm which had to be done.

At this time and for long after, all the people lived close together in a compact village, such farm buildings as they needed being adjacent to their houses and each homestead having a small croft, or paddock, behind it, in which such stock was run as needed more personal attention than could be given on the commons and wastes. Laxton, at the Domesday Survey, was a small community living in a village built along the road running through its northern part which links it to Ollerton, on the west, and to Tuxford, on the east. Behind the homesteads on either side of the road was a chain of grass paddocks, and beyond these, again, lay the ploughlands in the three Open Fields. Along the stream in the bottom was the meadow land, unfenced, and all round the occupied parts of the parish was a great area of woodland and waste.

The next document throwing light upon the economy of Laxton is a charter, dated 1232, confirming to Robert de Lexington certain gifts of land and other property within the manor and elsewhere. The part relating to Laxton runs:

Grant dated at Westminster 4 Feb. 1232 to Robert de Lexinton, his heirs and assigns, of the following gifts, grants and quitclaims:—

of the gift of Maud de Kauz (inter alia) a bovate in Lexintun with a toft and croft, which Hugh Mansel held, and three acres and a half in the field of Lexintun towards Osantun in the tillage called Tunstal.

of the gift of the same, four bovates of her demesne at Lexintun, each containing 10 acres, with a little meadow between the tillage of Cruchewelle and the brook that falls into the fishpond, 6 ac. of meadow in the meadow of Estkirk on the east side, two bovates which Robert son of Geoffrey the reeve held in Lexintun, a toft which Coleswanus held in Morhuses and all her wood there.

of the gift of John de Birkin, the hamlet called Moorhuses and the men dwelling there with all that goes with them and their goods; the meadow called Nabheng, which Geoffrey de Lond held, 12d. of service, which Hugh the clerk paid to said John yearly for 4 acres and the 4 acres; a toft formerly of Ranulf le Francers; 4 bovates of land which Geoffrey son of Roger and William son of Geoffrey held, with the tofts and crofts thereto belonging, and meadows called Fordayles.

of the quitclaim of said John, remission of two pounds of pepper which sd Robert used to pay to him for his holding in Lexintun and Newtun under the charters of Maud de Kauz:

of the gift of said John, 90 ac. by the perch of 20 feet, of his demesne in Lexinton, and all the meadow which he had in demesne in Estkirk, with 6s. 6d., which he used to receive yearly through the said Robert from the land of Alan son of Robert, and the land of the said Alan.

of the grant and quitclaim of said John, all his right in that part of the wood of Lexintun which is beyond Ballandebec on the south side; also licence to make exchanges of land with his men in Lexintun, both free and bond.

of the gift of Thomas de Birkin, all the wood called Knapenshay and all the meadow called Suthlund, and five sellions of demesne in Langhill; the homage and service of Engeram the cook of the holding held from the sd Thomas in Lexinton.

of the gift of Robert de Everingham and Isabel his wife, 100s. of land in Lexintun, that is the land which the said Robert de Lexintun formerly held for the term of 12 years under an agreement, made between him and Thomas de Birkin.

of the gift of Roger son of Geoffrey de Lexinton, 4 bovates of land in Lexinton.

of the gift of Alard de Lexinton, all his land in Lexintun, that is 3 bovates and 2 tofts, which he had of the gift of Maud de Kauz:

of the gift of John de Lascy, constable of Chester, two parts of the wood, which was in dispute between him and John de Birkin, that is the two parts lying nearer to the brook called Balandebec, and land in the fields of Lexintun which Ralph son of Stephen held;[1]

(also land in Egmanton, West Markham, Weston, etc.)

This charter, dated about 150 years after the Domesday Survey, enables us to draw a picture of a self-contained village community in full working. We know from other evidence that Laxton was now the head manor of a barony and that its lords had built a castle there, above the village, and a church upon the village street. Besides the lord, the other grades of a feudal community are disclosed. The charter itself is the first evidence of the creation of a large freehold, for which in later years the status of a sub-manor was claimed. There is evidence of smaller freeholds and of

[1] *Cal. Charter Rolls*, vol. i, 1226–57, p. 149.

ordinary villein tenure, and there is mention of the parish priest (Hugh, the clerk), of the reeve (Robert, son of Geoffrey), and even of the cook. As to the conditions of tenure, these again are representative, the large freehold or sub-manor being held, as we know from later evidence, by military service, the smaller ones by quit-rents, while the tenants of the manor held by services, or by money rents, or both.

There is evidence of the cultivation of the arable land in Open Fields, in the mention of some of the furlongs within them. Several of the names in the charter recur in Mark Pierce's survey and map of 1635, while some are still in use today. The 'tillage of Cruchewelle' is Crouchwell Furlong in the West Field, and the 'five sellions of demesne in Langhill' are lands in Langwell Syke Furlong in Mill Field, both of them being ploughlands near the village. The 'tillage called Tunstal' has not been identified, but 'the field of Lexintun towards Osantun' in which it was, must be the South Field.

There was meadow land, both open and inclosed. Meadows mentioned in the charter, which can be identified by their names, are situated on the south boundary of the manor ('Nabheng'), or adjacent to the hamlet of Moorhouse, on the east ('Estkirk'). This is the first mention of Moorhouse, and the hamlet 'and the men dwelling there, with all that goes with them and their goods' were granted to Robert de Lexington and formed the nucleus of his sub-manor.

Perhaps the most interesting evidence in the charter is that which concerns the lord's demesne. At some previous date, presumably when the castle was built, the family of de Caux had inclosed, as part of their demesne, land on the northern boundary of the parish, between the West Field and the wood designated East Park Wood in the survey of 1635. It is probable that all this land was once part of the wood, and the demesne closes created out of it were grass closes. Below the castle and close to it was a spring which fed a fishpond, the remains of which can still be seen. But the reference in the charter to 'five selions of demesne in Langhill', is evidence, confirmation of which is supplied in a later document,[1] of what is called scattered demesne. It is commonly stated that a distinguishing feature of the lord's land in the medieval manor was that he occupied it in severalty, by contrast with the freeholders and his tenants, who held their arable land and much of their meadow land in scattered strips in the common fields and meadows. At Laxton, at all events, the lord's arable land was scattered in the Open Fields with that of the other occupiers, and evidence from other places can be cited which suggests

[1] See p. 80, *post*.

that, at one time, this was general throughout the country.[1] The practice of inclosing the arable as well as the grassland of the demesne began, however, at an early date.

Finally, the picture of the manor is completed by the reference to the woods, all of them lying on the boundaries, and available, as will presently appear, for extensions of the farming area as the community grew.

It is not possible to reconstruct the rents and services from the details given in the charter. The customary holding of land at the date of the charter was the bovate or oxgang, 'each containing 10 acres', but if these were estimated 'by the perch of 20 feet' they would be about 30 per cent. larger by standard measurement. This unit of land was held generally with a toft and croft, a toft being a house which carried grazing-rights upon the wastes of the manor, and it should be noted that, at all events at a later date, such rights were not necessarily attached to every farm within the manor.

Another clause of the charter which calls for comment is the licence to Robert de Lexington 'to make exchanges of land with his men in Lexintun, both free and bond'. This appears to recognize the possibility of greater convenience in farming through the re-allotment of strips, and possibly through some measure of consolidation. Indeed, a licence such as this foreshadows the slow process of inclosure by voluntary agreement which was going on centuries before parliamentary inclosure, evidence of which is afforded by the history of the Laxton Open Fields themselves.[2]

At the time of this charter, then, Laxton was a village community living under the shadow of the Norman castle of its lords, with an outlying hamlet, Moorhouse, on its eastern border. There were demesne closes round the castle, there were open arable fields to the west, south, and east of the village, occupied in common by the lord, the freeholders, and the tenants. There was meadow land, some of which was occupied in common and some inclosed. There were extensive woodlands, particularly on the south side of the manor. There was almost certainly a mill.

A big freehold, having the status of a sub-manor, had been created by grants of succeeding lords, with the hamlet of Moorhouse as its nucleus, its lands, both arable and grass, being intermingled with those of the lord, of the smaller freeholders, and of

---

[1] See, for example, *Essex: Anham (? Henham)*, 4 *John, Ped. Fin.*:

A moiety of Thomas Ivelchild's demesne	1½ roods at the windmill
6 acres in Hofeld	2½ acres in la Brome
3 acres under Langeheg	1½ acres in Ho
4 acres in the Broadfield	½ acre meadow in Frithewade.
1½ acres of land under Langeheg	

[2] See p. 110, *post.*

the lord's tenants. Indeed, the outstanding feature of the agricultural organization of Laxton is that except for the demesne closes
and, perhaps, a few other inclosures of grassland and the little
paddocks adjacent to each homestead, all the people of Laxton
—the lord, the sub-lord, the small freeholders, and the tenants—
occupied their arable land and their meadow land in intermingled
holdings, each one of them rigidly bound by the code which
regulated the common use of the land.

Speaking broadly, the medieval manor was made up of the
lord's demesne, of the messuages and lands of the freeholders and
of the tenants, of the holdings of the cottars, and of the woodlands
and waste.

The lord's demesne included the castle or manor-house, if he
were resident, with its appurtenant buildings, often with some inclosed fields round it. Like the freeholders and tenants, his living
was derived from his land, and so he occupied strips in the open
arable fields which were cultivated for him. He was also the
owner of the waste.

The freeholders, or yeomen, stood next below the lord. In
effect, they were hereditary tenants, owing certain duties to the
lord but having security of tenure and the right of disposition of
their lands so long as these duties were fulfilled. They had their
houses, their strips in the arable fields amongst those of the lord
and of his tenants in villeinage, their doles of meadow land, and
grazing and other rights on the lord's waste.

The holdings of the unfree tenants resembled those of the freeholders in structure, but the tenure differed. The tenant in villeinage had no power of disposal, and on his death his lands escheated
to the lord. Until the commutation of service rents, it was this
class of the village community upon which devolved the work of
cultivating the lord's land.

The cottars were more than mere cottagers, but though they
had some land they did not occupy full-time holdings in the Open
Fields.[1]

During the next 400 years information about Laxton and its
economic and social life is derived mainly from the Inquisitions
post mortem on the passing of the lords and sub-lords. These were,
in effect, probate valuations made on the death of the lord. They
differ very much in the amount of information they supply. The
name of the deceased lord is given, together with the name and
age of his heir, and the service by which the manor was held. The

---

[1] This is a mere skeleton of the social structure of the manor. For a full account of the
various classes of village society and their economic and social status, see Vinogradoff and
other standard writers.

PLATE 12

a. THE CASTLE MOUND, LAXTON

b. LAXTON MILL, 1916

value of the manor is generally given, the extent of the demesne land, and the value of the rents or services of the freeholders and tenants. There is often a good deal of miscellaneous information, such as the value of the perquisites of the court, and of the mill, fishponds, dovecotes, &c.

For the manor of Laxton, held in chief of the king, there are eleven inquisitions during the period 1252 to 1606, in which there were thirteen lords.

Descent. The chief manor passed eight times to the eldest son, once to two nieces, and once to four granddaughters. The only break in the descent occurred in 1476, when the manor was given to Thomas Rotherham, Archbishop of York, but it returned to heirs of the grantor's family in 1501, by a marriage with the archbishop's niece. When the manor passed to coheiresses it does not seem to have been divided but it became the portion of one of them, the other or others taking, presumably, other property, for Laxton was only one of several manors held by the descendants of Geoffrey Alselin.

Tenure. Laxton was held of the king in chief by knight's service and this is specified every time from the year 1287. In 1433 it is stated to be a twentieth part of a knight's fee, and so it continues all through the sixteenth century, except that in the inquisition taken on the death of Archbishop Rotherham, in 1501, it is said to be by service of $1\frac{1}{2}$ knight's fees.

Value. Little can be deduced from the figures given for the annual value of the manor, which range from a maximum of £50 in 1501 to a minimum of £6. 13s. 4d. in 1606. A variation from £20 on the death of Adam de Everingham in 1281 to £45. 11s. 4d. on the death of his son Robert, six years later, suggests that the valuations are not comparable. On three occasions values are not specified.

The Lord's Demesne

The Capital Messuage. The court and garden, with herbage, worth half a mark, are mentioned in the year 1252. In 1287 it is recorded that the capital messuage was not sufficient for the lord's sustenance by the year. Its equipment included a grange, cattle-shed, stable, and other houses, worth 4s., and two gardens with herbage and fruits, worth 5s. As owners of other manors, the de Everinghams had no need to rely upon Laxton for their subsistence the year through. In 1388, indeed, upon the death of the last Adam de Everingham, it is recorded that the site of the manor is worth nothing, and it is probable that the family had ceased to live there. Upon the death of John de Etton, in 1433, who had succeeded through his marriage to Adam's granddaughter, it was recorded again that the site of the manor was worth nothing, 'because it is ruinous'. This marks the end of the Norman castle.

The Land. The extent of the arable land of the lord's demesne is given sometimes in acres and sometimes in carucates. In 1252 it was 254 acres, each worth 6*d*. In 1287 it was 240 acres, and in 1341, upon the death of the second Adam de Everingham, it is put at 300 acres, worth 5*d*. per acre, coupled with the interesting note that two parts of it were sown and the third lay waste, the herbage being worth nothing because it lay in common. Here is further and direct evidence for scattered demesne lands. Clearly the lord's land lay in the Open Fields, one-third being in winter corn, one-third in spring corn, and the other third in fallow (waste) and subject to common grazing.

In the years 1281, 1388, and 1433 the arable lands of the demesne are given as 4, 3, and 4 carucates respectively. Peter Roos, in 1606, had 300 acres of ploughland in his demesne.

The meadow land of the demesne, that is to say, grassland for hay-making, is difficult to estimate. In 1252 there were 34 acres in the common meadows and two meadows inclosed. There is little change until the end of the period under review, when Peter Roos is found to have 100 acres.

Grazing, apart from the aftermath of the meadows and the stubbles and fallows of the Open Fields, extended over the wastes and a few closes. Herbage and pannage are mentioned in the three earlier inquisitions, otherwise there is no separate mention of it until 1521, when Humphrey Roos is said to have had 160 acres inclosed by hedges. Probably most of this was represented by the demesne closes round the site of the old castle. In 1606 his grandson, Peter, was said to have 300 acres of pasture.

The Laxton woodlands were extensive, but there is no complete record of those belonging to the main manor in the years under review. There is no mention of any between the Domesday Survey and 1388, when 'wood containing 80 acres, worth 26*s*. 8*d*.' is recorded; in 1433 the same acreage is said to have been worth 20*s*.

Other Property of the Demesne. Other items of value included in the inquisitions are the advowson of the church of Laxton, the mill, the fishpond, and the dovehouse.

The advowson is mentioned in 1287 as being worth 40 marks, and in 1433 as being worth nothing, because it was not vacant. In 1476 the advowson passed to the College of Jesus, Rotherham, with whom it remained until the college was dissolved, when it passed to the Crown, and early in the seventeenth century it was acquired by the family of Pierrepont.

The windmill is recorded in 1252, when it was worth 15s., but in 1341 it was worth only 6s. 8d. 'because it is broken and ruinous'. In 1388 the value was only 4s. The mill was standing in 1606, when Peter Roos died, and it continued in use, grinding corn for the people of Laxton, until 1916, when it was blown down, and it has never been rebuilt.

The fishpond, of which the first mention occurred in Robert de Lexington's charter of 1232, was said to be worth 2s. in 1287, on the death of Sir Robert de Everingham.

There is no mention of the dovehouse until 1606.

The Tenants and Freeholders

Only in the first inquisition, that of the year 1252, are the number of tenants and their holdings specified; there were 8 free tenants holding 12½ bovates, who paid 38s. 10d., an unspecified number of villeins holding 35 bovates, each worth half a mark (6s. 8d.), and 20 cottagers paying 36s. 7d. The difference in the rental between 1388 and 1433 is striking. At the former date, tenants at will paid £20 and tenants in bondage 10s. At the latter date there were free tenants paying 10s., tenants at will paying £5, and tenants in bondage paying 20s. Was this due to changes in agrarian conditions following the Black Death?

The Manor Court and View of Frankpledge. In the years 1252 and 1287 the pleas and perquisites of the court were worth half a mark, but thereafter the value steadily declined. The view of frankpledge is mentioned, both in 1388 and in 1433, as rendering to the king 5s. yearly and worth nothing beyond.

Turning now to the sub-manor, knowledge of the two moieties is derived from Robert de Lexington's charter and again from the Inquisitions *post mortem*, of which there are fourteen during the period 1256 to 1528.

Descent. The sub-manor descended through the de Lexington family, till in 1288 it passed to two co-heiresses, who married respectively into the de Bekering and de Longvilliers families. From that time, until a piecemeal dispersal began in the early seventeenth century, it passed in two equal parts.

Tenure. The sub-manor was held of Adam de Everingham and his heirs, by half a knight's fee and payment of a penny, before its partition in 1288. Thereafter, until 1352, the family of de Bekering are recorded as holding by knight's service, but the service seems to have been uncertain after this date, and in 1426 the jury inquiring into the value of the estate of Thomas de Bekering the younger said they were utterly ignorant by what service it was held. Subsequently the tenants of both moieties are recorded as holding by payment of 1*d*. or 1½*d*.

Value. As with the chief manor, little can be made of the values recorded in the Inquisitions *post mortem*. Before the partition they vary from so little as £16. 13*s*. 11*d*. on the death of Henry de Lessington, in 1258, to so much as £34. 2*s*. on the death of his heir, Robert de Markham. After the partition the moiety taken by the family of de Bekering is valued at £11. 18*s*. 9*d*. in 1326, but at no more than £6 in 1458. The part taken by the family of de Longvilliers, on the other hand, is valued at £18 in 1297, and at the same figure in 1528.

The Capital Messuage. There is no mention of a manor-house until 1326, when the first de Bekering had one, and he may have built it. In the years 1376 and 1387 it is said to be worth nothing, and there is no further mention of it. Thomas de Longvilliers had a messuage and other property in Laxton Moorhouse, and it is recorded, in 1374, that he had held of Adam de Everingham by an eighth of a knight's fee.

The Land. The records of the family of de Longvilliers and their descendants when considered in conjunction with those of de Bekering, which are more numerous, are insufficient for any reconstruction of the sub-manor. Some points, however, can be noted. It is twice recorded that the herbage on the arable land of the de Bekering demesne was worth nothing because it lay in common, a further proof of scattered demesne lands. In 1426 a great increase occurred in the extent of the arable land in the occupation of Thomas de Bekering, a change which is to be observed about the same time in the lands occupied by John de Etton, the lord of the main manor. The meadow land shows a similar tendency. It is recorded, moreover, that Thomas de Bekering had twelve messuages which were worth nothing, being ruinous, while John de Etton's rents showed likewise a remarkable reduction. Once more the question arises: Had an epidemic reduced the population of the village, or is this reduction accounted for by the social changes following the Peasants' Revolt and the Statute of Labourers?

The grazing seems to have been shared by the two lords of the sub-manor. Woodland is first mentioned in 1352, when Thomas de Bekering had a certain inclosed wood, worth nothing because it had been cut down. There is mention, also, of the sale of underwood from a wood called Esthod,[1] and, in 1426, Thomas de Bekering had 60 acres of great wood worth nothing.

The Tenants. The inquisitions distinguish between different kinds of tenants only on two occasions. In 1289 Robert de Mark-

---

[1] Mentioned under the name of Estoved in the Charter of 1232.

ham had rent of assize from free tenants, £7. 3s. 10d.; villeins, £4. 4s.; and cottars, 73s. 6d. This was the undivided sub-manor. In 1297, after the partition, John de Longvilliers had:

24 free tenants holding 16½ bovates and paying £4. 2s. 5d.

5 neifs holding 6½ bovates in villeinage and paying 1s. 8d.

12 cottars holding 12 cottages and paying 23s. 6d.

Later inquisitions give the rent of assize generally as one total.

From earliest times it had been customary for the routine work on the farms of the lords of manors to be performed by their tenants as a condition of their tenure. They had to plough the land; to harrow it down after the seed had been broadcast on the furrow by the lord's servants; to go weeding during the growing-season; to cut and carry both hay and corn, and, later, to thresh the corn. Before the days of a money economy, and afterwards, when money was still scarce, it was the obvious means by which the landlord could get a rent from his tenants.

The number of days' work to be rendered throughout the seasons was definite, but it might not be enough for the work to be done, and the lord could call upon his tenants for additional services, called *precaria*, for which an acknowledgement was paid, sometimes in the form of food and drink while the work was in progress. At the inquisition on the death of Adam de Evering-ham, in 1281, there is a reference to the value of the works of the villeins at Laxton, and six years later, on the death of his son Robert, the jury found

that the customary *precaria*, as in ploughing, harrowing, cartage, mowing of meadows, reaping corn and the cocks of the place are worth by the year £6. 5s. 3d.

In 1326, in the inquisition on the death of the first Thomas de Bekering, the services due from the neifs, or villeins, are recorded in detail:

. . . the aforesaid neifs of Laxton shall do yearly, for ploughing, in all xii works, with the food of their lord, and xii works for harrowing the land, and each work for harrowing the land is worth beyond food iid. and the work for harrowing the land id. Sum iiis. Also the neifs shall weed for two days and a half, and the work is worth by the day ½d. And four neifs shall mow the meadow of the lord by vii works, price of a work iid. Sum xivd. Also . . . works, to wit the hay of the lord, by xxx works, price of a work id. Sum iis. vid. Also the said neifs shall reap the corn of the lord by xlii works, with the food of the lord once in the day, price of the work beyond the food id. Sum iiis. vid. Also the four neifs shall carry the hay and corn of the lord for x dàys, price of the work beyond the food is Sum xxd. [*sic*].

The origin of these services is easily understood, but they were irksome to all but the recipient and every opportunity was taken to commute them, whatever they were, for money payments. At Laxton it is interesting to note that the last mention of the value of rents and services on the main manor in the Inquisitions *post mortem* was in 1287. Nothing is said about the value either of villein work or *precaria* at the death of the next lord, the second Adam de Everingham, in 1341, while the rents of all classes of tenants from that time onwards are stated in money and they were payable half-yearly, generally at Martinmas and Pentecost. Thus it would appear that on the main manor commutation was arranged early in the fourteenth century. How soon the services on the sub-manor recorded in Thomas de Bekering's inquisition, in 1326, were commuted has not been determined, but there is no mention of them after this date. The sums recorded for each of the operations, 2*d.* for ploughing, 1*d.* for weeding, and so on, are not payments made to the villeins, but the jury's estimate of the value of the work to the lord.

The onerous nature of the work is evident when it is realized that it amounts to about 100 days in the year for each villein. This was the equivalent of more than two days' work in each week, and allowing for Sundays and holy days it must have taken the villeins, or members of their families, away from their own holdings for nearly one-half of their working time.

It is of interest to note that ploughing and mowing are valued at 2*d.* a day, and all other work at 1*d.* except weeding, which was priced at $\frac{1}{2}d$. Ploughing and mowing are skilled operations, performed, no doubt, by the villein in person, whereas much of the other work could be delegated to his sons, and things such as weeding and haymaking to his wife and children. Food was given to the men when ploughing, harvesting, and carrying hay and corn, that is to say, on sixty-four of the days.

Returning now to complete the abstract of the evidence of the Inquisitions *post mortem* referring to the sub-manor, it had its own windmill in 1289, which stood in the South Field. The profits of the mill were shared between the families of de Bekering and de Longvilliers and their descendants. In 1352, on the death of the second Sir Thomas de Bekering, it was described as being decayed and ruinous. The de Bekerings had also a dovecote.

There is no mention of a separate manorial court for the sub-manor until 1297, when it is recorded, on the death of John de Longvilliers, that the pleas and perquisites of the court were worth 5*s.* According to Vinogradoff, it was the recognized right of every lord to hold a court, for the settlement of the disputes of his tenants,[1] but at Laxton the lord of the main manor was careful to see that his jurisdiction in other matters was not infringed by

[1] Vinogradoff, P., *The Growth of the Manor*, p. 363.

the court of his sub-lord. In 1313 the second Adam de Everingham and Clarice his wife were summoned to answer a charge of
illegal distress, having taken and detained the cow of one William
Vesey, of Laxton. They said that at the view of frankpledge it was
found that William had brewed and sold beer against the assize
and he was amerced 12d., for which they took his cow. William
said that he never went to Adam's and Clarice's view of frankpledge, but to that of Thomas de Longvilliers and Cecily de
Bekering, lords of a moiety of the vill of Laxton, to which Adam
and Clarice replied that Thomas and Cecily had no view of frankpledge in the vill.[1] In 1339 there was another case, exactly similar,
Adam de Everingham having distrained upon the ox of William
de Marischal, of Laxton, who had been amerced 6d. at Adam's
view of frankpledge for an offence against the assize of ale. He,
too, claimed that he was not in Adam's frankpledge, but in that of
Thomas de Bekering and Thomas de Longvilliers.[2] Ten years
before, however, when, under a writ of *Quo Warranto*, these two
had claimed freewarren in Laxton through the Royal Charter of
Henry III granted to their ancestor, Robert de Lexington, it was
established that while they had used their rights properly and
their claim must be allowed, they were in mercy for a false claim
to amend the assize of bread and ale.[3]

There is no mention of the court of the sub-manor later than
the inquisition on the death of Sir Thomas de Bekering, in 1352.

---

[1] *De Banco* Rolls, No. 201, Notts., m. 55.
[2] *De Banco* Rolls, No. 318, Notts., m. 2 d.
[3] *Placita de Quo Warranto*, 3 Edw. III, p. 57.

VII. THE SURVEY OF 1635

IN 1625 the main manor of Laxton had been bought from the
Duke of Buckingham by Sir William Courten, Kt., a merchant of the City of London. In that year the duke had
employed Francis and William Mason to make two plans
and terriers of Laxton and of the adjacent manor of Kneesal, and
ten years later, upon the instructions of Sir William Courten,
these were revised by one Mark Pierce, who prepared one map
for the two manors and one 'Booke of Survaye', or terrier. Both
map and terrier were preserved in the muniment-room at Thoresby
until 1942, when they were sold to the Bodleian Library. The
map, done on sheepskins to a scale of 8 inches to 1 mile, delineates
with great accuracy and detail not only every house, building, and
inclosure in the two manors, but also every strip of ploughland in
the Open Fields and every dole of grassland in the meadows.
Each inclosure, strip, and dole is numbered, and the numbers
have reference to the terrier, in which is recorded a description
of each parcel, with the owner, occupier, and acreage.

The Laxton portion of this beautiful map, which is embellished
with many agricultural and sporting scenes, has been reproduced,
half-scale, for this work, from a faithful tracing of the original,
which, though in a fair state of preservation, could not be reproduced by photography. Where the reference numbers are missing
in the reproduction they were illegible in the original, but they
can usually be supplied by numbering onward or backward from
the adjacent ones. In the corners of the map are a north-point,
a scale, a coat of arms, that of Sir William Courten, and a beautifully decorated title which reads as follows:

A PLAT AND DESCRIPTION OF THE WHOLE MANNOR & LORDSHIP of
Laxton with Laxton Moorehouse in the County of Nottingham and also
of the Mannor & Lordship of Kneesall lying adiacent to the aforesaid
Mannor of Laxton & within the said County Which Suruey was first taken
and two seuerall Platts thereof made by Francis Mason & William Mason
in the year of our Lord 1625 by the apointment of the Right Honᵇˡᵉ the
Duke of Buckingham & then possessor of these Mannors And Reviewed
perfected and this one intire Platt & Booke of Suruey made of both the said
Mannors by Mark Pierce in the yeare 1635 by the apointment of the Right
worshipfull Sir William Courten of London Knight Purchaser & Possessor
thereof In the description of all & euery parcell of which Lands there is
placed certaine numbers which are to be refered to the correspondent numbers in the booke of Suruey which sheweth the name of euery Comon Field
& of euery close & furlong therin with the name of euery Tenant & Freehold
erto which each parcell belongeth & the measure thereof And at the end of

PLATE 13

a. HAWKING, LAXTON, 1635

b. STAG-HUNTING, LAXTON, 1635

the particulars of the Lands belonging to these seuerall Mannors there is placed the Collections or Totall Summes of Meddow Pasture & Arable houlden by euery Tenent & Freehoulder therein With all the seuerall Tenements of Lands lately purchased by the said Sir William Courten now Lord of these Mannors of Mr. Augustine Hind Esq Francis Rosse Esq within the Mannor of Laxton and of Mr. Samwell Hartup within the Mannor of Kneesall knowne & distinguished in the Platt by a light yellow colour And at the end of the Totall Summes of the Lands of all the Tenants & Freeholders there is placed the Totall Summe of each Mannor And after the Summe a Summarie or generall Totall of both the said Mannors are placed Tables of Parcells seruing for the more speedy findinge out of the Lands belonginge to euery perticular Tenement Besides the distinction of colours whereby the Demesne & Tenement lands are seuered from the Lands of the Free Tenents which are all left white All which numbers before mentioned both in the Booke of Suruey and in this Platt are equally correspondent the one to the other as by comparinge them together plainly apeareth.

For convenience of study and publication, the map has been divided into five sections, which follow the main divisions of the manor:

(i) Laxton Town, the demesne closes and woods, the East Field, and the Long Meadow.
(ii) West Field and Westwood Common.
(iii) Mill Field, and various closes and meadows.
(iv) South Field, and other woods and closes.
(v) The Hamlet of Laxton Moorhouse and its fields, both open and inclosed.

There are 3,333 parcels of land. The holdings of freeholders are uncoloured in the original, those of the tenants being red, and the lands mentioned in the title as having been bought from Mr. Hinde and Mr. Roos, yellow. All the furlongs in the Open Fields are identified by capital letters, which are repeated, together with their names, or descriptions where unnamed, in the *Booke of Survaye*.

The scenes of rural life are clear and vivid. Most farming operations are portrayed: ploughing, sowing, harrowing, and harvesting; mowing, haymaking, milking, and shepherding. The plough-teams are always made up of two bullocks with a horse in the lead, and the wagons resemble the 'hermaphrodite', a two-wheeled cart fitted with a movable fore-carriage, which has been in general use at Laxton until today. The sporting scenes include stag-hunting, hare-hunting, and hawking, and these and the agricultural pictures illustrate both the methods and the costume of the time.

The object of a map and terrier of a manor was to account for all the property within it, both that of the lord and of those claiming freeholds. Only in this way could the lord of the manor define his own estate, for everything—woodlands, wastes, roads, water—which was not claimed by the freeholders, by the church, or by charitable trusts, was directly under his control.

The manor of Laxton with Laxton Moorhouse extended to 3,853 acres, and, while Sir William Courten acquired the manorial rights over the whole, the extent of the lands coming under his direct control was little more than one-half of this. The rest, amounting to 1,910 acres, was held by the freeholders, about twenty-five in number, the largest of whom were Peter Broughton and Augustine Hinde, esquires, who were holders of moieties of the old sub-manor, each of them having about 600 acres. Some of the others were yeomen, holding up to 75 acres, while a dozen or more held little freeholds of no more than an acre or two, and some even less than one acre.

Shortly after his purchase of the manor, Sir William Courten bought five farms, part of Mr. Augustine Hinde's freehold, and thus began the process of consolidation which was carried on by the lords of the manor, by purchase and exchange, throughout the next three centuries. The lands included in this purchase, about 300 acres, are distinguished in the *Booke of Survaye* by a note against each, 'late Hindes'. At the same time he bought two other freeholds, those of Mr. Francis Roos and Mr. Edward Snow, together about 73 acres. Thus, at the time at which the survey was made, Sir William had about 2,316 acres in Laxton and Laxton Moorhouse under his direct control.

The *Booke of Survaye* is a folio, bound in parchment, with the arms of Sir William Courten on the cover, and the title-page reproduced as the frontispiece to this volume follows closely the legend on the map. The plan is to give, first, a complete schedule of the 3,333 parcels of land of which the manor was composed, as delineated on the map, with the name of the freeholder, or of the tenant, of each, and its acreage. Then follows a summary of the meadow, pasture, and arable land as reserved in the hands of the lord of the manor or as let by him to each of his tenants, or as held by each of the freeholders of the manor, together with their yearly rents or chief rents. Last come the 'Tables of Parcelles serving for the redy finding out of all the parcells of land houlden by every tenant and Freehoulder within the manor of Laxton and Laxton Moorhouse'—a register of their names followed by the map numbers of each parcel of the land held by them, and the field, or place, in which it lay. In the following pages a detailed examination of the *Booke of Survaye* and of the map to which it refers is made.

Taking the *first section* of the reproduction of the map, which includes Laxton Town, the demesne closes and woods, the East Field, and the Long Meadow, an inspection of it shows the way in which the demesne and village were laid out, and their general conformity to the conventional descriptions of the typical manor. On the high ground to the north of the village are the remains of the keep and bailey of the Norman castle. To the south of it stands the Tudor manor-house with its outbuildings and gardens, 'the Gatehouse, brewhouses, Stables, Cowhouses, two Dove-houses, Court, garden, Mount Orchard, vineyard orchard, two barnes, one hempyard, and the Hall Lound', in fact all the appurtenances essential to the self-contained life of a landowner of the times (No. 2998).

On each side of the house and extending to the northern boundary of the manor are some of the demesne closes. The names of some of them suggest that they had been reclaimed from woodland or waste: the Mowing Butwood (No. 3006), the Bryerie and the Little Butwood (No. 3004 and 3005), the various Breck Closes (Nos. 3014 and 3021) to the north-east. The names of others, again, suggest their uses: the Farther and Hither Conygrey Meadows (Nos. 3007 and 3008), formerly perhaps the rabbit-warrens of the lord; the Great and Little Pond meadows (Nos. 3000 and 3002), containing fishponds; the Horse Close (No. 3003). The most westerly of the closes, lying between the road and the big wood, was known as the Justing Close (No. 3009), probably nothing to do with the tourney, but a corruption of 'agisting' close, a field into which stock could be turned at a charge for grazing.[1]

Eastward from the Justing Close is the big East Park Wood (No. 3022), of 136 acres, and farther eastward and south of the wood down so far as the Long Meadow which borders the stream are more closes, some demesne, some sub-manor, and some in the occupation of tenants. On the extreme north-west corner of this section of the map of Laxton are the Cruchewell Closes (Nos. 294 to 303), which formed part of the sub-manor; and at the extreme south-east, at the end of the Long Meadow, are two closes called Tharkholme (Nos. 2728 and 2729). Below the church are three more closes (Nos. 3033, 3034, and 3035), once part of the demesne.

South of the manor-house and immediately below it lies the village, displayed on either side of the road which runs east and west from Tuxford to Ollerton, and on the road south from it which goes to Moorhouse. Near the junction of the roads and in the centre of the village stands the church of St. Michael. No. 1 in map and Terrier is the church and churchyard, and

---

[1] There was another of the same name in the hamlet of Moorhouse.

the village holdings number on to No. 124, each number being followed by the name of the tenant or freeholder, together with a description of the holding and its acreage, thus:

Number	Name	a	r.	p.
44	John Jepson a cottage and yard			38
63	Thomas Freeman a Toft and cloase	4	0	1
76	Christopher Salmon a Messuage house, yard and			
	Croft close at his backe side	1	0	35
100	Robt Shipton a Messuage and yard *Free*	1	3	35

Freeholds are so described in this and in all the other sections of the terrier. There are, in all, 31 messuages, 6 houses (including the vicarage and the chantry house), 7 cottage houses, and 43 cottages, adopting the classification of the Terrier, a total of 87 dwelling-houses of all sorts. The other entries in this section are either crofts, closes, or tofts, and the total extent is 156 a. 1 r. 6 p.,

All the houses and cottages adjoin the roads, and those of them that are farmhouses have their yards and buildings behind them. Each of these, too, has behind it a croft or inclosure of grassland. Except for 'a Cottage and little croft incloased in the Westwood Common' (No. 124), which appears in the second section of the reproduction of the map of Laxton, there was no habitation of any kind outside the village, nor was there any building other than those in the village, except for the windmills (Nos. 2404 and 1069) which stood on the high ground in Mill Field and in South Field.

The East Field lies, as its name indicates, on the east side of the village, between its houses and crofts and the closes below East Park Wood. This is the smallest of the open arable fields, and at the time of the survey it was farmed, in the rotation, together with the West Field, the acreage of the two together being roughly approximate to that of either of the other two fields. It is 134 a. 3 r. 16 p. in extent, divided in 13 furlongs, containing together 241 parcels of land, numbering from 617 to 857 in the map and Terrier.

This section of the map is completed by a long strip of grass-land on the south, bordering the stream—the Long Meadow. In any manor bounded or intersected by a stream, the low-lying land adjacent to it, where grass grew well and arable cultivation might be difficult, was generally assigned to the common meadows, and the Long Meadow at Laxton comprised the largest part of the mowing ground. It was 67 a. 3 r. 13 p. in extent, divided into four parts, each of them allocated amongst the freeholders and tenants in strips known as doles. They number from 2,472 to 2,727, making 256 separate parcels in all. Some of the parcels, however, comprise two or more doles, and a single dole is generally

PLATE 15

Laxton Demeisnes

No.	Description	a	r	p
2998	Mr Samuell Stanford houldth (at the will of the Lord of th^{is} Man^{or}) Laxton Hall, or the Mann^o house, wth the Gatehouse, brewhouse, Stables, Cow house, two Douehouses, Court, garden, Mount orhar, somevard orchard, two barnes, one hempyard and the Hall yeaund, rontayning togethd	7	2	26
2999	Stanford afores^d houlath ye Hall meddow —	15	0	15
3000	Willm Challond, the Great Pond medow —	6	1	30
3001	Thomas feneuere Robt feneuere & Henry Pith togeth^r hould ye North bush wood —	19	0	10
3002	Tho: feneuere & predict: The Little Pond	4	1	21
3003	Mr Stanford afores^d. The horse Clasc —	4	3	30
3004	Mr Stanford & late, Willm Graisbrough, Barrerie Butwood —	24	2	27
3005	Zacharry Woulflete & Peter Poss^e The Little Butwood meddowe —	9	3	17
3006	Christopher Blonket Willm Graisbrough & Chrstr Bitney, The moving Butwood —	19	1	19
3007	Richard Whalehead Henry Pith and Peter Smith, the farther Conygrey medd	4	3	1
3008	Mr Stanford afores^d hith Conygrer medd	4	3	20
3009	Stanford afores^d hould ye fushing Clasc —	9	2	32
3010	The said Stanford, houldth newdik rlaisc —	14	1	9
3011	New dike Close late, m ffraunp Eß ßten —	18	3	36
3012	Mr Stanford & Willm Salmon late, Onas wyldsmith, west fnger rlosc meds	18	2	4
3013	Tho: Tailer Senr woddow Harpham & Willm Dickinson the Neither New dike rlaisc —	23	3	37
3014	Thomas feneure South Brerke rloasc —	2	0	21

FROM THE *BOOKE OF SURVAYE OF THE MANOR OF LAXTON*, 1635

about half a rood, the smallest of them being no more than 8 perches.

At the western end of the Long Meadow is Laxton East Moore (No. 3032), a piece of common grazing of 7 acres. A road from the village led across it, giving access to the South Field on the other side of the stream.

The *second section* of the reproduction of the map comprises the West Field and the Common.

The West Field adjoins the village and the Cruchewell Closes on its east side, while the northern limits of the manor, the Common, and the road from Ollerton form its boundaries on the north, west, and south. As noted above, it was farmed in the rotation as one with the East Field.

The open ploughlands of the West Field are 318 a. 3 r. 5 p. in extent, divided into 28 furlongs and 466 parcels. The parcels are numbered in the terrier from 125 to 616, including the Cruchewell Closes, which appear on the first section of the map, and some other inclosures, amounting in all to 88 a. 0 r. 37 p.

This section of the map shows very clearly a particularly interesting feature of the Open Fields. Running across the arable land of the West Field, from south-west to north-east, are two broad belts of land known as 'sykes' or 'sikes'[1] upon which stock are depicted grazing. These are Rodbeck Syke (No. 615) and North Howbecke Syke (No. 616), containing respectively 14 and 11 acres. Similar features will be noted presently, both in the Mill Field and in the South Field, and their occasion and uses will be discussed later.[2]

The Common, known as Westwood, or Cocking Moor (No. 3031), forms the north-western extremity of the manor. It is 88 a. 3 r. 22 p. in extent, and except for the 7 acres in Laxton East Moore it supplied all the common grassland of the manor. Its name suggests that it was once woodland, and the small inclosure in it (No. 124) is known in some documents as 'The Assarts'.

South of the West Field and Laxton town is the next great Open Field, the Mill Field, contained in the *third section* of the reproduction of the map. The parcels in it are numbered from 1606 to 2404 in map and terrier, and its total extent is 833 a. 2 r. 2 p. Of this, just 400 acres are closes and waste, leaving 433 acres in the common arable field. There are several sikes (No. 2403), amounting altogether to nearly 25 acres, and another portion of the common meadow land occurs along the stream, at the middle of the eastern boundary. This is the Shitterpool Meadow (Nos. 2405 to 2471), of 15 a. 1 r. 30 p., comprising no fewer than 82 doles.

---

[1] Pronounced 'seeks'.   [2] See p. 97, *post*.

The large block of closes forming so much of the western and southern portion of the field should be noted (Nos. 1606 to 1623, 1923 to 1937, and 2017 to 2022). The two little furlongs on the extreme east of the map (Nos. 858 to 895 and Nos. 896 to 913) belong to the South Field.

The *fourth section* of the reproduction of the map includes all that part of the manor which lies south of Long Meadow and the village. On its west is the Mill Field and the manor of Kneesal, and on its east the hamlet of Moorhouse and the manor of Ossington.

The South Field proper (Nos. 858 to 1605)[1] comprises the northern half of this section. Its total extent is 507 a. 2 r. 35 p., of which about 50 acres are closes and 30 acres sikes and waste, leaving 428 acres in common arable cultivation, divided into 25 furlongs. It may be noted that this compares with an extent of open arable land of 433 acres in the Mill Field and of 445 acres in the West and East Fields together. Thus, each area applied to the practice of the three-field farming system was approximately equal.

Several big sikes will be observed in this field.

There are a few closes included in the field, the Harwick Closes (Nos. 1097 and 1099), and Munkbrigg Close (No. 1098), on the north-west, in one of which a harvesting scene is depicted. There is also another group of closes in this section of the map, not included in the acreage of South Field. These are Copthorne Close (No. 3023) and the Porters Wong Closes (Nos. 3041, 3054, 3055), which are in the north-east corner.

Apart from the furlongs and these few closes, the most striking features of this section of the map are the broad belt of woodland which runs across it, and the girdle of large closes which surrounds it on the east and south. There are three woods, Bollam Becke (No. 3024), of 65 acres, Middle Springe (No. 3025), 45 acres, and Sawood (No. 3027), also 45 acres, while the close between the two last named, the Cork Gload (No. 3026), 15 acres, was evidently once part of the woodlands. The three woods and the close all form part of the main manor, as do the row of small closes immediately above them, the Stubbin Closes (Nos. 3028 to 3030, and 3037), and the long, narrow close, Hardy Springe (No. 3038) immediately below them. But the long stretch of large closes on the north-east and south were all of them part of the sub-manor, and at the date of Robert de Lexington's Charter, 1232,[2] they were woodland. Those on the north-east (Nos. 3042 and 3056) were known as the Stubbin Closes at the time of Mark Pierce's

---

[1] Nos. 858 to 913 appear on the Mill Field (third) section.
[2] See p. 74, *ante.*

survey, a name which suggests their reclamation from woodland. The next five, going southward (Nos. 3057, 3058, 3043–5), were the Knapney Closes in 1635, and they represent, almost certainly, 'the wood called Knapenshay' in Robert de Lexington's Charter. The two large closes forming the southern end (Nos. 3049 and 3059),[1] in which a hawking scene is depicted, are both called Hartshorn in the *Booke of Survaye*, and they are clearly 'that part of the wood of Lexintun which is beyond Ballandebec on the southside' in the same charter. The Inquisition *post mortem* of Robert de Markham, 1289, mentions 'a little park called Herteshorne' as part of his inheritance in Laxton.

One other portion of this section of the map remains to be described. In the extreme north-east corner are three areas contained within hedges. The first is called South Lound (Nos. 2911 to 2968), containing 46 a. 0 r. 24 p., a stretch of 57 arable strips in the occupation of the cottage tenants.[2] The second is South Lound Meadows (Nos. 2730 to 2739), 22 a. 3 r. 6 p., being eight small and two larger parcels of meadow land. Adjoining these on the west is the third, South Lound Meadow Doles (Nos. 2740 to 2800), 13 a. 2 r. 23 p. (the name does not appear on the map), which were part of the common meadow land.

The *fifth and last section* into which the reproduction of the map of Laxton has been divided includes the hamlet of Moorhouse with its own open arable fields, its meadow land, its commons, and its closes. It will be observed, too, that the manor had some detached parcels of land, about 12 acres in all, in the adjoining parish of Ossington (Nos. 3317 to 3333). Where a manor included one or more hamlets besides the main village, each detached settlement seems commonly to have had its own field system. This was natural enough if the hamlet represents a proportion of a growing village community which had hived off, for very practical reasons, into one of the remoter parts of a large manor, there to develop a separate economic life instead of extending the bounds of the parent settlement to inconvenient distances. The same would be true if it were an original independent settlement made for the same reasons.[3]

---

[1] The irregular numbering of the closes often makes them difficult to find on the maps. Mark Pierce numbered the parcels of arable land in the Open Fields consecutively in furlongs, but the closes of the lord's demesne and of the sub-manor are grouped and numbered at the end of the *Booke of Survaye* in sequence of ownership instead of location.

[2] See p. 121, *post*.

[3] An example from another part of the country is provided in 'The Viewe and Survey of the Mannor of Mudforde and Hinton in the Countie of Somersett' made in the year 1554, which reads: 'The Mannor of Mudford . . . is devyded into too severall hamlets, that is to saye, Mudforde and Hynton. And every of the said hamletts or villagies have thre common feildes, wherin the tenaunts of the same have ther londes lyinge intermedled, as in all other common feildes. . . . None of the hamletts do intercomen with the other, but every hamlet

There was a chapel at Moorhouse (No. 3086) and about twenty dwelling-houses scattered along the roads that traverse the lower part of the hamlet. There was a grass common, Laxton Moorhouse Towne Gate, of 17 acres, in the middle of the village (No. 3299), and another, Moorhouse Hill Common, of 19 acres (No. 3297), at the northern boundary, where it joined the common of the neighbouring parish of Weston. There was a small extent of meadow land, in doles, scattered round the south-western corner (Nos. 3223 to 3244).

That there was an open-field arable system here is obvious, both from the map and from the record of the distribution of holdings in the *Booke of Survaye*. It would be very difficult, however, to reconstruct the division of the land for the working of a three-field system from the information available. Two arable fields only are mentioned by name, the North Field, containing, with closes, about 50 acres, and Hew Croft, containing about 27 acres; and there are also the arable strips in Ossington Fields referred to above. The north-eastern corner of the hamlet consists of a block of closes (Nos. 3290 to 3296), all of them freehold and belonging to the sub-manor, which look as if they had formed part, at one time, of Moorhouse Hill Common.

In the extreme south-east of the hamlet lay East Kirk Ing (Nos. 2801 to 2910), a stretch of meadow land of nearly 40 acres, most of it allotted in the customary small doles, almost all of which, curiously enough, were held by the freeholders and tenants of the manor of Laxton, not of Moorhouse. Excluding this area, Laxton Moorhouse extended to 333 a. 1 r. 30 p.

Mark Pierce's survey shows demesne lands and woods, leasehold tenements, freehold lands, and commons in Laxton to the total extent of 3519 a. 3 r. 13 p., made up as follows:

	a.	r.	p.	a.	r.	p.
The Land of Sir Wm. Courten:						
Pasture and Arable	1,527	2	2			
Meadow	174	2	33			
Commons	186	3	15			
Demesne Woods	292	2	5			
				2,181	2	15
The Lands of the Freeholders:						
Pasture and Arable	1,272	2	21			
Meadow	65	2	17			
				1,338	0	38
				3,519	3	13

hath their fildes devyded to themselves as if the same were severall mannors and severall parishes.' Tawney, R. H., and Power, Eileen, *Tudor Economic Documents*, vol. i, pp. 60–61 (1924).

For Laxton Moorhouse the analysis is:

	a.	r.	p.	a.	r.	p.
The Land of Sir William Courten:						
Pasture and Arable	86	1	25			
Meadow	10	0	27			
Commons	38	3	12			
				135	1	24
The Lands of the Freeholders				198	0	6
				333	1	30

The combination of 'pasture and arable' in this schedule is interesting. The total extent of lands thus described in Laxton is 2,800 acres, of which some 1,300 acres were the ploughlands of the Open Fields, while the remaining 1,500 acres were contained in closes, some of which were under the plough while the rest were used for grazing. The contribution to the grazing made by the meadow land was slight, for it extended only to 240 acres, and it was shut up during the best part of the season. The arable land, on the other hand, made a material contribution to the available grazing, for the right to turn out stock upon the stubbles, after harvest, and upon the fallow field for a longer time, was highly valued. It was this practice of grazing the Open Fields, and the importance of it, which led, no doubt, to their inclusion with the pasture closes in the classification 'pasture and arable' adopted by Mark Pierce.

VIII. THE STRUCTURE OF
THE FIELDS

BEFORE passing to examine the system of ownership and occupation of the lands of the open-field manor, as exemplified by Laxton, some study of the structure of the fields themselves is needed.

In the previous chapter it has been shown how the lands of the manor were made up of the village with its crofts and tofts, the common arable fields, the common meadows, the closes of arable and grass land, the commons, and woodlands. It will be remembered that the extent of land lying in open arable cultivation was about 1,300 acres, thus:

	a.	r.	p.	a.	r.	p.
West Field	318	3	5			
East Field	126	2	21			
				445	1	26
South Field				428	0	19
Mill Field				433	2	20
Total				1,307	0	25

Let us take section ii of the reproduction of the map, namely, that which shows the West Field and Westwood Common, and examine its principal features.

Obviously, the most striking feature of the Open Fields is provided by the furlongs, to which the name 'flatts' is sometimes given in the terrier, and which are known also in some places as 'shotts'. In Latin documents of medieval times they are called *culturae*.

Here, as in the other fields, the furlongs have pushed outward from the village as the community grew in size, encroaching all the time on the wastes or woodlands. In the West Field this encroachment was arrested by the need of the community to preserve a certain minimum area for common grazing, the Westwood Common.

The first thing that strikes the eye is the great diversity in size, shape, and direction of the furlongs and the parcels of land within them. It would have been far more convenient for distribution amongst the farmers, as well as for cultivation by them, if the parcels could have been laid out in furlongs similar in size and direction, following one another in parallel lines across the field. And why were they not? The answer is that both the shape of the field and its contours made this impossible. If the Open Fields had been laid out on flat land or on land with a uniform slope, such an arrangement would almost certainly have been made, but these conditions are found rarely, if ever, in England. The ploughman knows that he must take advantage of the natural slope of the land if he is to secure drainage, and this is especially important on the heavier soils, such as that at Laxton. As a consequence, the parcels of land for ploughing have to be fitted into fields with irregular boundaries and inclining in different directions at different points. The act of ploughing cuts a shallow trench in the soil, and throws up a furrow-slice above it from which the rain runs into the bottom of the furrow. If, therefore, the ploughman set out his work across the slope of the field, the rain-water would accumulate in his furrows, to drain with difficulty from one furrow to the next one below it, until the lands ploughed across the lowest part of the slope became completely waterlogged. Instead, lands were, and they still are, laid out and the furrows were, and are, ploughed up and down the slopes, so that water can run down each furrow independently, to get a discharge into a stream or ditch at the bottom.

So, while the arrangement of the parcels in furlongs on the map appears, at first sight, to be quite arbitrary and even absurdly inconvenient, the reason is obvious when they are studied on the ground, or when a map of an Open Field is considered in relation to such changes in its contours as can be identified. It is seen at once that the furlongs and the strips within them follow the fall of the land.

Prominent in the map of the West Field are two broad belts of land (Nos. 615 and 616), the sikes mentioned above.[1] In an area of this size in undulating country, tracts of land are almost certain to occur which, for one reason or another, are unfit for tillage. It may be that they are low-lying and wet, or they may be too precipitous for ploughing. These sikes, as they were called, were left in their natural state. In the West Field there are two of them, being little valleys running north-east, the land between them rising to a little watershed. It will be seen that all the lands in the furlongs on either side of each of them are laid out to drain naturally into them, until we get to the heads of these little valleys at their south-western ends, when the direction of the furlongs turns round and is at right angles to those below, so that the lands within them may likewise get the best discharge for their drainage water.

It must not be supposed that the sikes served no other useful purpose. On the contrary, they were turned to account in several ways. After the harvest, and also when the land was being fallowed in preparation for the wheat crop, the fields were thrown open

[1] See p. 91, ante.

for common grazing, and the grass of the sikes was a valuable addition to the somewhat sparse keep afforded by the cultivated land. In West Field, for example, the sikes amounted to some 25 acres, and stock are depicted in the map as grazing upon them. Before harvest, while crops were growing in the fields devoted to winter and spring corn, free grazing was impossible, of course, and stock were tethered daily upon the grass on the sikes. At some date before the nineteenth century, however, though how much before has not been determined, the practice of tethering was abandoned, and instead the custom of selling grass by auction to the highest bidder began, and it still continues. The various sikes in the cornfields of the year are lotted, as well as any grass-land worth mowing along the road-sides, and the buyers are under obligation to mow the grass and carry the hay by the time of the harvest, so that the aftermath may be available for the stock turned out on the stubbles. The proceeds of the auctions are divided between the lord of the manor and the freeholders in proportion to their holdings in the Open Fields.

Again, such natural features as the sikes greatly facilitated the laying-out of the Open Fields, by the ready access which they afforded to the land to be cultivated. They were natural occupation roads. Moreover, they helped the cultivators to get through the work in the quickest way and with least inconvenience to each other, for the ploughman could plough his furrows through and turn his team on the sike, thus obviating the need for a headland.

If the reader will consider the positions of some of the furlongs in the middle of the region between the two sikes, the difficulty of getting to the individual strips without passing across those in other furlongs is apparent. This was overcome by the provision sometimes of balks (small strips of land unfit for cultivation), sometimes by making the outermost land of the boundary strip of the furlong a headland, and more commonly, perhaps, by customary arrangements between neighbours. By such arrangements access to a parcel might be given down an adjacent land, but it created no customary right. A revision of the by-laws of the manor, dated 1789, mentions specifically certain lands over which attempts had evidently been made to claim a right of way, for it laid down, for example, 'that none do make a way up or down Wm. Pinder's acre at the top of the West Field. Fine 3s. 4d.' Where consent was given, it was expected that any consequent damage to the tillage should be made good.

The intricacy of these communications and arrangements appears extreme when an Open Field is considered in its final state, but it must be remembered that the fields were never planned in their entirety, but that they grew, furlong by furlong, as the

PLATE 16

a. A COMMON WAY IN MILL FIELD

b. A SIKE IN WEST FIELD

communities that they served increased in numbers. So it was simple to arrange the access to each as the need arose, taking advantage of a common balk here and laying out a common head-land there, and the access to most of the parcels of land in the manor of Laxton can be traced from the map and terrier. Clearly the matter was one of first importance to the lord and to the tenants, and Mark Pierce was careful to record the headlands and balks in his *Booke of Survaye*.

In a great many instances, however, there are no obvious arrangements at the lands' ends to enable the teams to turn. The lands of one furlong abut direct on to those of another, or they finish at right angles to the outside land of the next furlong, with-out the intervention of any common balk or headland. This situa-tion was met by a custom to which every one had to conform. Where the lands met end to end, the last $2\frac{1}{2}$ yards of each of them constituted what is known today as a 'stintin' and in Mark Pierce's survey as '$\frac{1}{2}$ balks'. Either cultivator had the right to tread that far on his neighbour's lands, for the purpose of cultivating his own, for carting manure on to them, and for carrying his harvest away. Where the lands of one furlong finished at right angles to the outermost land of another, the farmers of the first had a simi-lar right to go upon this land in the performance of their opera-tions. These rights arose from necessity, as being the only way in which the work could be done without loss of land by leaving uncultivated strips. The occupier's right to the use of the half-balk, or of the outside land, was otherwise unaffected, and when his neighbours had finished their work he would cultivate it and sow it, for harvest in due season with the rest.[1] Where the lands were narrow, and it happened very often that they were only a few yards wide, it was impossible to cultivate the half-balks with the plough, for the team and the plough itself would be nearly as long as the bit of land to be cultivated. In these circumstances the stintins or half-balks had to be dug with the spade, and this is the process described by William Langland in *Piers the Plowman*:

> Now Piers and his pilgrims to the plough are gone;
> To plough his half acre there helped him full many;
> Dikers and delvers, they digged up the balks . . .[2]

It must not be supposed that the arrangement always worked smoothly. A dilatory farmer could hold up the work of his opposite neighbour, both at seed-time and at harvest, and the recollection of such difficulties survives today, when other arrangements have been made. But they were a petty annoyance to the more efficient

---

[1] From information supplied by Laxton farmers.
[2] *The Vision of Piers the Plowman*, passus vi, ll. 107–9 (Skeat's Modern English version).

farmers rather than a serious handicap, and delinquents were never brought before the manor court to answer for them.

Except for the few common balks in the Open Fields, some of which were named and were no other than occupation roads, and except for a very few balks in individual occupation, which provided access to particular furlongs (see Section II, Nos. 340 and 352), the only balks mentioned in Mark Pierce's survey are the '½ balks' described above, which were not balks at all as the term is generally understood. Seebohm's narrow strips of unploughed turf which separated each acre from the next are quite unknown.[1] The outside furrow-slices of each parcel, turned away from each other, drew a well-marked border line between them, and they were supplemented by landmarks, posts driven in under the direction of the juries of the manor court, at the corners of each man's parcel. 'Ploughing his neighbour's land' was an offence for which men were presented at the court, and the by-laws of the manor prescribed a fine of £1. 10s. 'if anyone remove his neighbour's Land Mark'. A suggestion that the parcels might have been separated by balks at some earlier date was ridiculed by farmers in the Laxton Open Fields today, on the grounds that they would have been unnecessary, and impossible to maintain in the face of every man's desire to plough as far as he could. These men know their own lands as a shepherd knows his sheep. A Laxton farmer ran over the location of each of the twenty strips held by his father in the Mill Field, which he had cultivated as a young man over thirty years before. 'Start in Holme Side furlong, plough two lands, miss three, plough one more, go on to Foxmore furlong . . . etc. . . .' He said that the only time that he had made a mistake was once when ridge and furrow were alike obliterated by snow, and he had carted manure on to a land adjacent to his father's. The assertion that there were unploughed balks between every strip in the Open Fields can no longer be maintained.

The structure of the furlongs and of component strips should be considered. At Laxton, at all events, neither had anything approaching that rigidity which is attributed to them by Seebohm. He says that the shotts or furlongs were 'always a furrow-long in width'.[2] This might have been possible on flat ground or on ground with one uniform slope, but remembering that the fields

---

[1] See p. 43, ante. Tawney and Power quote presentments in 1548 for the offence of ploughing up balks, all of them roadways or paths:

'Mr. Muryell hathe plowed uppe certayne bawlks and carte wayes in the fealde. . . .'

'Mr. Byerdyck hath plowed uppe the more part of a bawlke behind the Black Freers of vii foot brode, betwyxt Jesus College grownde and Myhell House grounde. . . .'

'There is another bawlk enclosed at both ends and plowed uppe, that leadeth from the forenamed bawlke directly crossing the hyghewaye into Barnwell cawsey and Jesus Greene.' *Tudor Economic Documents*, vol. i, pp. 45–46.

[2] *The English Village Community*, p. 4.

extended often to hundreds of acres, such conditions must have been rare. In other circumstances the width of the furlongs was controlled by the slope of the ground, and its upper limit, the furrow-long of about 220 yards, which was the most that a plough-team could work without a halt, was reached only if the slope allowed it. A glance at the map of the West Field of Laxton shows that the furlongs were of many widths within this limit, and an examination of the terrier reveals that they varied in size from 2 acres to 23 acres, while in the Mill Field and in the South Field the range was even greater.

The furlongs were made up of 'lands' of ridge-and-furrow, the formation of which by the operation of ploughing has been described already.[1] Nor had the land any fixed or absolute size. Its length was determined by the furlong, its width depended upon the nature of the soil, narrow lands with frequent water-furrows being ploughed in wet, heavy soils, and wider ones in lighter soils. Where the field was flat and the soil light, the land might be the full furrow-long of 220 yards and the full width of 22 yards, which fix its upper size-limit of 1 acre. At Laxton these conditions never occurred, and the land was sometimes so little as a quarter of an acre.

The strips, or parcels, as shown upon the map, were composed of one, two, three, or of many lands. A typical example is provided by Radwell Gapp Furlong, numbered A in the Terrier, in the extreme south-east corner of the West Field, the first four entries reading:

No.			a.	r.	p.
125	Widdow Tailer	5 lands	0	3	34
126	Mr. Hinde	4 lands *Free*	0	3	33
127	Willm. Challond	1 land	0	1	12
128	Anthony Whalehead	1 land	0	1	12

This extract shows not only the diversity in the number of lands which make up the parcels, but also the variety in the size of individual lands. Thus, Widow Tailer has five lands, whereas William Challond and Anthony Whalehead have only one each in their parcels, while Mr. Hinde has as large an area in his strip of four lands as Widow Tailer has in hers of five. In the absence of continuous evidence from an earlier date, it is only possible to speculate upon the reasons for the diversity in the sizes of the parcels as they appear in 1635. It has been suggested that in the origin of the Open Fields, an allocation was made to individuals in strips of one day's work. If this be true, it is clear that there had been a great deal of consolidation, at Laxton, as time went by, and indeed, this must have been inevitable. We know that so

[1] See pp. 32–35, *ante.*

early as 1232 Robert de Lexington's charter confirming to him his sub-manor gave him 'licence to make exchanges of land with his men in Lexingtun, both free and bond',[1] and if he took advantage of it, some consolidation of strips would follow. Again, the lands held by the lord's tenants reverted to him, as escheats, at death, and if there were no son to succeed, the strips in the Open Fields may have been granted to the adjacent occupiers, which would explain some of the variations in the sizes of holdings at Laxton by the time that Mark Pierce's survey was made.[2] Further, we know that at one time the ploughlands of the lord's demesne were distributed, with those of his tenants and of the freeholders, throughout the Open Fields, and that later they were consolidated, while the same applies to those of the two largest freeholders, the representatives of the sub-manor. The allocation of these old demesne strips may help, also, to account for some of the diversity in size of parcels. Indeed, despite the absence of documentary evidence, it would be the more surprising if conditions so late as 1635 did not reflect the natural inclination of the tenants and freeholders of the manor to add to the size of their parcels as opportunity offered, both for convenience of working and for economic advancement.

There is no evidence at Laxton to support Seebohm's statement that 'taking them [the strips] generally and comparing them with the statute acre, it will be seen at once that the normal strip was identical with it'.[3] Here is a schedule of the lands held by a farmer in the Mill Field in 1635, being part of his holding of 29 acres.

Hugh Tailer. His Holding in Mill Field, 17 parcels

No.	Furlong	No. of Lands	a.	r.	p.
2281	Curtious Leys (JJ)	2 lands	0	1	11
2298	Holme (KK)	1 land	0	0	32
	then back to road to				
1963	Furlong over Kneesal Way (V)	1 narrow land	0	1	12
2233	Langwell sike (GG)	1 land	0	0	19
	back to Kneesal Way and down and across to				
2158	Mayden roods (DD)	3 lands and ½ balks	0	1	30
2150	Fox Moore syke leys (CC)	2 leys	0	1	6
	by Fox Moore sike to				
2068	East Shitterpool Hill (Z)	2 lands	0	2	4
	down common way on east boundary to				
2320	Brockley Side (MM)	2 lands	0	1	5
	back to				
2023	Moorelands (Y)	2 lands	0	1	7
	up Kneesall way to				
2004	Pudding Roods (W)	3 lands	0	1	30
	up Kneesal way and along Stony balk to				
1809	Middle Furlong (N)	7 lands	1	0	26

[1] See p. 75, *ante.*   [2] See p. 109, *post.*
[3] *The English Village Community,* p. 2.

PLATE 17

Mill field.

1910	Mr Broughto̅ a rlose at West end of those Lands Free	1	0	12
1911	Humphrey Hopkinson gt 16 lands pigore Lat. Hindp	2	2	34
1912	The said Humphrey gr̅ hould also a rloase at East end of those Lands, late Mr Hindp	1	0	18
	Suma ---	7	2	0

Pony hole furlong begin at North side; S

1913	Richard Pinder one rlose late Hindp	1	0	31
1914	Mr Broughton 1 land Free ---	0	0	36
1915	Mr Broughton 1 land m With castlen Fre	0	0	35
1916	Mr Stanford 1 land late Hindp ---	0	0	34
1917	Mr Hinde 3 lands Free ---	0	2	17
1918	Mr Broughton 4 lands Free ---	0	3	1
1919	Hum: Hopkinson gt 3 lands late Hindp	0	2	2
1920	Mr Broughton 3 lands Free ---	0	2	0
1921	Hum: Hopkinson gt 3 lands late Hindeb	0	1	37
1922	Mr Broughton 3 lands Free ---	0	1	35
	Suma ---	5	0	28

Certaine Closes begin wth hall ffloores. T

1923	Tho: Hunt one fourth pte of y hall floores	11	1	13
1924	Alex: Tailer 4th pt of hall floore late Powland	13	3	24
1925	Christo: Salmon ½ y hall floore lying in 3 rlose	21	1	36
1926	Rich: Shawe pony hole rlose late Poss	1	2	4
1927	Hum: Hopkinson gt 2 littlerloses late Hindeb	0	3	32
1928	Richard Sharxe one rlose late Poss	0	3	16
1929	Mr Broughton, floule syke rloase Free	12	1	7

FROM THE *BOOKE OF SURVAYE OF THE MANOR OF LAXTON*, 1635

1821	Clay Sticks Furlong (O)	3 lands	0	3	1
	very close to				
1763	Foulding Roods (K)	1 land and 1 short land at East end	0	1	16
	up Hall Flower Sike to				
1703	Acre Edge Corner Side (E)	4 lands and ½ balks	0	3	13
	across sike to				
1670	Last strip in Furlong lying above Hall Flower (C)	3 lands next the hedge	0	2	20
1687	Long lands above Hall Flower (D)	1 land and ½ balks	0	1	20
1624	Furlong butting on Freerfull (B)	7 lands and gores	0	3	34
			8	0	26

(Total, 8½ acres in 17 strips, consisting of 44 lands, 2 leys, a gore, 3½ balks. Though this works out at an average of ½ acre per strip, only 2 strips are ½ acre; the rest are ¼ or ¾ acre.)

The division of a furlong into lands for ploughing necessitated, sometimes, cutting off an odd bit in which the lands set out were very short. Such were called 'butts'. In the map of the West Field there is a parcel, No. 269, between the furlongs K and M, described in the Terrier as being '8 little Butts', and their total extent is only 1 r. 38 p. Wherever the ends of the furlongs were not parallel, short lands running off to a point had to be laid out to fill up, and these were called 'gores' or 'gore acres'. Sometimes ploughing began along one of the sides of such a furlong, the lands being laid out parallel to it, which left a triangle, the gore, at the other side. The strip No. 452 in furlong Y is an example; it is unnumbered on the map, but it can easily be identified, being the extreme outside strip at the northern apex of the field. Sometimes ploughing began at each of the unparallel ends of the furlong, which left a gore or gores in the middle of it, where the lands from either end approached each other. The strips Nos. 594 and 595 in part of the large furlong FF are good examples of this.

The common meadows at Laxton extended to about 130 acres in four blocks, thus:

Names	Section of map	Identification numbers	Acreage a. r. p.
Long Meadow . . .	I	Nos. 2472–727	67 3 13
Shitterpool Meadow . .	III	Nos. 2405–71	15 1 30
South Lound Meadow .	IV	Nos. 2740–800	13 2 23
East Kirke Inge . .	V	Nos. 2805–910	34 1 23
			131 1 9

It will be remembered that the total extent in common arable cultivation was 1,307 acres,[1] so that the area of the common

---

[1] See p. 96, *ante*.

meadows was about one-tenth of that of the ploughlands. This is important, because this ratio applied not only to the lands of the manor, but roughly, also, to the holdings within it. The medieval farm, whether oxgang or bovate, virgate or yardland, or whatever its denomination, was an economic unit, containing arable, meadow, and common pasture in certain proportions.

Like the ploughlands, the meadows were held in strips, each consisting of one or more doles.

Besides the furlongs of the Open Fields, and the meadows and the woodlands, the map of Laxton contains many closes. An inspection of the sections as reproduced shows that, with the exception of the demesne closes immediately round the castle, all the larger closes have been taken in on the outlying portions of the manor and those most remote from the village. This is particularly striking in the sections reproducing the South Field and the Mill Field. It is obvious that cultivation spread outwards from the village, and the tendency to inclose the more remote wastes rather than to bring them into the Open Fields in the form of new furlongs arose partly, no doubt, from practical difficulties, but chiefly from the growing realization of the advantages of farming in severalty rather than in common.[1] For although the big closes are mostly on the boundaries, or obviously late reclamations from woodland such as the field called Middle New Dyke (Section I, No. 2997) and the others adjacent to it, there are several references in the Terrier to the inclosure of parcels of strips. In the West Field, for example, each of the parcels Nos. 608 to 612, in furlong FF, are described as so many 'lands inclosed'. In the northern apex of this field the parcel No. 454 in furlong Y is described as 'late inclosed'. The other fields supply further examples, and although so large a part of the Laxton Open Fields have survived until this day, the tendency to inclose, which was manifest so long ago as 1635, has characterized every change which has occurred in the manor since that date.

That the desire to inclose was strong at that time is shown by a report to the Privy Council made by the Justices of Nottinghamshire, in 1631, recording the extent of recent inclosures in the parishes of that county. In Laxton they were few and unimportant, but elsewhere the process was going on extensively.[2]

Inclosures were made indifferently both for arable and for grass farming. To the progressive farmer they meant liberty to crop as he pleased and complete control of his land, free from the exercise of common rights by his neighbours. For the less progressive,

---

[1] On this, see Tawney, R. H., *The Agrarian Problem in the Sixteenth Century*, pt. i, ch. iv.
[2] See p. 109, *post*.

PLATE 18

Laxton South Pound medows

South Pound, begin at east end.

No.	Description			
2730	M⁻ Bmde one acre peere Free - - -	o	3	27
2731	Hum Hopkinson & 1 acre peere late Bmde -	o	3	4
2732	M⁻ Bmde 1 acre Peere Free - - -	o	3	4
2733	Humphry Hopkinson & 4 acres late Bmde	3	1	24
2734	M⁻ Bmde one acre peere Free - -	o	3	32
2735	Humphry Hopkinson & 1 acre peere late Bmde	o	3	26
2736	M⁻ Bmde two acre peeres Free - -	1	3	o
	Begin at east end & south side of these acres			
2737	The Parsonaige one close - - - -	1	.2	22
2738	John Chapell one close Free - - -	1	2	o
2739	M⁻ Broughton, the eleuen acre peere lyng on the south side of & Acres aforeste	10	o	27
	Suma totalis - -	22	3	6

Doles, Begin at the East side

No.	Description			
2740	Thomas Hunt 1 Dole - - - - -	o	o	33
2741	M⁻ Broughton 1 Dole Free - - -	o	o	32
2742	M⁻ Bmde 1 Dole Free - - - -	o	o	30
2743	Christo: Salmon 1 Dole - - - -	o	o	31
2744	M⁻ Broughton 1 Dole Free - -	o	o	30
2745	Robt Holben 1 Dole - - - -	o	o	30
2746	Thomas Cullm 1 Dole Free - - -	o	o	29
2747	M⁻ Broughton 1 Dole Free - - -	o	o	29
2748	Broughto aforest 1 other Dole Free -	o	o	29
2749	Alexand⁻ Tailer 1 Dole Chantry - -	o	o	28
2750	Jo Chapell 2 Doles Free - - - -	o	1	15

FROM THE *BOOKE OF SURVAYE OF THE MANOR OF LAXTON*, 1635

farming still in the traditional way, an inclosure by his neighbour meant the withdrawal of these same rights. So there were the two forces at work, pulling in opposite directions, and the rate at which inclosure proceeded, both before and after resort to private Acts of Parliament, was the measure of the strength of either of them.

IX. FREEHOLDERS, TENANTS, AND THEIR HOLDINGS

THE lordship of a manor did not necessarily imply the full rights of ownership as they are understood and exercised by the agricultural landlord of today. It is true that the lord of the manor was the owner of it under the Crown, and there were large parts of it occupied either by himself—the demesne lands—or by farmers and others holding direct from him—the tenements. But the creation of freehold within the manor was a common incident of the manorial system. Freeholders owed suit and service to the lord, which took the form, ultimately, of a token payment, a chief rent, but they enjoyed the property in their land for the purposes of husbandry, and could occupy, lease, or even sell it, at their pleasure.

The extent of the manor in the hands of the freeholders varied very greatly. At Laxton, in 1635, the freeholders held no less than 1,338 acres, all of it houses and agricultural land, by contrast with 2,181 acres, which included nearly 500 acres of commons and woods, retained by the lord. At Laxton Moorhouse the position was even more striking, the freeholders having no less than some two-thirds of the agricultural land.

Freeholders, however, differed in status. There were the subinfeudators, little landlords themselves, owning a sub-manor within the manor, who owed suit to their superior lord but who acted, otherwise, as lords themselves, often holding manor courts, occupying some of their lands and letting the rest of them to tenants. At Laxton, as has been shown already, there was originally one such large freehold, held under the charter of 1232 by Robert de Lexington, which came to be divided into two moieties by descent from coheiresses, and in 1635 these were held by Mr. Peter Broughton and Mr. Augustine Hinde.

Then there were the yeomen, who might be described as owner-occupiers, men differing little, if at all, from the better-class tenants of the manor, farming, as some of them did, freeholds smaller than the holdings of the larger tenants.

Other freeholders owned only a few acres of land, insufficient to support them. These men supplemented their own holdings by renting land from the lord or from one of the sub-lords, or they hired themselves to others.

Again, there were other freeholders, neither sub-lords nor occupying-owners, who had generally no more than small acreages of land which they let to tenants. Often, the owners of such free-holds were religious houses, or the Church, to which grants had been made. At Laxton, for example, the Dean and Chapter of Southwell, Ferriby Abbey, Laxton Church, and the Chantry therein, were all of them freeholders of this type, though there were a few others in 1635, private persons, the origins of whose grants have not been traced.

Then there were the tenants, persons holding from the lord, from a sub-lord, or from some other freeholder. The conditions under which they held varied from tenancies at the will of the lord for service rents and payments in kind, in the earlier days,[1] to leases for a term of years or for life or for two or more lives, in return for money rents, as the social and economic organization of the manor developed. Upon the death of a tenant in villeinage, his holding escheated to the lord, who, though he might grant it where he liked, was restricted, naturally, in his choice in a self-contained village community, and widows often succeeded to husbands and sons to their parents.

By 1635, when Mark Pierce wrote his *Booke of Survaye*, there are no records of tenancies at will and one only of a rent in kind. Widow Tailer, who occupied a tenement of 32 acres,[2] paid a yearly rent of £6, 'with a load of Coles and a cupple of Capons'. Otherwise, service and produce rents had all been commuted.

Freeholders, of whatever standing below that of sub-infeudator, often rented additional land. Moreover, whatever may have been the size of the economic holding in earliest times, either of free-men or of bondmen, whether it were the oxgang of 15 acres or the virgate of 30 acres, at Laxton, by the time of the first complete survey, there had been much redistribution, both by subdivision and engrossment, by additions from the waste, and by letting the demesne lands.

Let us deal first of all with the lands in the occupation of the lord and of the sub-lords. In the time of Adam de Everingham there is evidence that the lord of the manor occupied parcels of arable land scattered amongst those of his tenants in the Open Fields.[3] By 1635, however, all the demesne land, extending to 350 acres excluding woodlands, was inclosed, and Sir William Courten, the new lord, had let the whole of it. His steward, one Samuel Stanford, occupied Laxton Hall, rent free, and he held, as tenant, about 123 acres of the demesne. Incidentally, this was only a part of his holding, for he rented also a tenement in the Open Fields of 68 acres, and, together with one Humphrey

---

[1] See, for example, p. 83, *ante*, for the services due from Laxton villeins in 1326 to Thomas de Bekering, lord of a moiety of the sub-manor.
[2] See p. 116, *post*.
[3] See p. 76, *ante*.

Hopkinson, he was joint tenant of the glebe lands of some 50 acres. At the time of the preparation of the Terrier he was in the act of taking over the 30-acre tenement of Edward Kelsterne. As Sir William Courten's agent he transacted all the business of the manor, and the miscellaneous character of the large area which he farmed suggests that he himself took over any lands coming in hand.[1]

The rest of the demesne closes, of varying sizes, some arable and some meadow, were let to tenants of the manor.

Both of the sub-lords, Mr. Peter Broughton and Mr. Augustine Hinde, occupied considerable parts of their freeholds. Mr. Broughton had in his own hands what was known as 'the great farme', extending to 314 acres, mostly in closes, but with 73 acres of arable and pasture in the Open Fields, and meadow. Further, he occupied 68 acres in six closes, being part of the Laxton demesne lands which he had purchased from Gilbert Roos, and a holding of 51 acres of arable and pasture, common meadow and closes, at Moorhouse. He lived and died at Lowdham, about fifteen miles away, and it may be assumed that these lands in Laxton were farmed for him by a bailiff. The rest of his moiety of the sub-manor of Laxton, consisting of lands scattered throughout the Open Fields and meadows, was distributed amongst twenty-five tenants.

Mr. Augustine Hinde had 201 acres reserved to his own use, consisting of ten large closes, a wong of 8 acres in Mill Field, and two small parcels of meadow in East Kirk Ing. He had, also, a holding in Moorhouse of the same size and character as that of Mr. Peter Broughton. He had lately sold 300 acres of his freehold to Sir William Courten, and the rest of it, most of which alternated with Mr. Peter Broughton's strips in the Open Fields and meadows, was let to twelve tenants.

The other freeholds were relatively small, and two only call for special mention. The first comprises the land, 69 acres in extent, formerly part of the possessions of Ferriby Abbey. It lay in five closes, Freerfall Closes, on the west side of Mill Field, and in 1635 it was the freehold of James Bacon, Esq. In 1664 William Pierrepont, Esq., bought it, and it was absorbed into the manor.

The second was 20 acres of arable land in Moorhouse, held by the Dean and Chapter of Southwell. It included one large block of 17 acres in the North Field, and three little closes. This freehold continued in the possession of the chapter until 1852, when it was sold by the Ecclesiastical Commissioners to John Evelyn

---

[1] Upon the sale of the manor, in 1640, to the Earl of Kingston, Samuel Stanford continued to be steward.

PLATE 19

Of Laxton Tenents:

Tables of parcells.

Serving for the redy findinge out of all the parcells of Land & houses
by the severall Tenants of the Manno of Laxton aforesaid,
viz.

Alexand. Tailer Sat Lowland Within the towne 32. 34. 80.
84.7 within west ffield 227. 235. 258. 267. 285. 323. 346. 349. 403. 410.
417. 495. 508. 5411. In East ffield. 640. 680. 692. 708. 722. 724. 772. 822. 837.
In South ffield 864. 885. 968. 979. 991. 1015. 1038. 1065. 1136. 1155. 1196. 1209.
1216. 1261. 1316. 1324. 1363. 1377. 1403. 1411. 1435. 1472. 1497. 1534. 1541. 1564. 1589.
In Mill ffield 1610. 1645. 1674. 1719. 1736. 1774. 1782. 1789. 1853. 1858. 1880. 1885.
1924. 1944. 1977. 1979. 2024. 2055. 2089. 2094. 2122. 2124. 2148. 2167. 2174. 2181. 2205.
2240. 2266. 2283. 2321. 2335. 2341. 2353. In Shitterpoole meddow 2406. 2450. 2470.
In the Long meddow 2481. 2486. 2520. 2549. 2594. 2617. 2652. 2656. 2686. 2698. In
South Sound meddow 2754. 2762. In East firk ing 2832. 2851. 2906.

Thomas Tailer 85. In west ffield 153. 171. 188. 225. 361. 402. 443.
490. 528. 551. 554. In east ffield 643. 657. 678. 703. 729. 750. 755. 778. 800.
802. 810. 824. 827. In South ffield 880. 883. 898. 902. 916. 946. 990. 1036.
1045. 1143. 1179. 1189. 1220. 1230. 1269. 1292. 1310. 1327. 1332. 1413. 1433. 1439.
1446. 1474. 1500. 1509. 1567. 1599. In Mill ffield 1630. 1639. 1673. 1678. 1689.
1742. 1832. 1891. 1942. 1949. 1954. 2000. 2020. 2027. 2036. 2049. 2059. 2101. 2136. 2156.
2202. 2220. 2228. 2319. 2356. 2362. 2383. In Shitterpoole meddow 2433.—
In Long meddow 2482. 2521. 2565. 2574. 2592. 2632. 2640. 2699. 2704—
In South Sound meddow 2751. 2767. 2790. In East firk inge 2830. 2842.
2877. 2909.

Christopher Salmon –6.– In west ffield 146. 179. 190. 230.
245. 278. 290. 321. 439. 489. 478. In East ffield 639. 693. 714. 717. 738. 746. 759.
776. 780. 783. 785. 804. 831. In South ffield 872. 957. 970. 1016. 1020.
1078. 1120. 1128. 1145. 1147. 1162. 1179. 1204. 1232. 1265. 1309. 1470. 1483.
1525. 1539. 1582. 1590. In Mill ffield 1613. 1654. 1657. 1694. 1699. 1702.
1765. 1767. 1803. 1834. 1838. 1887. 1925. 1968. 1990. 1995. 2087. 2149.
2191. 2218. 2264. 2294. 2296. 2316.– In Shitterpoole meddow 2461.
2469. In Long meddow 2476. 2515. 2529. 2554. 2591. 2621. 2655. 2663.
2717. 2722. 2726. In South Sound meddow 2743.– In the East firk
ing 2815. 2895. 1– The Cork aforesaid 3026 at my Lo graunt.

FROM THE *BOOKE OF SURVAYE OF THE MANOR OF LAXTON*, 1635

PLATE 20

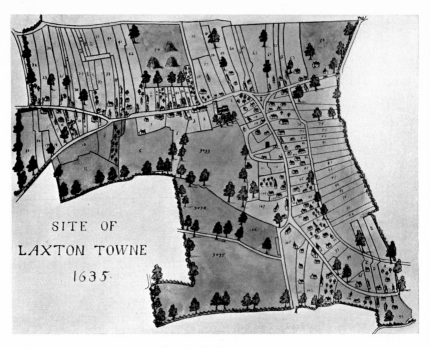

a. LAXTON TOWN, 1635

b. LAXTON TOWN, 1935

Denison, Esq., of Ossington, and it is held today by his descendants.

The rest of the occupiers of land in Laxton were all of them working farmers, village craftsmen, or cottagers, and they may be considered together, both freeholders and tenants of the main or of the sub-manor. In the lists which follow, compiled from information contained in the Terrier, the farms are classified in size-groups as they were held in 1635. The analyses of acreage include not only land held in the Open Fields and the meadows, for some of the occupiers held also one or more of the demesne or other closes. The rents paid are available only for lands held from the lord of the manor. Mark Pierce's survey was made for Sir William Courten, and while he delineated and enumerated every strip and close of the lands of the sub-manor and of the other freeholds, he was not concerned to record their rents.

Considering the holdings irrespective of the nature of the tenure, great variations in sizes are to be observed. A community of people identical in economic status, with holdings roughly equal in acreage, is not the condition of things disclosed at Laxton in 1635. The process of evolution, however, may be reconstructed. Upon the assumption that the Open Fields developed naturally as the community grew and plough was added to plough, nevertheless a distribution of strips between man and man mathematically precise could not long be maintained. Escheats had to be allotted, and if there were no heir, nor other claimant, a natural course was to add such a holding to that of another family. This may explain the holding of John Chappell, of 33 acres, for his portions of arable land in the Open Fields are very often in blocks larger than those of his neighbours in the same furlongs: if the average strip of the furlong is one of two lands, his contain four, or if they are one-land strips, his are two. It may explain, also, the farm occupied by Robert Shipton, of 76 acres, for he has, almost invariably, two separate strips in each furlong. As Robert had also two houses and yards, there are good grounds for assuming that his farm represented two separate holdings, each of about 38 acres, which had been put together.[1] It may be noted, too, in support, that J. Chappell's chief rent was 6s. for 34 acres, while R. Shipton paid 12s. for 76 acres.

Or an escheated holding may have been allotted amongst several tenants, which would explain not only the variations between farm and farm but also the fact that individuals sometimes have more arable land in one of the Open Fields than in the others.

Again, on the medieval manor, there were a number of part-

[1] For schedules of Robert Shipton's and John Chappell's holdings see pp. 112 and 116, *post*.

timers, the cottars, working most of their time on the demesne; the village craftsmen, occupied mainly at their trades; and some of the servants of the lord to whom a little land had to be assigned, but not full-time holdings. There are examples in the ranks of the Laxton tenants of holdings such as these.

The farmers occupied, each of them, a house, buildings, and yard in the village, arable land distributed in strips fairly evenly over the Open Fields, and a due proportion of doles of meadow. Most of the farms had also some small closes. In the Laxton Terrier, descriptions such as 'a close', or '4 lands inclosed', often appear, applied to one or more parcels, generally at the top or at the bottom of a furlong. See, for example, Mill Field, furlongs B, Nos. 1624 to 1636, and BB, Nos. 2106 to 2146, or LL, Nos. 2305 to 2315, where No. 2305 is described as—'Mr. Broughton, a close newly inclosed, *Free*. 2a. 2r. 25p.' Sometimes a whole furlong is inclosed, as in Mill Field, A, Nos. 1606 to 1623. How these inclosures came to be made can only be conjectured. There is no doubt, however, that the tendency to inclose was strong about this time. Amongst unpublished papers in the Record Office are some certificates by the Justices to the Lords of the Privy Council, dated 1631, of all inclosures of arable land made within the two years last past. At Laxton one inclosure of 2 acres was reported, and of four others, varying from 3 acres to 1 acre, the record is 'attempted to inclose'. A note appended by the Justices of the County of Nottingham to their certificate states that they 'are of Opinion that the severall Inclosures of 5 acres and under are in no way prejudiciall to the good of the Commonweale, or tend to depopulation, but are very necessary for the maintenance of tillage'.[1] Many of the Laxton closes are of the same character, and it is likely that they were made about this time. It is noteworthy that local opinion favoured rather than deprecated them. All of them are in the more remote parts of the fields, and evidently it had been found convenient to withdraw such strips and furlongs from common cultivation.

I. *Holdings 200 acres and more*

There are three, only, of these, the farms of the two sub-lords and the miscellaneous holding farmed by Sir William Courten's steward. They have been described already.

II. *Holdings 70 to 200 acres*

The nine holdings in this group extend from 188 acres downward, but the range in size of farms is not so wide, perhaps, as it

---

[1] S.P.D. Car. I, 16/192, H. 173–4–5. Com. Nott. The authors are indebted to Mr. W. E. Tate, F.R.Hist.S., for this reference and transcript.

LAXTON FARMS

Abbreviations: M = Tenant of the Manor; B = Tenant of Mr. Broughton; H = Tenant of Mr. Hinde; C = Tenant of the Chantry; F = Freeholder.

I. HOLDINGS 200 ACRES AND OVER

Name	Status	Holding	Rent £ s. d.	Arable and pasture a.	Meadow a.	Closes a.	Closes No.	Total acreage a.	General Total a.	Notes
Mr. Peter Broughton	F	Great farme	: :	50	23	28	(6)	101		
„	F	Land late Lord Vaux	: :	: :	: :	213	(12)	213		
„	F	Late Gilbert Roos	: :	: :	: :	68	(6)	68		
„	F	Moorhouse	: :	25	3	23	(4)	51	433	
Mr. Augustine Hinde	F	Reserved to own use	: :	8	2	191	(10)	201		
„	F	Moorhouse	: :	17	1	33	(9)	51	252	
Mr. Samuel Stanford	M	Demesne	36 4 0	: :	: :	123	(10)	123		No rent paid for Laxton Hall and one meadow.
„	M	Parsonage Farm	90 0 0	38	6	6	(3)	50		The Glebe land, including the Tithes of Laxton, paying yearly rent to the king £23. 10s.
„	M	Ten. late Hinde	16 0 0	28	2	38	(8)	68		
„	B	Land	: :	2	: :	: :	: :	2	243	
				168	37	723		: :	928	

II. HOLDINGS 70 TO 200 ACRES

Name	Status	Holding	Rent (£ s. d.)	Arable and pasture (a.)	Meadow (a.)	Closes (a.)	Closes (No.)	Total acreage (a.)	General Total (a.)	Notes
Humphrey Hopkinson (jointly with (R. Whitlam)	M	Tenement	3 0 0	42	4	21	(6)	67		H. Hopkinson paid £12 and R. Whitlam £10.
,,	M	2 Ten. late Hinde	22 0 0	71	8	18	(6)	97		Not including acreage of Parsonage Farm held with Mr. Stanford.
,,	B	Tenement	..	22	2	..	..	24	188	
Thomas Tailer, sen., maltman	M	Ten. and ox-gang	10 0 0	48	4	47	(8)	99		The rent is made up of £3 for the Tenement, £6 for Brecks close (34a), and £1 for an oxgang of land.
,,	M	Demesne	5 8 0	..	..	24	(1)	24		
,, (with others)	M	Demesne	6 6 8	..	..	14	(1)	14	137	
W. Woulflet	B	Tenement	..	40	3	11	(4)	54		
,,	H	Tenement	..	44	5	1	(1)	50	104	
Widow Rosse	M	Tenement	4 0 4	46	5	6	(2)	57		Lease for 2 lives, widow R. aged 40 and son Francis, aged 17.
,,	M	Demesne	..	..	..	41	(2)	41		
,,	B	Meadow	..	..	1	..	..	1	99	
William Urry	M	Tenement	1 18 4	3	1	15	(2)	19		A note that the value of the Moorhouse tenement is £15 p.a.
,,	M	Ten. in Moorhouse	3 0 0	36	4	24	(7)	64		
,,	B	Tenement	..	5	1	9	(2)	15	98	
Christopher Salmon	M	Tenement	4 0 0	44	4	24	(2)	72		
,,	M	Demesne	3 10 0	..	..	16	(1)	16	88	
Alexander Tailer	M	Tenement	5 0 0	32	18	25	(2)	75		
,,	C	Chantry land	..	4	1	..	..	5	80	
Robert Shipton	F	Freehold	12 0 0	62	6	8	(5)	..	76	This holding includes two houses and yards.
James Bacon, Esq.	F	Tenement	..	..	..	70	(5)	..	70	Late lands of Ferriby Abbey.
				499	67	374	..	..	940	

looks, as seven are composite holdings, combining two or more farms, or a farm and some demesne closes. Groups I and II together account for about one-half of the agricultural land of the manor.

III. *Holdings 40 to 70 acres*

This group contains twelve holdings, aggregating some 675 acres. Most of them are normal holdings, with their proportion of strips in the three fields and their meadow land. Thomas Cawdaile, however, occupied two virgate holdings, one of 35 acres, rented of Mr. Augustine Hinde, the other 27 acres, rented from Sir William Courten, and William Bedam had a freehold farm of 15 acres—an oxgang—and 34 acres of demesne.

The rents of the holdings in this group and in Group II are of some interest. Dealing with the farms, as distinct from the demesne closes, it is seen that except for five of them, the rents range from £3 to £5, irrespective of size. The five exceptions have rents ranging from £8 to £12, that is to say, more than double. Now these five holdings were all of them purchased by Sir William Courten shortly before the Terrier was prepared,[1] four from Mr. Augustine Hinde and one from Francis Roos, and they disclose, quite clearly, the estate policy of the London merchant. The old tenants of manor holdings were paying customary rents which could not be varied until their tenancies expired, but the new landlord was resolved upon rent revision whenever opportunity offered. Of the farms which he purchased, three were at once re-let to new tenants, to Humphrey Hopkinson and his partner, Richard Whitlam, to Mr. Samuel Stanford, and to Richard Pinder, for more money, and there are notes in the Terrier against the other two, to the effect that the rents are to be raised upon the expiration of the current leases. This marks, probably, the first serious attempt to introduce economic rents into the manor. The old rents, bearing little or no relation to the size of the holdings, had their origins in the commuted values of services. Sir William Courten was determined to relate rents to the values of the holdings, and he made a start with these farms purchased from Mr. Augustine Hinde and Francis Roos. After his death, in 1636, the policy was developed by his son, who re-let many holdings at higher rents, and later, by his successors in title, until the various tenements of the manor came to be let at rents based upon their size and quality and all of them at figures representing economic rather than customary values.

Sir William Courten's introduction of business methods into estate management is well illustrated by his parcelling and letting

[1] Thoresby Deeds, Nos. B 43, 47, 49, 50, 65.

III. HOLDINGS 40 TO 70 ACRES

Name	Status	Holding	Rent £	s.	d.	Arable and pasture (a.)	Meadow (a.)	Closes (a.)	Closes (No.)	Total acreage (a.)	General Total (a.)	Notes
Robert Holbem	M	Tenement	4	0	0	29	5	15	(1)	..	49	
William Challond	M	Tenement	4	10	2	53	6	2	(1)	61	67	
"	M	Demesne	5	0	0	..	..	6	(1)	6		
Thomas Hunt	M	Tenement	5	0	0	41	4	22	(5)	..	67	
Richard Shaw	M	Ten. late Mr. Rosse	8	0	0	54	5	7	(6)	..	66	Farm and Laxton Mill thereon purchased from Francis Rosse in 1630.
Thomas Cawdaile	M	Tenement	2	0	..	22	1	4	(2)	27	63	
"	H	Tenement				16	5	15	(2)	36		
Thomas Freeman	M	Tenement	4	..	0	52	3	6	(2)	..	61	
Abraham Tailer	B	Tenement	..	..	0	50	4	4	(5)	58	59	
"	M	Toft & 3 crofts	4	..	0	..	..	1	(1)	1		
Richard Pinder	M	Ten. late Hinde	10	0	0	41	4	6	(2)	..	51	
Thomas Hassard	M	Ten. late Hinde	9	0	0	34	3	13	(3)	..	50	
Michaell Tailer	B	Tenement	2	..	0	27	2	11	(2)	40	49	
"	M	Westwood Close				..	..	9	(1)	9		
William Bedam	F	Freehold	..	..	0	14	1	..		15	49	
"	M	Demesne	5	4	0	..	..	26	(1)	26		
(with R. Shaw)	M	Westcroft med.	5	0	0	..	..	8	(1)	8		
John Freeman	M	Tenement	4	0	0	32	2	10	(2)	..	44	Acreage includes a close of 7a in Kneesal Park.
						465	45	165	..	..	675	

of the demesne..So far as is known, it had remained in the occupation of successive lords until the sale of the manor by Gilbert Roos, in 1618, to the Earl of Buckingham, and possibly until the sale by him, in 1625, to Sir William Courten. His policy, as an absentee landlord, was to let the lands in hand. The Terrier records that every close was separately valued. The best grasslands, Great Pond meadow, for example, were let for so much as 30s. an acre, and the average for the whole of the demesne, arable, pasture, and meadow, was about 7s. an acre. These figures contrast with customary rents, paid by the tenants of the old tenements of the manor, ranging from about 1s. 2d. to 2s. an acre.

This tendency towards commercialism on the land seems to be discernible, at the same time, in some of the larger farmers. Humphrey Hopkinson, for example, was evidently an enterprising man, prepared to take on more and more land as opportunity offered. His original holding was one of 67 acres, for which he paid £3. He was joint tenant of two others with Richard Whitlam, paying £12 for his share, while Whitlam paid £10. With Mr. Stanford he rented 50 acres of Parsonage lands and collected the tithe, paying £90 for the whole to the lord of the manor and £23. 10s. to the Crown; and he was a tenant of 23 acres of Mr. Broughton's moiety of the sub-manor at a rent not stated. His total occupation of 239 acres, including his joint tenancies, comprised no fewer than 260 parcels, and there was hardly a furlong in the Open Fields in which he and his partners had not one or more strips.

Thomas Tailer, senr., the maltman, the next largest tenant, held 138 acres in all. He had a tenement and an oxgang, together 65 acres, and three demesne closes, for two of which he was joint tenant with others. Robert Shipton, a freeholder, had two tenements, together 76 acres. These three men, and Alexander Tailer and Thomas Hunt, tenants respectively of 75 acres and 67 acres, both of them holdings above the average in size, were the five named in the Justices' Certificate to the Privy Council, in 1631, as 'attempting to inclose'.

IV. *Holdings 20 to 40 acres*

The next group in this arbitrary classification of the open-field farms comprises those between 20 and 40 acres. It might have been expected that these would be the most numerous class, as derivatives of the 30-acre virgate or yardland, which, according to Seebohm, was once the commonest unit of occupation. But it is evident that by 1635 there had been so much redistribution of land, with a general tendency towards larger holdings, that few of the old virgate holdings remained in their integrity. The freeholds

IV. HOLDINGS 20 TO 40 ACRES

Name	Status	Holding	Rent £ s. d.	Arable and pasture a.	Meadow a.	Closes a.	Closes No.	Total acreage a.	General Total a.	Notes
Widow Tailer	M	Ten. late Hinde	£6 & a load of coles and 2 capons 6 0	29	2	2	(1)	..	33	
John Chapell	F	Freehold	..	24	4	5	(2)	..	33	3 houses in Moorhouse with this tenement.
John Rosse	F	Freehold (Moorhouse)	..	21	3	7	(4)	31	32	
	B	Tenement	..	1	..	..	..	1		
Edward Kelsterne	M	Tenement	2 0 0	28	2	1	(1)	..	31	
George Salmon	F	Freehold	..	1	..	..	..	1	31	
"	F	Freehold (Moorhouse)	..	19	1	10	(4)	30		3 lands in West Field in questio. for Freehold. Also had a Freehold cottage and yard.
Hugh Tailer	C	Chantry land	..	25	5	..	..	..	30	
Thomas Greene	M	Tenement	..	1	..	..	..	1	28	
"	M	Demesne	2 16 0	..	..	13	(1)	13		
"	B	2 closes	..	..	..	14	(2)	14		
Robert Rosse	M	Tenement	..	14	2	10	(3)	..	26	Tenement in questio. for freehold messuage & 3 cottages.
Thomas Jenevere	M	Tenement	12 0 0	2	..	..	..	2	25	
" (with others)	M	Demesne	4 10 0	..	..	23	(2)	23		
Christopher Betney, joiner	B	Tenement	..	17	1	5	(4)	..	23	
Widow Hassard	F	Toft	..	..	..	1	(1)	1	21	A note that the value of this tenement is £5 p.a.
"	M	Ten. (Moorhouse)	3 10 0	12	3	4	(2)	19		
"	M	Tenement	2 0 0	1	..	..	..	1		
Bryan Smith	F	Freehold	..	17	1	2	(2)	..	20	
Dean & Chapter of Southwell	F	Freehold (Moorhouse)	..	17	..	3	(2)	..	20	
				229	24	100	..	..	353	

of John Chappell and Hugh Tailer and the tenements of Widow Tailer and Edward Kelsterne may be virgate survivals. It should be noted, too, that there are more freeholders in this size-group than in any other.

V. *Holdings 9 to 20 acres*

The fifth group includes the farms from 9 to 20 acres. This is more interesting, for it contains the half-virgate or oxgang holdings. One, that of Samuel Holbem, consisting of 13 acres of arable and pasture, 1 acre of meadow and a small close, making 16 acres in all, is actually described in the Terrier as 'an oxgang of land', and the holdings of James Lees, Anthony Whalehead, and John Nicholson, are similar in size and construction. Those of George Smith, Peter Parnell, and Henry Inkersell[1] are only a little smaller, and the rents are comparable with that paid by Samuel Holbem. They differ from the others, however, in that half their land is enclosed.

VI. *Holdings 5 to 9 acres*

There are two clearly marked types of holding in this group. All the Chantry land holdings and those occupied by Francis Wyldsmith and Rowland Taylor are open-field farms in miniature. Each has its strips in the three fields, and, with one exception, its doles of meadowland. If there were ever half-oxgang holdings, these would be typical. William Diconson, for example, had a freehold house and yard together with 2 acres of land in each arable field, eleven parcels in all, and five bits of meadow in East Kirk Ing, amounting to 1 acre. It is a perfectly regular holding, and the others are very similar.

The rest of the holdings in this group are a mixed bag, and it is not possible to find any principle in their construction.

VII. *Holdings below 5 acres*

This group includes:

(*a*) *Cottage farmers.* These must have filled up their time by working for the lord in the woodlands or elsewhere, or for some of the larger farmers. Some of the holdings, like Thomas Cullin's freehold of 4½ acres, were perfect miniature farms. He had a cottage and yard, about an acre of arable land in each of the Open Fields, and half an acre of meadow. Others, like Robert Jenevere, the tenant of a holding of about the same size, had no land in the Open Fields, but a collection of four crofts in the town, a strip of

---

[1] Henry Inkersell appears in the rental but is omitted from the Tables of Parcels—one of Mark Pierce's rare lapses.

V. HOLDINGS 9 TO 20 ACRES

Name	Status	Holding	Rent £ s. d.	Arable and pasture a.	Meadow a.	Closes a.	Closes No.	Total acreage a.	General Total a.	Notes
Christopher Blonket (with others)	M	Demesne	7 10 0			19	(1)		19	Also cottage and yard, Chantry.
Robert Tailer	B	Tenement				16	(3)		17	
Samuel Holbern	M	Oxgang	1 14 0	13	1	1	(1)	15	16	
	B	Arable land		1				1		
John Nicholson	M	Tenement		11	1			12	16	'Tenement in Mortmain, wch. ye Lord may cease on to his own use.'
"	M	Arable		4				4		3s. 6d. per ann. paid for it to Parsonage of Laxton.
Anthony Whalehead	M	Arable	8 0	2			(1)	2	15	
"	B	Tenement		11	1	1		13		
Anthony Tailer jun. of Moorhouse	M	Ten. Moorhouse	19 0		1	7	(2)	8	13	
" " "	M	Arable	1 0	5				5		
James Lee, Shoemaker	F	Freehold	1 2 0	11	1	1	(1)		13	
Henry Challond	M	Tenement	1 9 8	8				8	12	All the land of this Tenement in South Lound.
"	M	Demesne	1 4 0			4	(1)	4		
George Smith	M	Tenement	1 6 8	5	1	5	(1)		11	
Thomas Tailer jun.	B	Tenement		4	1	2	(1)	7	11	
" "	H	2 Tofts, &c.		1	1	2	(2)	4		
Richard Whalehead	M	Tenement	1 4 0	5	1			6	11	
"	M	Demesne	3 0			5	(1)	5		
Edward Snow	F	Freehold, Moorhouse	1 13 4	10	1				11	Nearly all in Ossington Fields.
Peter Parnell	M	Tenement	4 0 0	4	1	5	(1)		10	
Zachary Woulfete (with P. Rosse)	M	Demesne	1 1 0			10	(1)		10	
William Cawdaile	M	Tenement	3 0 0	4		3	(1)	7	10	
"	M	Meadow			3			3		
William Nicholson	B	Tenement	2 10 0	5		5	(1)		10	Land mostly in East Inger Close.
William Graysbrough	M	Tenement		8	1				9	
Robert Harpham	B	Tenement	1 16 8	8	1				9	
Henry Inkersell	M	Tenement		8	1				9	
Fulk Cartwright, Esq.	F	Freehold		7	1	1	(1)		9	
				135	18	87			240	

VI. HOLDINGS 5 TO 9 ACRES

Name	Status	Holding	Rent £ s. d.	Arable and pasture a. r. p.	Meadow a. r. p.	Closes a. r. p.	No.	Total acreage a. r. p.	General Total a. r. p.	Notes
John Cawdaile	F	Freehold	..	2 0 0	..	..	..	2 0 0	8 2 0	
,,	H	Tenement	..	..	..	6 2 0	(3)	6 2 0		
Edward Tailer	B	Tenement	1 10 0	2 0 0	..	6 0 0	(3)	..	8 0 0	
William Skaith	M	Tenement	2 .. 0	4 2 0	1 0 0	2 2 0	(1)	..	8 0 0	
George Smalpage	M	Tenement	..	2 0 0	1 2 0	4 2 0	(2)	..	8 0 0	
Francis Wyldsmith	H	Tenement	1 1 0	4 0 0	1 0 0	2 0 0	(1)	..	7 0 0	All in South Lound.
Rowland Diconson	M	Arable	.. 7 4	5 2 0	..	..	..	5 2 0	7 0 0	
,,	M	Meadow	..	..	1 2 0	..	..	1 2 0		
William Diconson	C	Chantry land	..	6 0 0	1 0 0	..	..	..	7 0 0	Also a freehold house and yard in Moorhouse.
Henry Kirkby	B	Close	..	..	..	7 0 0	(1)	..	7 0 0	Close on Kneesal border.
Widow Harpham	M	Ten. Moorhouse	1 13 0	4 0 0	..	..	..	4 0 0	6 0 0	Also held land in Kneesal.
,,	M	Land	.. 11 0	1 3 0	0 1 0	..	..	2 0 0		
Michael Betney	M	Tenement	2 0 0	5 0 0	1 0 0	..	..	..	6 0 0	
Robert Cadman	C	Chantry land	..	6 0 0	..	..	..	..	6 0 0	
Jane, Countess of Shrewsbury	F	Freehold	..	6 0 0	..	..	..	..	6 0 0	
Rowland Tailer	F	Freehold	..	5 2 0	0 2 0	..	..	..	6 0 0	
Ralph Gaskin	B	Land	..	2 2 0	..	2 2 0	(1)	..	5 0 0	
William Chapell	C	Chantry land	..	4 0 0	1 0 0	..	..	..	5 0 0	
Charles Cawdaile	M	Tenement	8 0	4 2 0	0 2 0	..	..	..	5 0 0	
				65 1 0	9 1 0	31 0 0	..	..	105 2 0	

VII. HOLDINGS UNDER 5 ACRES

Name	Status	Holding	Rent (£ s. d.)	Arable and pasture (a. r. p.)	Meadow (a. r. p.)	Closes (a. r. p.)	Closes No.	Total acreage (a. r. p.)	General Total (a. r. p.)	Notes
Thomas Cullin	F	Freehold		4 0 0	2 0				4 2 0	Arable land all in East Inger.
Robert Jenevere	M	Tenement	1 0 0	2 2 0	2 0	1 0 0	(4)		4 0 0	
Christopher Hassard	B	Tenement		4 1 0	1 0				4 2 0	Formerly held big farm now held by R. Pinder. No house.
Thomas Tailer, sen., of Moorhouse	F	Freehold	2	1 1 0				1 1 0		
„ „	F	Freehold in Moorhouse		3 0 0				3 0 0	4 1 0	
Thomas Parker	M	Tenement	1 0 0	4 0 0	1 0				4 1 0	
Roger Turner	H	Tenement		2 3 0	1 0	1 0 0	(1)		4 0 0	No house.
Robert Chapell	B	Land			2 0	2 3 0	(1)		3 1 0	Late Widow Nicholson.
John Jepson	M	Tenement	1 5 0	2 2 0	2 0				3 0 0	Town barne & house on waste (in mortmain).
George Hinde	M	Tenement	8 0	2 2 0	2 0				3 0 0	
Thomas Colt	M	Tenement	14 0 0	2 2 0					2 2 0	
William Bull	M	Land	2 0	1 3 0				3 0		Lands & meadow in South Lound, with cottage in Moor-house.
„	H	Cottage & Yard		1 3 0				3 0	2 2 0	
James Dawson	H	Tenement		1 2 0	3 0				2 2 0	
William Treswell	F	Freehold		2 1 0					2 1 0	10 lands in West Field belonging to Egmanton. No house.
Nicholas Pawlthrop, tailer		Tenement	1 5 0	1 3 0	2 0				2 1 0	
John Tailer	M	Tenement	8 0			2 0 0	(1)			Lands in Middle New Dike close, late W. Urry's.
„	M	Demesne							2 2 0	
Edward Harrison	M	Cottage & Croft	6 8			2 0 0	(1)		2 0 0	Cottage & Litle Croft inclosed in Westwood Common.
John Bullivant	M	Tenement	1 6 0	1 3 0	1 0				1 3 0	
Edward Doncaster	B	Tenement		3 0	1 0	3 0 0	(1)		1 3 0	

Name		Holding					Remarks
Widow Harson	M	Tenement	10 0		2 0	(4) 1 0 · 1 3 0	Lands & grass in South Lound. No house.
William Gilbert	M	Land	5 0	3 0		1 3 0	
John Hurst	F	Freehold		3 0		1 3 0	No house.
William Flinton	H	Land			2 0	1 2 0	No house.
Widow Betney	M	Tenement	8 0	1 1	1 0	1 2 0	Lands in South Lound, old way to the Mill, & Cottage on Moorhouse Common.
Nicholas Tailer, tanner	F	Freehold		2 0		1 2 0	Lands in South Lound, and House and yard on Moorhouse Common, rent 1s. 3d. p.a.
Anthony Salford	M	Tenement	4 0	1 1		1 1 0	
William Cartwright	M	Land	2 6	3 0	3 0	1 0 0	
,,	B	Cottage & yard			1 0		
Thomas Godfrey	M	Ten. in Moorhouse	9 0	2 0	2 0	1 0 0	
Thomas Rosse, labourer	M	Tenement	7 4	0	(2)	1 0 0	4s. for Cottage & yard, 3s. 4d. for arable land sometime belonging to Cottage in Westwood Common.
Jonas Diconson	M	Land	2 6	3 0		3 0	Lands in South Lound. No house.
Abraham Marshall	F	Freehold		3 0	1 0	3 0	No house.
George Page	M	Cottage & yard	10 0		1 0		
,,	B	Land		2 0	2 0		
Rowland Dawson	H	Meadow		3 0		3 0	No house.
William Talbut	M	Tenement	8 0	2 0	1 0	3 0	4s. for Cottage & yard on waste, 4s. for 2 lands in West Field.
			52 0 0	6 3 0	11 1 0	70 0 0	

meadow in Long Meadow, and three parcels, two of them arable, in East Inger Close.

(b) *Village tradesmen*, such as Nicholas Tailer, the tanner, and Nicholas Pawlthrop, the tailor, who had odd pieces of land, here and there, which could not be described as farms.

(c) *Farm workers*. Thomas Rosse, for example, who died in 1669, is described in the Parish Register as 'labourer'. He had 3 roods of land, 2 in West Field, and 1 in Mill Field. Perhaps the great value of a holding such as this was that it gave the tenant the right to turn out stock in the Open Fields, for this has proved to be the first rung of the agricultural ladder for many Laxton men.[1]

(d) *Miscellaneous holdings*. The largest number of holdings under 5 acres are quite indefinite in character. A few are occupied by widows, while one at least, that of Christopher Hassard, is the holding of an old man who had given up one of the large farms. If the occupations of all the men were known, it would be found, in all probability, that most of them belonged to the class just named, being labourers with a strip or two of land. Some of the surnames will be found amongst the tenants or freeholders of larger farms, and it may be that Robert Chapell, for example, who occupied 3 acres, was the son or brother of John Chapell, a freeholder of 30 acres, and worked for him. There was much intermarriage and most of the people were related to each other, either closely or at a few removes. There is the possibility, too, that some of these farmers of minute holdings in Laxton may have worked them in conjunction with other lands held by them in adjoining parishes, as, for example, did W. Treswell.

There is a curious disparity in the rents paid by these small tenants. While most of them pay only a few shillings, there are five who pay £1 or more. John Jepson, who paid £1. 5s. for 3 acres, had only recently taken over the holding from Widow Nicholson, and if the tenants of the other more highly rented holdings were in like case, these rents would provide further examples of Sir William Courten's policy of changing customary into economic rents.

Cottagers with no land

There were seven of these, one of them a freeholder in Moorhouse. Of the others, three had cottages on Moorhouse Common, or on the lord's waste, and three in Laxton town. They paid rents ranging from 1s. 3d. to 8s. a year.

Then there was the miller, John Brooke, tenant of both mills, for each of which he paid £4.

[1] See p. 172, *post*.

Lastly, there were ten freeholders and tenants whose holdings do not fit into any of the above categories. Some had a close or two, others a close and a few strips of arable land. One, at least, had a farm in Kneesal and held Laxton land on his boundary, but it is not easy to see how most of these holdings were assembled. None of them had houses attached to them. In the aggregate they account for 88 acres. One small freehold may be mentioned, belonging to Jane, Countess of Shrewsbury. It consisted of 6 acres, all arable land in the Open Fields, which must have been let in conjunction with another holding.

The following is a summary of those owning land in Laxton and Moorhouse in 1635:

		Acres
Sir William Courten		2,317 (including Commons)
Mr. Peter Broughton		754
Mr. Augustine Hinde		362
Robert Shipton, yeoman		76
Mr. James Bacon		69
Chantry Lands		54
Dean and Chapter of Southwell . . .		20
Vicar of Laxton		3
25 small freeholders		197
Total		3,852 (including Commons)

About four-fifths of the farmed land, exclusive of the demesne and Mr. Broughton's and Mr. Hinde's inclosed farms, was occupied by about one-third of the people of Laxton in holdings from 20 acres upwards. Another third of the people occupied holdings between 5 acres and 20 acres, being one-tenth of the area, while the other third were the cottage tenants, averaging 2 acres of land apiece, who, together with the miscellaneous holdings, accounted for the other tenth. There were only eight of the inhabitants who did not hold any land.

An analysis of the rental of the manor of Laxton in 1635 reads as follows:

	£	s.	d.
Chief Rents	1	6	2
Laxton Demesne Lands . . .	104	15	8
Laxton Tenements . . .	253	13	10
Moorhouse Tenements . . .	9	16	0
Total	£369	11	8

X. FARMING AND ADMINISTRATION

THE lands of the manor were divided into the lord's demesne, the freeholders' lands, and the lands of the lord's tenants. There is some evidence at Laxton that, except for the big freehold of the Lexington family, which was virtually a manor within the manor, medieval holdings, whether free or bond, were small. This is only what might be expected if we can assume that the opportunities for commercial farming were few or none, and that the land was occupied mainly for self-supply. Further, the demands made upon the villein tenants for services upon the lord's demesne, amounting, as has been shown, to so much as 100 days in the year,[1] would prevent them from farming on any extensive scale on their own account. The evidence of the Inquisitions *post mortem*, which furnish practically the only information about land-holding at Laxton until the end of the sixteenth century, is not enough to allow of any reconstruction of the various holdings. We do not know how the small freeholds were created, nor when, nor any of the processes of grant, sale, assembly, or division of parcels of land which had resulted, by the year 1635, in the distribution disclosed in Mark Pierce's *Booke of Survaye*.

From this time onwards, both the farming and the administration of the manor have been recorded, virtually without a break up to the present day. The two are disclosed as interlocking so completely as to be quite inseparable, so that it is impossible to think of the farming system apart from the administrative machine, or to consider the system of estate management and local government apart from the farming practice. Since the inclosure of the Open Fields, farming and estate management in other places have been no more the joint concern of the village community. They are pursued as separate enterprises in which it is not always easy to find community of interest, while the State has had to step in to determine many questions arising in their practice, which were decided at Laxton by the common consent of the people. Whatever may have been the position of the people of the manor in the days when their lord enacted service rents which took them from their own holdings for a large part of the year, by 1650 the economic organization of the place is revealed as being controlled entirely by the community, and it is of real interest and impor-

---

[1] See p. 83, *ante*.

tance to observe that amid all the great social inequalities of the
time, the principle upon which life and work in the Open Fields
was based was the principle of the same law for all. In the practice
of agriculture, the lord and the people were, all of them, equal.

The system of farming was that of the Common Fields; the
system of administration was that of the Manor Court. The two
together determined and directed the entire economic and social
life of the community. The Open Fields would have been impossible apart from the sanctions of the Manor Court. The court
baron would have been almost a superfluity apart from the administration of the Open Fields.

A little reflection will show the imperative need for the regula-
tion of farming in the Open Fields by the authority of the people
themselves. On the enclosed farms of today, farming is regulated
by agreements between landlord and tenant. The course of cropping is prescribed, the responsibility for the maintenance of house
and buildings, for hedges and fences, for ditches and watercourses,
for proper cultivation and manuring—all of these and other things
are matters of arrangement and bargain. While the intention is
to ensure the proper maintenance of the holding, the neglect,
either voluntary or permissive, of the tenant to observe these
covenants, can damage no one, as a rule, except himself and the
landlord. If his fences be neglected, if he fail to cultivate properly,
if he sub-let his grazing instead of stocking it himself or sell his
hay instead of consuming it on the farm, the landlord suffers by
the deterioration of his farm, and sooner or later the tenant will
suffer too. But no one else is affected.[1] Broken gates, overgrown
hedges, dirty or starved ploughlands may reduce the rental value
and the productivity of the particular holding, but the farmers on
the surrounding land are not prejudiced. In the Common or Open
Fields, however, there was little room for bargaining between the
lord and any of his tenants as to the conditions of tenure and their
mutual rights and liabilities. The system of farming, and the
diffusion of holdings all over the fields, made differential treatment between tenant and tenant impossible, alike as to the farming system and as to the responsibility for the maintenance of the
holding. When the whole field was open to common grazing after
harvest, a common system of cropping was necessary. When the
lands bordering a ditch, hedge, or watercourse were occupied by
every farmer of the manor in alternating strips a few yards wide,
it was necessary that all should be under the same obligation to

[1] Since the Second World War the national need for maximum food production has led
to the intervention of the State to enforce better estate management and farming. As
between landlord and tenant, and farmer and farmer, in the Open Fields, the argument
as stated is unaffected.

scour or to repair, for one man's neglect would recoil not only upon himself and the lord, but upon all his neighbours. In 1635 Mr. Peter Broughton, the freehold occupier of the inclosed Greate Farme, might elect to burn his hedge trimmings on his adjacent grassland, and no one would suffer; but if Samuel Holbem, the tenant of an oxgang, were to do this in the Open Fields he destroyed grazing which he shared in common with others. Mr. Broughton might leave his stock to graze on the land which he would mow, later, until whatever date he pleased; but if Holbem left his stock on the common meadows after the date fixed for 'driving' them (i.e. removing all stock to allow the grass to grow for hay) he was stealing his neighbours' herbage. Mr. Broughton might take a short cut across one of his fields to reach another; but if Holbem drove his plough-team from one of his strips to another, or if he carted dung from his homestead to his strips, without taking care to go round by the roads, by the common balks, or by the common headlands arranged to give access to them, he did damage to his neighbours' crops or cultivations. Broughton might graze his pastures as he pleased; but if Sam turned his horses on to the cow-pasture or his stallion upon the mares' common, or if he allowed a rig sheep to stray among everybody's ewes, then obviously he was offending against the common weal.

Even if every one farming in the fields had been the tenant of the lord, it is clear that daily supervision so close as that which was entailed by a system involving so much joint responsibility, could never have been exercised by the lord's steward. When it is remembered that a proportion of the farmers were freeholders and not subject to his jurisdiction, it is obvious that the difficulty of administering the common system of husbandry from above would be insuperable. The system could function without friction only if the administration were vested in the people themselves, both freeholders and tenants, to make regulations by common consent governing the common practice, and with authority to enforce them.

This, in fact, was the position. With authority derived from the lord and exercised through the machinery of his court baron, the farming system was defined and its observance was enforced by a panel of those who owed suit and service to the lord—that is, the freeholders and the tenants together. It is no part of the present purpose to trace the evolution of the manor court and its jurisdiction from earliest times. Its legal status and its relation to the judicial system can be studied elsewhere. It is the Court in action with which we are now concerned. The fine series of Laxton Court rolls begins in 1651 with 'the Court Leet and Court

Baron of the honble William Pierpont Esq.', and they continue, with only an occasional break, up to the present day.[1] The procedure at the court was and is as follows:

The court was presided over by the lord's steward. He fixed the dates on which it should be summoned, and these were half-yearly, in April and October, until 1684, after which the court sat once a year only, in October, November, or December. It was the duty of the Bailiff to summon the court, and every one whose name appeared on the suit-roll, whether freeholder or tenant, was bound to appear in person, unless essoigned on payment of a small fine. The bailiff opened the court by calling over the suit-roll, to check the attendance of the homage, and from those present a foreman was chosen and a jury was empanelled and sworn. In the earlier years the court, sitting as the court leet, then proceeded to hear civil cases. Very occasionally these were for disorderly conduct, as in 1651, when Peter Roos, gent., was fined 12d. 'for an affray upon Lawrence Bretton'; other offences in this category and the fines imposed were for 'making an affray in the alehouse, 6s. 8d.' (1660); 'for scoulding and disturbance to the neighbours, 3s. 4d.' (1661); 'bloodshedding upon Adam Chapell, 3s. 4d.' (1682). More frequent were claims for debt, which either were withdrawn or an attachment was made out, as the case might be; and most frequent of all were cases in which it is recorded that so-and-so complained against so-and-so, the offence not being stated and the case withdrawn. After the year 1682 civil actions were heard no longer at Laxton.

Fines were imposed on those absent, not having been essoigned, when the roll was called. The fine was commonly 6d. or less, but for a few years at the end of the seventeenth century, freeholders of standing, like George, Earl of Halifax, and Sir Brian Broughton, might be fined so much as 2s. 6d.

The court then proceeded to the appointment of officers. These were (i) the *Bailiff*, who seems to have been a go-between for the steward and the homage at this date.[2] His appointment is recorded only occasionally in the Laxton rolls, and the office was one which might be held for a period of years.

(ii) The *Constable* and the *Deputy Constables*, usually two, called

---

[1] There is some variety in the title of the court as given in the Rolls. Between 1651 and 1660 there is, of course, no mention of the king, and the inscription is in English. At the October court, 1660, it is in Latin, and the steward followed the general practice of counting the date of the King's Accession from the year of the execution of King Charles I. The Rolls continue in Latin until 1732, after which date they are always written in English, thus: 'Court Leet of our Sovereign Lord the King and Court Baron of . . .', &c. The presentment papers of the Jury were always written in English, in the hand of the Foreman.

[2] Before the commutation of service rents, it was the duty of the bailiff to supervise the work of the villein tenants upon the lord's demesne. See Lipson, E., *The Economic History of England*, vol. i, p. 53, 5th ed.

Thirdboroughs until 1754. The constables and deputies rarely held office for more than one year.

(iii) The *Pinder* (Lat. *Imparcator*), whose duty it was to impound stock found straying in the Open Fields and to hold them until the appropriate fines were paid for their release, besides serving in other ways as related later. He is named and sworn nearly every year, but he might hold his office for a term of years upon the confirmation of his appointment by each succeeding court. This office was held, now and again, by a woman. In 1754 Mary Palfreyman was pinder; Mary White held the office from 1761 to 1769, while Elizabeth Hempseed was pinder for three years from 1801. In the nineteenth century two pinders occasionally were appointed. The pinder was entitled to collect dues from every suitor in the manor, at Christmas, as his wages, and he received payment according to a scale of charges which were fixed by the court together with his wages, from time to time, for every straying animal impounded.

Other officers, whose appointments are mentioned only occasionally in the rolls, were:

(iv) The *Overseers*; mentioned three times only, in the seventeenth century, and their duties not stated.

(v) The *Head of the Frankpledge* (Lat. *capitalis plegius*); not appointed after 1723.

(vi) The *Burleymen*; men appointed, apparently, to secure the observance of the by-laws made by the court baron, from time to time, to regulate the use of the Open Fields, &c.—the 'by-law men'. There were six or eight of them, possibly two for each field, as they are always coupled when referred to. Only one appointment is recorded in the rolls and there is no indication of the method of their selection. Sometimes the Overseers of the Highways served also as Burleymen.

The hamlet of Moorhouse had its own set of officials, rendered necessary by its separate identity and open-field system. It had no bailiff, of course, as its people attended the Laxton court. Except for the period from 1756 to 1795, its constable enjoyed only the status of Thirdborough, or deputy. The hamlet had its own pinder until 1852, after which the office seems to have lapsed.

Following the appointment and swearing of the officers, the next business of the court was the admission of new freeholders and tenants. Every heir succeeding to a freehold, every purchaser of a freehold, and every tenant entering upon a holding under the lord, had to attend at the next court to do fealty. A fee of 3*s*. 4*d*. was payable to the lord of the manor on each admission. In 1886 a suitor attending the court declined to do fealty; the jury ordered that he should do fealty and pay 3*s*. 4*d*., but the practice by this time had clearly no significance, and, in 1890, the court resolved that in future it should not be required of new-comers.

There is a good deal of disparity in the numbers of admissions of freeholders and tenants at different periods. From 1658 to 1700 the average is two a year; from 1701 to 1800 it is five a year, but during the six years 1726 to 1731 there were sixty-three admissions, averaging more than ten a year. This was the period, as will appear presently, when some inclosure was carried out in the outlying parts of the manor, involving some redistribution of holdings.[1] From 1801 to 1887 the average is between two and three a year.

The court then proceeded to receive and to endorse the presentments made by the jury. The duties of the jury were both general and particular. It was concerned in general with all matters affecting the well-being of the community, both in its social life and in the pursuit of husbandry. While, however, it secured the due observance of all the rules and by-laws made at the court, from time to time, in the interests of community farming, it had a particular responsibility for one field in the rotation, namely, that sown with wheat. The jury had to go round the wheat field of the year to see that the boundary stakes marking each man's strips were in position, and to replace any that were missing; to note whether any man had encroached upon the sikes and patches of common grassland on to which many of the furlongs abutted; to note whether ditches had been scoured and fences repaired, and many other acts of omission and commission contrary to the by-laws and to the detriment of good farming. In this way, each of the Open Fields of the manor was thoroughly inspected once in three years, and the standard of farming was maintained by presenting and fining all delinquents.

By-laws made by the jury at the Laxton Court have survived only for the years 1686, 1688, and 1789 (these last having been revised in 1821), 1871, and 1908. They are printed in full at the end of this chapter, and a glance through them shows them to be a curious medley of fundamental principles and things of importance only at the moment; of things which every member of the community must observe and things personal to individuals. This is true, particularly, of the two seventeenth-century sets of by-laws. For example, 'Imprimis: It is pained that noo one shall carry any fire betwixt Neighbour and Neighbour uncovered in paine of any offending 5s.'—and again, 'That the foot-way at the Bottom of Christopher Salmon's yard be made passable before the 24th of this Instant, in paine of not so doing to pay 3s. 4d.' Or these, 'That everyone shall wring their swine betwixt this and the

---

[1] See p. 162, *post.*

20th of this Month and so keepe them from time [to time]; in paine of any offending: 3*s*. 4*d*.'; and 'That Mr. Stephenson cut his crabtree tops in High Lane'. The explanation is, of course, that while the jury had to make by-laws affecting the community in general, individual cases had also to be covered by *ad hoc* by-laws, the jury being the only responsible authority.

The presentments at each court were those of the jury appointed at the previous court. The presentment paper was signed by each member of the jury, those unable to write, and they were very few, making their mark.

An analysis of the presentments throws much light upon the social life of the place and particularly upon the farming system. Presentments for social offences are confined to the earlier years, and they disappear from the rolls after the middle of the eighteenth century.

From 1651 to 1697 each presentment paper begins with the names of persons who had broken the Assize of Bread and Ale. In the earlier years these offenders number about ten. They decline gradually to three, and there are none at all after 1697.

The danger of fire in a township of timber-built and straw-thatched houses, closely set as they were and each of them backed or flanked by its farm buildings and stacks, was very real, and the by-law which forbade carrying naked lights 'between neighbour and neighbour' led to presentments and fines (1668 and 1731). A fine for 'not repairing his chimney according to the laws of the Court' (1731) refers to the same danger.

Obstructions of one kind and another were the occasion of intermittent presentments, such as that for 'laying wood in the Towne strete and hindering the hiewaie' (1662), and for 'throwing noysom carrion into the strete' (1684).

'Carrying false weights and using same' (1675) is an isolated presentment of an enterprising merchant, but there are a few others for unlawful appropriations of various kinds. Between 1651 and 1673 seven persons were fined for removing wood, cutting thorns, mowing bracken, taking stone out of the highway, &c.

Driving a neighbour's heifer out of the parish (1779) refers evidently to some personal difference. Presentments in the three years 1682–3–4, 'for breaking the Statute for killing calves under 5 weeks old', have reference to a statue of 1 James I, cap. 22, sec. 3, which was enacted in the interests of 'Tanners, Curriers, Shomakers and other Artificers occupying the Cutting of Leathers'. These are the only presentments for the offence, though why there are such only in these years and none before or after is not clear.

As elsewhere, the administration of the Poor Law at Laxton

fell heavily upon the unfortunate, every parish being anxious to escape responsibility for the destitute. In 1653 two persons were presented 'for harbouring beggars'; in 1690 two for 'lodging wanderers'; in 1698 six 'for lodging travellers'; and in 1710 three 'for harbouring strangers that Gleaned Corn from our own Neighbours in time of harvest'. A by-law made in 1789 ordered 'that none lodge any travellers more than one night, if they do not give an account from whence they came'. The fines for these offences were relatively heavy. In 1779 a fine of £1. 19s. 11d., the highest recorded, was imposed on one of the people for 'keeping a servant girl contrayry to the laws of our Court when she is likely to become chargeable to the Parish and he has been admonished and been told of the same by Wm. Cocking by order of the officers if he dont turn her away by Michaelmas next'. In 1794 a woman 'belonging to the House' was presented 'for not being Drest'.

It was necessary, of course, that the dignity and the authority of the court and of the jury should be maintained, and the following presentments illustrate action taken against those who disobeyed the court, or its officers; they are comparatively rare:

1653   'concealing his goods due to the Churchwardens by Ratment, 6d.'
1678   'not obeying Jury's order, 2s.'
1729   'not obeying the foreman, 2s. 6d.'
1750   'not obeying the Jury, 1s. 6d.'
1764   'neglect of taking up his land and setting the Jury at defiance, 2s.'
1795   'not paying pinder his Christmas due, 6d.'

But the great interest of the Laxton Court Rolls lies in the light that is thrown by the presentments of the jury upon the practice of husbandry there, during the last 300 years. We have seen that at the time of Mark Pierce's survey holdings were of various sizes ranging from 200 acres downwards and farms were made up of strips of arable land in the Open Fields, doles of meadowland in the common meadows, grazing on the sikes or stubbles of the open arable fields; together, for many of the people, with closes, some of them arable, some of them grass, some of them inclosed on the outsides of the big fields, others forming part of the demesne, all of which were occupied in severalty. Let us see how their farming was organized and controlled.

Open-field farming, like all mixed farming today, was concerned with the production of crops and livestock. These branches of husbandry were equally important. The general principles of the three-field arable farming system are well understood, and the particular ways in which it was developed at Laxton under the by-laws of the court will be described presently. The system by which the Open Fields and the common grazings were used for the maintenance of livestock is less well known, and it is impossible to describe a typical Laxton farmer's agricultural year until its principles are understood.

In the early days, when the population of the country was small, there was grazing and to spare. The ploughlands round the village community encroached only a little on the woodlands and wastes, and there was ample range for livestock. If the population grew, and cultivation had to be pushed farther and farther afield, woodlands were grubbed and wastes were ploughed up, until, as at Laxton by 1635, plough farming could expand but very little more. Indeed, the self-sufficing village communities may often have been in something of a dilemma at the end of the Middle Ages. They needed more and more arable land on which to grow bread for their increasing numbers, but this could only be provided by leaving themselves less and less grassland which they needed just as much, for the production of meat, milk, and wool. Their necessities led them to evolve an elaborate system of controlled grazing, designed to make the utmost of their limited resources.

At Laxton, and in many other places no doubt, the grass keep was of three kinds. There were the commons, which were what was left of the waste, together with odds and ends of grassland beside the green roads which led to the Open Fields; there was the aftermath of the common meadows; there were the sikes, balks, roadsides, and stubbles of the Open Fields themselves. There is some evidence that the right to graze the commons was reserved to the smaller inhabitants who had no land in the Open Fields. If they were not to depend for their living entirely upon work for wages (and such people were a very small class in the rural community before the eighteenth century), they must have had some opportunity for part-time farming, and it was provided by a cottage holding, with grazing on the commons.

The Laxton commons, Cocking Moor, or Westwood Common, in the north-west corner of the manor [No. 3031], of 89 acres, and the East Moor or Towne Moor, at the bottom of the village [No. 3032], of 7 acres, were the principal grazings in this class, and little bits here and there, on the waysides and elsewhere, brought the total up to 108 acres. The grazing on this was stinted, that is to say, the number of animals which might be turned out on them was restricted. The toft rights, as they were called, were attached to certain houses, and the cottage farmers who occupied or owned them appear to have been entitled each of them to put on 20 sheep, or their equivalent in beasts or horses, and this rule remained until 1908, when the numbers were reduced by one-half, namely, to 10 sheep, 3 beasts, or 2 horses.

These grazing rights were highly valued and jealously guarded. The commonest offence in connexion with them, for which men were presented and fined by the jury, was that of turning on more stock than the toft right allowed:

1662 'oppressing the Commons, 1s.'
1667 'over stocking the Comons with his sheepe, having moore in sumer then he maintains in Winter, 5s.'
1718 'tethering her cow upon Laxton Common, 6d.'
1814 'stocking our commons without common right, 5s.'
1814 'bringing Edward Hunt's ass, of Kirton, on our Commons, 2s. 6d.'
1875 'stocking Common without a right, 10s.'

The presentment of 1667 about sheep refers to a custom which restricted those with common rights to keeping on the common no more than the breeding-stock which they were able to winter, together, of course, with their progeny of the year. This man had evidently bought extra sheep to put on the common in summer.

Other regulations were directed towards preventing injury to the commons themselves. The earliest by-laws extant (1686) provided 'that everyone shall wring their swine betwixt this [8th October] and the 20th of this Month and so keepe them from time to time, in paine of any offend: 3s. 4d.' Taking soil from the commons was another offence, and so jealous were the people of their rights, that when the Duke of Portland's keepers came to take ant-hills, presumably for his young pheasants, they were presented and fined. Examples are:

1662 'not felling his part of thistles on the Towne Moore, 6d.'
1790 'suffering his pigs to go unwrung, 1s.'
1804 'her pigs turning up the swarth on the moor, 6d.'
1816 'digging earth of Common to make a bank in Garden, 1s.'
1850 'paring Comon and taking it away, 1s.'
1887 'Duke of Portland for leading soil of the Commons, 5s.'[1]

The presentment of 1662, for not cutting thistles, refers to a by-law which imposed on all those with common right the duty of cutting thistles before they should seed.

The aftermath of the common meadows—the Long Meadows [Nos. 2472–729], 67 acres, South Lound Meadows [Nos. 2740–97], 20 acres, Shitterpool Meadows [Nos. 2405–71], 15 acres, and East Kirk Ing [Nos. 2805–910], 34 acres, amounting in all to about 136 acres—was the property of those who occupied doles

---

[1] A note on the presentment paper adds: 'Took off ant-hills for eggs, but Mrs. Pinder says it was the D[uke] of N[ewcastle].'

within them. This was without doubt the best grazing in the manor. By custom, hay-making had to be finished at Lammas (1 August) and thereupon the meadows were 'broken', that is to say, they were thrown open for grazing. Stock could remain on them until 1 November, when it was the duty of the pinder to 'drive' the meadows so that they should not be damaged by poaching (trampling by stock), in the wet winter months. Lying along the banks of the stream, they would be very wet and soft. By this date, probably, all the surplus livestock, the year's increment in cattle, sheep, and pigs, had been sold in the nearest market town, except such as were required for breeding, or for slaughter and salting for the winter food-supply of the farmer's household. These were brought up to the homesteads and crofts in the village.

The third source of grazing was the Open Fields themselves. In the four of them, the grass on sikes and common balks amounted to no less than 82 acres. That this land had to be stocked, notwithstanding the difficulties which would be raised when horses, cattle, sheep, and pigs were to be turned on to fields the primary purpose of which was corn-production, shows the importance of making use of every rood of ground to a community which had grown to the utmost limits of the capacity of the land, and which had no means of subsistence apart from it. Let us take the year through and see how grazing in the Open Fields was regulated.

Directly after harvest was finished, the church bell was rung to announce that the fields were 'broken'. All those who had land in the Open Fields might then drive their stock on to the wheat and spring corn stubbles without any stint. This right was highly prized, and, owing to the very limited grazing-area of the manor, people sometimes anticipated the ringing of the church bell and turned their stock on before all the corn was carried. This was an offence, of which the Court Rolls furnish several examples:

1652 'tenting his bease in the Little [East] Field before it was Brooke, 2s. 6d.'
1663 'putting his beasts in the cornefield before the corne was led forth without the burleymens consent, 1s. 6d.'
1663 'tenteing his Cowes in the cornefield before the Corne was reaped, 2s.'
1686 'breaking the corn a week before the time, 6d.'
1696 'turning his horses loose in the stubble field before the field was broken, 3s. 4d.'
1802 'tenting his horses loose in the open field before the Harvest was got, 2s.'
1850 'eating Commons before crops removed, 20s.'

Grazing continued on the wheat stubble until 15 October. This field was then needed for ploughing in preparation for the next spring corn crop, and accordingly it was 'driven', that is to say, the stock were driven off by the pinder. The field carrying the stubbles of the spring corn was to be the bare fallow for the coming year, and unrestricted grazing might continue here until 23 November, when cattle and horses had to be taken away. From this date until October in the following year, when wheat-sowing on the fallow would begin, sheep only might graze in the fallow field, but the numbers were no longer unstinted. Each farmer was restricted to twenty sheep.

But the removal of stock from the new wheat field and from the new spring corn field, by no means disposed of these fields as potential grazing-areas. Although by springtime the corn was growing, so also was the grass of the sikes and common balks. From the presentments it appears that the practice in the seventeenth century was to tether livestock on these various parcels so that they could graze without damage to the growing corn, and, moreover, that each sike was earmarked for a particular class of animal. Sheep and pigs, of course, were excluded from these fields until after harvest, as they could not be tethered. One sike was reserved for mares and foals, another for stoned horses (stallions), a third for cows, while there was still another one for oxen. It was an offence to tether stock upon any other than the sike reserved for it. The right to this tether grazing was restricted, of course, to those who had land in the Open Fields. Moreover, from the evidence of the presentments, it is clear that this grazing was stinted, and the restriction took the form of the allotment to the farmers of 'gate rights',[1] which sometimes they exceeded. The following presentments serve to illustrate the use of the cornfields for tether grazing:

1652 'tethering his cowe of the horse commons contrary to a paine, 6d.'
1652 'tethering his mayres upon the horse comon, 2s.'
1663 'mare and foal on ston'd horse sike, 1s.'
1663 'tethering oxen on horse common, 1s.'
1667 'tethering horses upon the cow commons, 1s.'
1670 'teathering his mare on the Stond Horse Comons, 1s.'
1682 'tethering more horses than he had gates for, 3s. 4d.'
1714 'tethering more Horses then he had Gates, having let them to other men, 1s.'
1731 'tethering his horse so as he eat William Hunts corn, 10s.'

From the presentment for 1714 it appears that gate rights in

---

[1] *Gate.* A right to a run or pasturage for a cow, horse, &c., on a common field, representing a share of the joint ownership in the field (*O.E.D.*). There were 312 of these gates in the Laxton fields.

the Open Fields were transferable, but only to people within the manor. Letting gates to strangers was an offence:

1682 'letting his common outside the town, 6d.'
1791 'bringing Beasts out of other Parishes into our Open, 5s.'

The time at which tether grazing in the cornfields might begin was prescribed, and all stock had to be cleared off the sikes after Midsummer,[1] to avoid the risk of damage to the standing corn.

1667 'teathering his meares and Foals in the fields after Midsumer, 2s. 6d.'
1712 'tethering his mares in the Sicks afore the time was expired according to the paines provided for that purpose, 5s.'

Mark Pierce's map of the West Field shows cattle tethered on the two big sikes there. Animals going to the tether grounds had to be led, not driven, for fear of damage to the crops. A by-law of 1686 runs—'It is pained that noe one shall drive either horses or beasts either to the Tezer or from it in paine of any offending 3s. 4d.' Tether grazing, which is still a common practice in Denmark and other continental countries where fields are unfenced, has died out entirely in England, except for goats, and gipsies' horses by the roadside. Besides being necessary on unfenced grazing in the cornfields, it made more economical use of the grass.

One of the arguments always used against the Open Fields is that under a system by which everybody's stock roamed the fields and commons together, it was difficult, if not impossible, for the improving farmer to raise the quality of his livestock. Others would share in the services of his improved rams, while his improved cows and ewes might suffer from the attentions of the common bull and any type of tup that his neighbours cared to use. It is the more interesting to note, therefore, that, in 1787, the time when the news of livestock improvement by men such as Robert Bakewell, Robert Fowler, and others was beginning to filter through the country, the Laxton jury were enlightened enough to frame by-laws to regulate the use of bulls and rams, as well as to punish those who put animals suffering from infectious diseases upon the commons.[2]

At some time early in the eighteenth century the difficulties of grazing stock amongst the growing corn led to the abandonment of the practice. Moreover, the common meadows had been inclosed, and several small farms had been inclosed on the outlying portions of the manor[3] whereon the tenants had their own grass fields, while the area of the common grazing in the Open Fields was unaffected. Further, about 170 acres of woodland had been

[1] Old Midsummer, 6 July.
[2] See p. 151, post.   [3] See p. 162, post.

grubbed and made into grass closes. The grazing problem, there-fore, had become less acute, and the court resolved to abandon grazing in the cornfields, and to let the grass on the sikes for hay-making. The earliest reference to the practice is the record of a letting which appears in the accounts of the Overseers of the Highways for 1728. A by-law of 1789 enacted:

That the Commons be let to the highest bidder on the public day, and the money paid proportionably to the Gate.

This is still the rule, effect being given to it by a public auction of the grass wastes in the two fields of the year which are in crop, held before haytime, early in July, by which the sikes, roadsides, common balks, &c., are all of them lotted and the grass sold to the highest bidder. Each purchaser pays a shilling to seal the bargain, the money going to the cost of a supper held after the auction, while the proceeds of the sale are divided among the lord of the manor and other freeholders, proportionately to the number of their gates. In the early years of the nineteenth century these lettings sometimes reached a total of over £200, the highest being £211. 16s. in 1837.[1]

Buyers were bound to cut and carry the grass at fixed dates, which varied between 10 July and 1 August, and there are occa-sional presentments for neglect:

1849 'mowing grass on Commons after ensaltime, 5s.'
1880 'not mowing in proper times, 1s.'

At an earlier date the sale or removal of this hay out of the parish was forbidden by a by-law under a penalty of £1. 10s. for each load, just as the letting of grazing on the commons to any one other than a Laxton man was, and still is, prohibited. Fodder was too scarce, and if one man had a surplus it must be offered to his neighbours:

1745 'selling Common grass out of the parish of Laxton, after the rate of £1. 10. 0. a load.'

The by-law was still in force in 1821.

The difficulty of protecting the long, unfenced borders of the Open Fields must have been very great, and presentments for damage to the cornfields from trespass, sometimes accidental and sometimes deliberate, by livestock of all kinds are very numerous.

1663 'destroying corn in Whitmore with his swine, 1s.'
1670 'destroying the Corne with his swine, 1s.'
1727 'being a common destroyer of Corn in the Nights with his Swine, 2s. 6d.'
1749 'trespassing with his Geese and Swine and so forth, 5s.'

1 Parish Accounts.

1749   'driving horses through the cornfield, 1s.'
1785   'taking his horses loose through the corn field and tenting them, 1s.'
1791   'John Johnson of Kneesall, For horses getting into our Open, 2s. 6d.'
1793   'mare and ass trespassing in corn fields, 2s.'
1812   'Geese and Pigs trespassing in the Bean Field, 1s.'
1818   'for is Pigs be in White Corn field se in on them imself, 1s.'
1826   'Beasts and Pigs, repeatedly Trespassing in Wheat Field, 2s. 6d.'
1898   'pigs running in top [West] field after being driven, 2s. 6d.'

It may be remarked in passing that all presentments and fines by the jury for offences other than those in the wheat field of the year, which were their particular concern, came to their notice upon the report of the burleymen, whose duty it was to keep a look-out for all incidental offences. They were presented themselves sometimes, and fined:

1708   'Burleymen, (6) for neglecting their office, 2s. 6d. each.'
1710   'Burleymen, (8) for neglecting their office, 4s.'
1714   'for not looking to their Office as Burliemen, 4 at 6d. each.'
1715   'the Burleymen (4) for not doing their Office, each man Sixpence.'

It was the duty of the pinder to collect stock straying in the fields and to drive them into the village pound or pinfold. Here they were kept, to be restored to their owners only upon payment of the appropriate fines. These were taken by the pinder as the perquisite of his office. A by-law of 1789 reads as follows:

That the Pounder's wages be paid as follows, viz. for every score of sheep 2d. For the out of town's 4d. A sow and pigs 4d. A Horse or Beast 1d. For out of town's 2d. At Christmas every Farmer 2d. and every Cottager 1d. apiece.
'That the Pounder's wages be paid without any fraud.

Those living outside Laxton parish had to pay twice as much, and all fines were doubled by a by-law made in 1843.

Pound-breach, that is to say, breaking open the pinfold and removing the stock without payment of the fines, and Rescue, which was taking the stock away from the pinder while he was driving them to the pound, were offences not uncommon in the seventeenth and eighteenth centuries:

1679   'Taking his sheep from Moorhouse Pinder, 1s.'
1680   'Resisting the Pinder, 1s.'
1742   'Breaking the Pinfold and for repeated trespasses with his cattel, 3s. 4d.'
1786   'Refusing to pay the Pinder's wages, 6d.'

The pinder himself was occasionally presented for neglect of his duty, and fined.

Let us now trace the farming year in the Open Fields, by following the operations of a typical Laxton farmer in the year

PLATE 21

a. FALLOWJACKS IN LAXTON FIELDS

b. LAXTON PINFOLD

1635. Hugh Tailer was a tenant of the Chantry Lands, occupying a virgate of 30 acres divided as follows: messuage and yard ½ acre; 8 acres in 11 parcels, or strips, in West and East Fields; 8 acres in 17 parcels in Mill Field; 7½ acres in 16 parcels in South Field; and 5½ acres in 8 parcels in the common meadows.[1]

Let us suppose that the West and East Fields, which were farmed as one in the rotation, had been in wheat, that the South Field had been in spring corn, while the Mill Field rested in fallow. The farming year begins after harvest. Hugh Tailer had driven his stock on to the stubbles when he heard the church bell ring, and then he turned to his strips of fallow in the Mill Field, which he had been ploughing during the previous summer whenever he could spare time. He would now give them a final ploughing.

One of the criticisms of the Open Fields made by historians is the inconvenience and loss of time which the cultivation of many and widely scattered strips involved. In fact, this was not so great as might appear at first sight. An arrangement which gave a man 8 acres scattered in 17 small strips throughout a field of 433 acres might seem to carry its own condemnation. But an examination of the distribution on the map shows that, in practice, it involved very little handicap in the days when farm machinery was unknown. Taken in conjunction with the daily part-time work with livestock, most of the strips represented a day's ploughing. It would be immaterial in point of convenience whether the farmer took his team each day to the same part of the field or to different parts. He would leave the plough itself in the field, so that the only loss of time involved would be its removal from one strip to another. As to this, the whole layout of the system of roads, common balks, and common headlands throughout the Open Fields, intricate as it might appear to a stranger, was devised for convenience of access, and to trace the movements needed to take the plough at the close of one day's work to the next strip ready for the following day's work is to realize how slight the inconvenience really was. Moreover, strips lying in different furlongs might, and in Hugh Tailer's holding several of them did, abut one upon another, or lie quite close to each other, and operations such as broadcasting and harrowing could easily be performed upon each with little loss of time. At harvest, all the work was manual, and movement from strip to strip mattered little. There were no statutory minimum wage-rates to be paid, in fact no wages at all. Hugh Tailer was working for himself, and if his return home was delayed by ten minutes because his team had to drag the plough to another strip in preparation for tomorrow's work, what matter?

[1] See p. 102, *ante.*

The ploughing finished, the lands' ends might have to be shovelled in. If any of his strips abutted on the sikes, they were ploughed their full length, without a headland, and the plough, as it ran out of the ground at the end of the furrow and turned to come back, would throw up some soil. These accumulations, after several times ploughing through the summer, might be considerable. Good husbandry and the custom of the manor demanded that he should take a spade and shovel the earth back on to his own land. He might have manured his strips or carted lime on to them, and here again custom demanded that none of this must be left upon the sike to obstruct it or to damage the grass. If he were a good neighbour as well as a good farmer, it may be taken for granted that he would not have overrun his boundaries, either at the lands' ends or sides, when ploughing, nor removed his landmarks, for the common belief that each man's strip was divided from his neighbour's by balks of unploughed turf, is a mistake.[1] The boundary between them was no more than the furrow, with a heavy wooden stake driven in at each end of it. Large stones, called merestones, were also used where more permanent boundary marks were needed between furlong and common.

The last ploughing finished and the lands' ends shovelled in, Hugh Tailer proceeded to broadcast his seed wheat on the furrows, and to harrow it in at once. The work should have been finished during October.

His next task was to fence any part of his lands' ends in the wheat field which abutted on a highway, to prevent trespass and damage by passing livestock. A by-law made by the jury in 1686 laid down 'that all the Fences belonging to the Wheat field be sufficiently made betwixt this [8th October] and the 30th day of this month, in paine of any offending 3s. 4d. These fences were made of stakes driven into the ground at intervals of a few feet and laced with boughs.

Then the jury for the year descended upon the Mill field to make their inspection. The foreman fixed the day, the bailiff warned the jurymen, and summoned them when the day arrived by ringing the church bell. One of their duties was to check all boundary marks and to replace all stones or stakes that had been moved. Where the removal was deliberate or malicious, the offender was presented and fined heavily:[2]

1662   'removing a mearstone, 5s.'
1708   'taking up the mearstone the Jury set down, 10s.'
1750   'removing the stakes belonging to commons, 10s.'
1810   'pulling up stakes, 2s.'

[1] See pp. 43–51, ante.
[2] See the by-laws of the manor made in 1789, p. 150, post.

PLATE 22

PLOUGHING, BROADCASTING, AND HARROWING, 1635

PLATE 23

a. BROADCASTING AT LAXTON, 1935

b. PLOUGHING AT LAXTON, 1935

Next, the jury had to see whether any encroachments had been made upon the commons, that is to say, the sikes, common balks, &c., within the field, either by ploughing too far or by leaving heaps of earth, lime, manure, or ditch-scourings (gripings) lying upon them. Presentments for such offences do not occur in any number until the middle of the eighteenth century, when tether-grazing had been given up and the sikes had to be kept clear for mowing, but from that time onward to the present day they are frequent. Many of the sikes are roadways, and encroachments may interfere seriously with getting to and from the strips. Those in the later years specify the number of lands and the names of the sikes upon which the encroachments were made, but the fines were not very heavy except in bad cases:

1679   'ploughing beyond the Mearestone at Acre hedge corner 6*d*.'
1750   'encroaching on commons by ploughing, 5*s*.'
1768   'throwing the gripings from the lands ends upon heaps upon the Commons more than usual, 1*s*.'
1774   'laying manure on Commons, 1*s*.'
1779   'ploughing up balk and taking away soil from said balk to put on his land, 2*s*.'
1789   'Ploughing out too far, 1*s*.'
1793   'Ploughing up Commons in Langsike, 1*s*.'
1871   'cultivating beyond their boundaries, 6*d*.'
1887   'ploughing one furrow of grass, 2*s*.'
1887   'not cleaning lands ends, 6*d*.'

Very rarely the jury had to present a man for ploughing his neighbour's land, as in 1771, when a fine of 5*s*. was imposed for 'ploughing people's land away'. According to Marc Bloch, *mangeurs de raies* were frequent and serious offenders in the French Open Fields, but at Laxton there is only one presentment in the 300 years of Court records, and the inference is that public opinion, expressed in the by-laws and administered by the jury, made it impossible.

The next task for the jury was to enforce the rules for maintaining fences, hedges, and gates. As already noted, lands' ends abutting on a road had to be fenced, and where two boundary hedges came down to a road on either side, as on that between Mill Field and West Field, a gate was fixed across it to keep out straying stock. Certain people were charged with the responsibility for their repair, and to leave one of these gates open when carting manure, or at harvest, &c., was an offence. Examples of presentments in this category are:

1663   'wife carrying hedgewood to his house and breaking hedges, 6*d*.'
1663   'neglecting hingeing of Radle Yate, 1*s*.'

1666   'his sonne leaving the Corne feild yate open whereby the Cowse goot
        into the Corne, 6*d*.'
1673   'leaving Whitmore Gate open when he led manure into South
        Lound Cloase, 6*d*.'
1674   'neglect of acre hedge making, 6*d*.'
1680   'pulling down the Hedge to the cornefield and not making it up
        again, 1*s*.'

Presentments for failure to fence are rare after 1800 and there
are none after 1835. The responsibility of husbands and fathers
for the acts of wives and children may be noted.

Less urgent than the fencing, but equally important, was the
ditching. The occupier of any strips abutting on a ditch or watercourse was responsible for keeping his length of it scoured and
free from obstructions, and it was the jury's duty to inspect these
and present where necessary. There is a fair number of such
presentments during the seventeenth century, the fines varying
from 4*d*. to 1*s*., but very few in the next century and in the first
half of the nineteenth. In 1860, however, there was a movement
to secure better drainage, and two of the jury were ordered by the
court to 'inspect all the sewers and watercourses in this Manor
before next Court day and report to the Jury then assembled any
persons who have not properly cleansed such sewers and watercourses with the view of presenting and fining the defaulters'. In
the following year eleven people were presented and fined, one of
whom refused to pay his 9*d*. and so was fined an additional 4*s*. 6*d*.
at the next court. In 1865 it was reported 'that the sewers and
watercourses were all properly cleansed and in good order'. From
this date to the present day the rules for scouring ditches have
been rigidly enforced, amongst those fined being the lord of the
manor himself. So efficiently was the work done that the Southwell Court of Sewers exercised no jurisdiction and levied no rate
in Laxton until recently.

A minute of the Court held on 26 November 1936 records that
the Court no longer has powers to fine for failure to cleanse dikes,
'as the powers of the Court over dykes was taken away by the Law
of Property Act, 1922'.

This completed the work involved at the jury's annual tour of
the wheat field. Meanwhile, our farmer, Hugh Tailer, had not
been idle. When he had finished sowing his wheat and fencing his
lands' ends in the Mill Field, it was time to think of the spring
corn crop to be sown in the West and East Fields, which were
cultivated together as one field in the rotation. It is of some
interest to note that the field assigned to the spring corn was, and
it still is, known at Laxton and elsewhere as the bean field, beans
formerly being regarded as a spring corn crop.

PLATE 24

MEARSTONES AND BOUNDARY STAKES

It was the spring corn field, sometimes called also the breach field, that gave elasticity to the three-field system to an extent not always realized.[1] While wheat was grown almost exclusively as the winter grain, to provide bread, a considerable range of crops —beans, peas, barley, oats, vetches (tares), hemp, and later, clover to mow for hay—were grown in the spring corn field, according to each man's fancy. These crops were grown, in the main, to provide winter keep for the livestock. The idea that the spring corn crop consisted mainly of barley for brewing is certainly not borne out by the evidence of Laxton. In fact, to generalize, it would be more correct, instead of talking of the 'bread corn' and the 'drink corn', to speak of the 'bread field' and the 'fodder field'. To imagine that nearly half the sown land could be devoted to the production of a drink crop is to fail to realize the hard struggle for subsistence, both for man and beast, which life on the land imposed. Meat, milk, and wool were more necessary, if less exhilarating, than beer, and fodder crops were absolutely vital in the largest quantity in which they could be grown, to supplement the straw and the small supply of hay, the only other winter foods.

About 15 October, wheat-sowing being finished and the livestock grazing on the wheat stubble in the West and East Fields having been driven off, Hugh Tailer then started plough-ing his eight acres divided into eleven strips, in these two fields, in preparation for spring sowing. He would need about twelve working days in which to plough the stubble under, and his lands then lay until the spring, to be mellowed and broken by frost and rain. The rest of his time in the short winter days was occupied in tending his livestock, most of which would now be housed in the yards and buildings behind his house; in scouring his ditches, plashing or trimming his boundary hedges if he had any; in mend-ing his tools and implements; in threshing his corn, and so on.

In March his spring sowing would begin, to be followed, as in the wheat field, by fencing such of his lands' ends as were exposed.

With the coming of spring, livestock and grassland began to displace corn crops and ploughland in their claims upon the prin-cipal part of the farmer's time and attention. The stocks of winter food, mainly hay and straw, were nearly exhausted, and directly there was any sign of young grass, say towards the end of April, the stock was turned out to be tethered on the sikes. Some of the farmers had one or more closes, held in severalty, in which they could turn out stock, but Hugh Tailer and many others had

[1] As to this, see also Fussell, G. E., 'Farming Methods in the Early Stuart Period', *The Journal of Modern History*, vol. vii, 1935, p. 5, and *Robert Loder's Farm Accounts, 1610–1620*, Royal Historical Society, Camden Third Series, vol. liii (1936), p. xxxi.

nothing except the waste lands in the Open Fields until the aftermath of the common meadows was available.

During April and May our farmer was busy amongst his ewes and lambs, his cows and calves, and his farrowing sows; the rest of his time was employed upon his fallows in the South Field. Constant ploughing of the fallows killed the weeds and got the soil into condition for autumn wheat-sowing. Laxton farmers claim, too, that the custom of stocking the fallow field with sheep throughout the year contributes to the preparation, for they eat the weeds and keep them from seeding, while the treading helps to produce the firm seed-bed which the wheat plant enjoys. They point to a noticeable difference, today, between the comparative cleanliness of the West by contrast with that of the East Field, both of which are cropped as one in the rotation, but common grazing is practised now only in the West Field.

Towards the end of June the grass in the four common meadows was ready for mowing. It has been related already how the grass was allotted in tiny strips, or doles, one man's alternating with those of his neighbours upon the principle of the strips in the common arable fields. The average size of a dole was no more than 20 perches, and the suggestion is offered that they represented the two swathes which a man would cut as he worked his way across the meadow and came back to the starting-point. Most of the Laxton men occupied their meadowland in strips made up of one or two doles each, though the strips of a few contained more. Our farmer, Hugh Tailer, occupied 5 acres in 8 parcels, being fortunate in that he had one small close of 1½ acres, a parcel of 1 acre in Long Meadow, and 13 doles which lay together in South Lound Meadow. These blocks are larger than fell to the lot of most of the small farmers, his neighbour Christopher Salmon, for example, having 4 acres of meadow in all, contained in 16 separate parcels.

The value of the hay crop in the economy of farming in the Open Fields has been emphasized, and, at Laxton, by-laws were made and strictly enforced to protect it. In the by-laws of 1686:

It is pained that all they Hedges belonging to the Long Medow and East Ing be sufficiently made betwixt this [8th Oct.] and the 30th day of this Month and so kept from time to time in paine of Any one Offending £1. 19. 11.'

It is pained that the pinders shall pinn out of they Medowes after the first of Nov: next in paine of their not so doing 10s.'

It is pained that no one shall make a way over the Long Medow betwixt the breck wong and porter wong 10s.'

These are heavy fines. The by-law as to making the hedges was revised by the jury two years later, and the date extended to

PLATE 25

HAYMAKING, 1635

PLATE 26

HARVESTING, 1635

1 February. The instruction to the pinders to clear all stock off the meadows after 1 November was given to prevent poaching and damage to the grass during the wet winter months.

The by-laws made by the jury in 1688 confirmed those foregoing and added, 'that everyone scour all the ditches belong to the Long-medow, South-loon, and East-Ing, betwixt this [Oct. 8th] and the 10th of May next following in paine of not, etc. 3s. 4d.'

Presentments of offenders occur only during the first hundred years of the Court Rolls, as the common meadows were inclosed and re-allotted in severalty in the first half of the eighteenth century.

Haymaking was one of the many operations of the farm in which the women shared. The grass was laid in swathes with the scythe, and after turning, to dry it, the women helped the men to rake it up into cocks, preparatory to leading it to the homestead. The work had to be finished by 1 August, when the aftermath, like the stubbles of the arable fields, was 'broken' for common grazing until 1 November. The commonest offences in the meadows were turning out stock too soon, neglecting fencing, and trespass. There is some evidence, too, that the grazing was restricted to certain classes of stock:

1651   'putting ston'd horse in the Long Meadow contrarie to a Pain, 4d.'
1670   'his wife breakeing hedges in the meadow, 6d.'
1714   'not making his meadow fences in divers places, 2s.'
1714   'Edmund Hynde Gentleman for putting his Horses into the Long Meadow, 6s. 8d.'
1718   'breaking the East Ing without the Burleymens Consent, 6d.'
1727   'driving loose and wilfully eating people's grass, 2s. 6d.'
1729   'making a way through the hay, 1s.'

Haymaking ended, harvest came quickly upon the Laxton farmers. This was the climax of the year's work, and everyone, male and female, young and old, repaired to the fields. The first man to start in the wheat field cut and bound a sheaf and carried it immediately to the church. Here it was received by the parish priest, who laid it upon the altar, while the church bell summoned the people to a celebration of the Holy Communion. This ceremony is still observed.

The men, aided by their sons when they were old enough, cut their corn with reaping-hooks, each man on his own strips, while their womenfolk bound the sheaves and built them into stooks. The corn, when ready, was led in carts to the homestead and there stacked or stored in the barn, ready for threshing throughout the winter. Meanwhile, the cottagers and the humbler members of the community were busy gleaning upon the stubbles. Thoroton tells how the mother of Gilbert Roos, the last of his family to be lord of the manor, 'was reduced to so great poverty, that she gleaned corn amongst other poor people in Laxton field'.[1] The privilege of gleaning was reserved to Laxton people.

The corn was ground, until so recently as the year 1916, in Laxton windmill. It was a post mill, standing high, at the top of the Mill Field. In earlier days there had been a second windmill, in the South Field, belonging to the sub-manor. It was working in 1635, but all trace of it has now disappeared.

Thus, the year's work was over. The church bell rang again and the stubbles were broken. To prevent a general hold-up in the interests of a few laggards, it was and is a custom that the fields might be broken, if necessary, before the last two farmers had finished carrying their corn.

But work on the land never stops. So now the ploughs were got out again, and Hugh Tailer and his neighbours began their preparations for another harvest.

One aspect of the farming and administrative system of Laxton remains to be mentioned. Whatever may have been the practice in other places, the Laxton court leet and court baron from 1651 onwards has been no mere formal institution. There has been no dictation to the people by their lord. The record of essoigns, the fealties, the election of officers, were matters of routine, and they are recorded year by year in the same forms of words by the lord's steward. But the jury elected from the people was a living institution, intervening to regulate the economic and social life of the community by a system which required personal service from each man at frequent intervals. The administrative officers were drawn from the community, and the various offices rotated amongst its members. The decisions of the jury recorded by the Court were no mere stereotyped forms or repetitions; they made their presentments in their own hand and phrase, with vividness and spontaneity; they assessed the appropriate fines without fear or favour. The flexibility of the administrative machine was ensured by the powers of the Court to make new by-laws, year by year, and to vary the old ones, to a degree that is impossible in an agricultural community controlled, instead, by ancient customs or laggard statutes. A custom is not a custom until 'the memory of man runneth not to the contrary', and a statue never reaches the Statute Book until long after the need for it has arisen. The by-laws of the Laxton Court could be, and they often were, made and varied every twelve months. They extended to questions of agricultural policy affecting the whole community, as well as to matters of detail in which only individuals were concerned, and the emphasis

[1] Thoroton, *History of Nottinghamshire*, ed. John Throsby, 1796, vol. iii, p. 209.

was always changing to meet changing needs. Their administration cost nothing to the law-abiding.

Certain of the by-laws made at various dates have been preserved:

MANOR LAXTON CUM MOORHOUSE

Paines made by the Jury at the Court Leet & Court Barron of the Right Honble Will: Earl of Kingston holden for the Manor aforesd 8th day of October 1686

Impr: it is pained that noo one shall carry any fire betwixt Neighbour & Neighbr uncovered in paine of any offending   5   0

It is pained that all ye Ditches belonging to the Town Street Toad Lane & Robort Lane be sufficiently scowered, betwixt this & the 30th day of this Month in paine of any offending   3   4

It is pained that all the Fences belonging to the Wheat field & the pinfold be sufficiently made betwixt this & the 30th day of this Month, in paine of any offending   3   4

It is pained that all they Hedges belonging to the Long Medow & East Ing be sufficiently made betwixt this and the 30th day of this Month and so kept from time to time in paine of Any one Offending   1   19   11

It is pained that the pinders shall pinn out of they Medowes after the first of Nov: next in paine of their not so doing   10   0

It is pained that all the ditches betwixt Moorhouse Sheepdike by netherend of Ossington Medow be scowered the same as it was the last time betwixt this and the 20th day of May in paine of any one offending   5   0

It is pained that all the Ditches belonging Moorehouse More be sufficiently scowered betwixt this and the first June next in paine of any one offend: 3   4

It is pained that all they Hedges betwixt the field and Knapneys be sufficiently repaired and Amended betwixt this and the 25th of March in paine of any offending   3   4

It is pained that noe one shall make A way over Great Brockeley Close into Robert Skiner Close in paine of any offending   3   4

It is pained that Robert Skiner lope his hedges in back lane betwixt this and the first day of May next in paine of not doing soe   2   6

It is pained that all the Ditches in Shitterpoole lane be sufficiently scowered betwixt this and the 30th day of this Month in pain of any offending   3   4

It is pained that all the Acre Hedg be sufficly made and soe kept betwixt this and the second day of Febr: in paine of any offend: 3   4

It is pained that every one shall wring their swine betwixt this and the 20th day of this Month and so keepe them from time in pain of any one offend: 3   4

It is pained that all the fences belonging to the In field be sufficiently repaired and made betwixt this & the second day Feb: in paine of any offend   3   4

It is pained that noe one shall make a way over the Long Medow betwixt the breck wong and porter wong   10   0

It is pained that noe one shall tether any Horses either Stond or Gelt on the Mayre Sicks for the first week after the Comons be broake in paine of any one offending   5   0

It is pained that they Burleymen shall look to their Office in paine of any offending   3   4

It is pained that noe one shall drive either horses or beasts either to the Tether or from it in paine of any offending   3   4

Robertus Heron gent. Senll. Manerii.

Pains made at the Court Leet & Court Baron of the Right Honble William Earl of Kingston at Laxton Oct. 15th Anno Dom. 1688

Impr.   It is pained that every one make his fence well and sufficiently about the Wheat-field before the 23rd of this Instant in pain of not so doing   3   4

Item   That every one scour the ditches in the town street, Toad-Lane and Robert-Lane before the first day May in pain of not so doing   3   4

That no one shall carry fire between neighbour & neighbour uncovered in pain of not so doing   3   4

That Mr. Stephenson cut his crab-tree-tops in High Lane, & every one plash their hedges there in pain of not so doing   3   4

Item   That it be done before the first day of May next following, in pain etc.

That everyone make his hedges about the Long-meadow, South-loon, & Easting before the 2nd day of February next following in pain of not so doing   3   4

That no one tether gild-horses in the mare-syck for a week after it be broken in pain of so doing   3   4

That the Burley-men look to their offices & every one send sufficient Labourers to the Comon-work in pain of not so doing   3   4

That the fence be made between Cop-thorn & Long-meadow before the 24th day of this month in pain of not so doing   3   4

Item   That no man make a high way from the top of Thomas Hazard's Orchard down the Holmes but keep the usual way in pain of not so doing   3 4

That Char: Ingham lop or plash his hedge in the Hall-floor close next to Tho: Lee betwixt this and Candlemas in pain of not so doing   3 4

That no one make a way on Abr. Taylors lands above the Hall-floor in pain of so offending   3 4

That every one make their fences against Stubbins and Knapnayes betwixt this & the 20 of January in pain of not so doing   3 4

That Mich. Cawdwell plash his hedge in Brockley close betwixt him & Willim Whale-head betwixt this & the 2d. of Febr. in pain of not, etc.   3 4

That Bollom-beck-hedges be made betwixt Thos. Lees & the fallow-field betwixt this & the 2d of Febr in pain of not so doing   3 4

That every one ring his swines to keep them so from time to time betwixt this & the 24th of this Instant in pain of not so doing   3 4

That no one shall make a way betwixt Wm. Challands & Orchard-nook over the Holmes in pain of so offending   3 4

That every one shall scour their ditches betwixt the Over-end of South-loon Meadow & Cundrind betwixt this and the first of April in pain of not so doing   3 4

into

That no one shall make a highway *over* Robert Skinner's close over Brockley-close in pain of so offending   3 4

That all old pains stand in force

Item   It is further pained that Chr. & Richard Salmon make their fence well and sufficiently between their Crofts & Mr. Stephensons Calf-close betwixt this and the 22nd of this Instant in pain of not so doing   3 4

Item   further that everyone plash their hedges in Westwood lanes & Scour their ditches betwixt this and the 24th of this instant in pain of not so doing   [torn]

That every one scour all the ditches belonging to the Long-meadow, South-loon & East-Ing betwixt this & the 10th of May next following in pain of not etc.   3 4

That Abr. Taylor junr scour his ditch at Monkbridge-close betwixt this and the 24th of this Instant in pain last aforegoing.

That the Burly-men scour the ditch under, above & beneath the Monk bridge betwixt this and the 24th of this Instant in pain of not so doing   3 4

That the Burley-men do repair Whitmoor-bridge betwixt this & the 24th of this Instant in pain of not so doing   3 4

That the foot-way at the Bottom of Chr. Salmons yard be made passable before the 24th of this Instant in pain of not so doing to pay   3 4

That Mr. Hynd do make his fence between Thatch Holme & the Pingle in the place where it formerly stood between this & Martin-mas-day next in [torn]   1 10 0

Examined & allowed by Robertus Heron gent. Senll. *ibidem*

A Copy of By-laws for the Manor of Lexington and Moorhouse

S. Pinder.

At a Court Leet, held for the Manor of Lexington and Moorhouse, presentments and Bye Laws made at Court, October 19th 1789 and revised October 25th 1821 for the Earl Manvers as follows.

First,	we make a Law that none carry fire uncovered between neighbour and neighbour. Any one offending	
2nd	That none carry away or break the pinfold. Fine	
3rd	That every one make a sufficient fence between his neighbour	0: 3: 4
4th	That every one do ring his swine and keep them so. Fine	0: 3: 4
5th	That the fields shall not be broken without the consent of the Overseers of the Highways and at the tolling of the Bell	£ s d 1: 10: 0
6th	That the overseers of the Highways shall take upon themselves the office of Bye Law men, and have full power to pound the offenders	£ s d 0: 5: 0
7	That if any one have Cattle die he shall pit them according to the Magistrates directions. Fine	£ s d 0: 10: 0
8	That if any one remove his neighbours' Land mark, or mark belonging to the Commons	£ s d 1: 10: 0
9th	That the Commons be let to the highest bidder on the public day, and the money paid proportionably to the Gates. Fine	£ s d 1: 19: 11
10th	That none drive or redrive Horses loose through the Cornfields	
11th	That none make a Road over Paul Glazebrooks Homestead	
12th	That all persons who have bad chimneys shall immediately mend or repair them	0: 10: 0

		£	s	d
13th	That none do plough up the Commons. Fine	1: 19: 11		
14th	That none drive or redrive Cattle up or down the Woodbalk		s 3	d 4

Done at Court the 15th day of October 1787

15. For the better ordering of Rams or Tups upon the Commons. We make a Law that any one having a clear Tup, close Tup or Rigel Sheep do take them off the Commons, on or before the first day of September, and keep them off untill the 12th of October following, and that no one shall have a clear Tup on the Commons of less value than Two pounds during the riding season, also that any one having a close Tup or Rigel Sheep upon the Commons do take them off at the above mentioned time and keep them off until Christmas following, any one offending in either case shall pay a fine of

£ s d
0: 13: 4

16th That no one make a way from Longbalk at the top of Honey-hole-hill across the lands to the bottom of Honeyhole. Fine

£ s d
0: 3: 4

17 That none take a Bull out of his pasture without leave

£ s d
0: 5: 0

18. That none tether any Horse, Mare or Gelding upon the Commons during the time of Rolling. Fine

£ s d
0: 13: 4

19th That none tether or tend either Horse, Mare or Gelding in the Corn-field all night. Fine

£ s d
0: 10: 0

20th That none make a way over the Hall Orchard more than usual

£ s d
0: 3: 4

21st That none make a way over Robert Eyre's Easter Kings-Close more than usual. Fine

£ s d
0: 3. 4.

22nd That the pounders wages be paid as follow, viz: For every score of sheep 2d. For the out of town's 4d. A sow and pigs 4d. A Horse or Beast 1d. For out of town's 2d. and at Christmas every Farmer 2d. and every Cottager 1d. apiece. Fine

£ s d
0: 3: 4

23rd That the pounders wages be paid without any fraud. Fine

0: 3. 4

24th That the Beanfield shall be laid as soon as the people begin to sow. Fine

0. 3: 4

25th That none make a way over Thomas Jepson's Meadow more than usual. Fine

0. 3. 4

26th That none make a way over Geo. Taylors Ley-close more than usual

0. 3: 4

27th That none sell or carry Hay out of the Town i.e. that grows upon the Commons. Fine for every load

£ s d
1: 10: 0

28th   That none make a way up or down John Warren's Honey-hole acre

29.   That none lodge any Travellers more than one night, if they do not give an account from whence they came. Fine.

	£	s	d
30. That the Wheatfield shall be laid as soon as people begin to sow	0:	3:	4
31. That none make a way over Geo. Taylor's Croft from John Rose's House	0:	3:	4
32. That if any one have one or two sheep that is (or are) common trespassers in the Corn-field shall pay for every offence 1d. or forfeit	0:	3:	4
33rd. That none make a way up or down Wm. Pinder's Acre at the top of the West field. Fine	0:	3:	4
34. That none make a way over Geo. Lees Homestead or over his ploughed Close at the top of the West field either with Horses or Carriages	0:	3:	4
35th That none make a way over Wm. Peatfield's Brick-kiln Close	0:	3:	4
36 That none go down the foot balks from Mill-hill-Close to Little-dale with either horses or carriage	0.	3:	4

37th   That none make a way over William Nicholson's Newdike more than usual. Fine

38   That none make a way over John Pickin's Justing-close more than usual. Fine.

	£	s	d
39. That none make a way over John Pickins Inger or over his Meadow Close. Fine.	0:	3:	4
40. That none make a way over William Nicholson's Meadow. Fine.	0:	3:	4

41.   That if any one be taken breaking hedges, stealing wood, coal, or any thing belonging to any one of the parish, then the offender or offenders be punished as the Law directs at the expense of the Parish and the Informer to have five shillings to be paid by the Constable of the Parish for the information.

	£	s	d
42nd. That none make a way over Wm. White's Cop-thorn.	0:	3:	4
43rd. That none make a way over Charles Doncaster's Inger or Newdikes.	0:	5:	0
44th. That none make a way from the Holmes-nook to the Mill, with either Horse or Carriage, or the Miller to go on any but the right way. Fine	1:	3:	4
45. That none tend or tether any mare with foal in the Cornfields		3.	4

	£	s	d

46. That any person that does not scour and cleanse the great drain by the long meadow side and likewise bank up the watering places before the 29th day of May shall pay. Fine — 0: 10: 0

47th. That every one shall scour his meadow drain in the long Meadow between the 15th day of October and the 10th day of May following — 0: 3: 4

48. That none lay stubble or plaster upon the Commons so that the Commons are damaged thereby — 0: 5: 0

49. That none make a way over Geo. Lees Bollonbeck. Fine. — 0: 3: 4

50. That if anyone shall heir, [? hire] or have a scabbed sheep in the fields or upon the Commons, and at the same time the same to be so, shall forfeit for every such sheep the sum of — 0. 5. 0.

Signed this 25th day of October 1821 by us we being Jurymen in the parish of Laxton and Moorhouse

R. Keyworth	Geo. Bartle
Wm. Whittington	Wm. Bagshaw
John Rose	Geo. Taylor
William Hopkins	Wm. Pinder
William White	John Clark
John Kelk	Thomas Jepson
John Johnson	

In 1871 new by-laws were drawn up, though not by the jury on this occasion, but at a vestry meeting. A committee of six was appointed to carry them out, but offenders were to be presented at the Manor Court in the usual way, to be dealt with as the jury might decide.

LAXTON COMMONS AND FIELDS

At a Vestry Meeting held in the School Room at Laxton, on Thursday, the 2nd day of March, 1871, the following

RULES

FOR REGULATING THE STOCKING OF THE OPEN COMMONS AND FIELDS

WERE AGREED TO:—

The pasturing of THE COMMON from the 24th day of June, 1871, until the breaking of the fields, is to be limited to 20 sheep only for each Toftholder; and such right is to be exercised for one Toft only for each person.

On the breaking of the fields, the quantity of stock may be unlimited, as heretofore.

THE WHEAT STUBBLE FIELD is not to be pastured for more than 28 days, after the same is broken in the customary manner, or not later than the 15th day of October in each year, when such field is to be driven.

THE SUMMER FALLOW FIELD is to be pastured the same as the Common, until the 8th day of October in each year, when the same is to be driven; the stock may then be transferred to the Field which is in course for Fallow the next year.

In THE BEAN AND CLOVER FIELD, the quantity of stock is to be unlimited in the same manner as in the Wheat Stubble Field, from the time it is broken until the 23rd day of November in each year, when the limit of 20 sheep for each Toft-Owner, as for the Common, is to commence: lambs are to be considered as sheep after the 23rd of November.

No sheep are to be turned out on THE COMMON OR OPEN FIELDS until they have been dressed, as a preventive of scab, and every sheep shall be so dressed before the breaking of the Fields.

Every sheep turned out is to be first branded by a person to be appointed by the Committee hereafter named, with the letters L.C., and not more than 20 sheep belonging to one person shall be branded except by the instructions as of any two of the Committee.

No tup shall be turned out or allowed to run on the Common or Open Fields from the time of the breaking of the Fields up to the 15th day of October; or shall any tup be allowed to remain on the Common or Fields after the 23rd day of December in each year.

With a view to prevent the seeding of thistles, THE TOWN MOOR is to be Let for Mowing, and is to be driven on the 14th day of February in each year.

All persons breaking any of the above Rules will be presented at the Court of the Lord of the Manor, and dealt with as the Jury may decide.

The brander appointed by the Committee is Mr. JOSEPH MERRILLS.

The following persons are to be a Committee for carrying these Rules into effect:—

Mr. JOHN KEYWORTH	Mr. RICHARD HARPHAM
— GEORGE PECK	— CHARLES WILCOX
— WILLIAM PINDER	— JOHN ATKINSON

GEORGE BENNETT, Chairman of the Committee.

These rules remained in force, apparently, for the next thirty-six years. By 1907 it seems that the control, both on the commons and in the Open Fields, had got out of hand. Originally, the right to graze on the two commons, Cocking Moor and Town, or East Moor, was reserved to the cottars, or those who had no other land to pasture, and their grazing was stinted. Similarly, gates, or rights to turn out in the Open Fields, had been reserved to those who held land there, the little tenants or freeholders with no strips and the few tenants of inclosed farms having no gates. Complaints had been made for some time to the lord that people possessing no rights were putting stock both on the commons and on the

Open Fields, and, further, that the stints were not being observed. At a discussion of the situation between his agent and the other freeholders, the following agreement was reached:

1. That his Tenants only, who have land in the open Fields, but not otherwise, shall turn in there subject to the Rules enclosed herewith.

2. That the 'East Moor' is to be grazed with Cows only belonging to the present Freeholders other than himself, but that they may sublet this right to other Parishioners in Laxton for their own bona-fide stock.

3. That as regards 'Cocking Moor', Lord Manvers will retain 8 Rights, and the other Freeholders 8 Rights, such Rights to be limited to 10 sheep, 3 beasts, or 2 horses, there being no power to sublet these Rights. Lord Manvers will give the first offer of such Rights to his small Tenants who have no land in the open Fields, but if they decline to exercise them, then to some of his smallest Tenants in the open Fields.

The rules governing the stocking of the Open Fields referred to in clause 1 above are as follows:

RULES AND REGULATIONS FOR GRAZING LAXTON OPEN FIELDS

1. The open Fields are to be grazed by Earl Manvers' Tenants only. No Tenant, who has no unenclosed land, is to be allowed to turn any stock into the Fields.

2. A Tenant, whose holding does not exceed a total of 40 acres, may turn into the open Fields under the following regulations, though he may not have unenclosed land in each of the three Fields. Tenants holding over 40 acres can only turn into the Fields in which they have unenclosed land.

3. The Fields are to be stocked as follows:—

   (a) *The Wheat Field.* Unlimited stock from the breaking up of the Field to the 15th October in the same year.

   (b) *The Bean and Clover Field.* Unlimited stock from the breaking up of the Field to the 23rd November in the same year.

   (c) *The Fallow Field.* From the 23rd November in one year to the 8th October in the following year, twenty Sheep by each Tenant. No Cattle or Horses to be allowed in this Field during the time named.

4. All stock so turned in to be the bona fide property of the Tenant, and no joist stock to be allowed under any circumstances. Anyone transgressing this Rule will be liable to be fined by the Jury.

5. No Sheep to be turned into the Open Fields until they have been properly dressed, such dressing to be done before they are turned in.

6. No tup to be turned in to the open Fields before the 15th October, or to be allowed to remain there later than the 23rd December, in any year.

7. The Foremen of the Juries, and the Parish Pinder, are to see that these Rules are carried out, and are to report anyone breaking them to the Thoresby Estate Office at once, and anyone so reported may, after one caution, be given notice to quit his Farm.

Lord Manvers appeals to his Tenants, in their common interests, to help him and the Foremen of the Juries to carry out the above. He asks them specially to be careful to shut the Gates on the Commons when passing through them, and also the Gates on the lands which he has lately inclosed.

R. W. WORDSWORTH,
Agent for Earl Manvers.

Estates Office, Thoresby Park,
     April, 1908.

There was another organization in the parish, designed mainly for social administration, the vestry, which supplemented the work of the manor court. In fact, the vestry and the court were complementary one to the other, and it could happen that regulations were made by the parishioners at a vestry meeting, the enforcement of which was enjoined upon the jury appointed by the court. The officers of the vestry were the churchwardens, the overseers of the poor, and the overseers of the highways. The constable, though appointed by the court, presented his accounts, at all events during the eighteenth century and onwards, to the vestry meeting. Such of the accounts of the Laxton vestry officers which still survive are less complete than are the Court Rolls, nor do they begin so early, but there is a ten-year run from the year 1726, and they are fairly complete between the years 1785 and 1835. The accounts were beautifully kept, in great detail, and they were presented and audited annually. The officers were appointed for a year, and their service was extended only rarely for more than one year.

The constable was concerned, in the first instance, with the apprehension of persons who were guilty of breaches of peace. He had to send them in the custody of the Thirdboroughs to Retford or elsewhere, and he had to hand on any hue and cry that might pass through Laxton. But disciplinary duties were the least part of his work. He attended at the appointment and swearing of other parish officers, and made certain disbursements connected therewith, such as the fastening penny, a shilling in point of fact, paid to the man appointed for 'field tenting'. While he was responsible for the use of the stocks, the cucking-stool, and for whippings, he was also the dispenser of much charity to help all kinds of vagrants on their way, if necessary finding them a night's lodging and supper. He gave small sums to those who had suffered loss by fire, or other disaster, and were on the road. He was responsible for payments for the destruction of vermin,[1] and he collected the levy which was made upon the inhabitants for the money needed by him for his various activities. His accounts were presented annually and signed by the jury.

---

[1] Foxes, badgers, wild cats, foumarts (polecats), martens, moles, and sparrows.

The overseers of the poor were concerned with the care of Laxton paupers, rather than with the casuals looked after by the constable. This is hardly the place for a detailed study of their work, for it impinges only very slightly on the story of the Open Fields. They take their place, however, in the system of local administration. The cost of the relief which they disbursed, in money and in kind, was raised by a levy on the parish, and it is interesting to note how this cost rose as the degree of self-sufficiency which characterized the people during the early years of the records falls before the oncoming of commercial farming. Relief which cost the parish about £14 in 1726 amounted to £61 in 1786 and to £245 in 1826.

The work of the overseers of the highways was more closely related to the practice of husbandry. These parish officers, two in number, maintained the roads in some sort of order by getting stone and filling ruts. They repaired the bridges on public roads and footpaths, and scoured the ditches and watercourses wherever this work could not be laid upon the occupiers of adjacent lands. They were responsible, also, for fencing in like circumstances, and for some of the gates across the public roads which prevented stock from straying. In the early part of the eighteenth century the cost of their work, which amounted to about £3 a year, was met by the money received from the sale of mowing grass on some of the commons and from the rent of a paddock belonging to the Town, supplemented by a levy on the parish when necessary. The annual amount spent on the highways increased steadily as time went on, and in 1826 it was £120, the levy being 6d. in the pound.

The remaining officers, the two churchwardens, were concerned almost exclusively with the repair of the church and of church property and furniture, the purchase of bread and wine, the expenses of visitations, and so on. They had a small income from town land, and above this their expenses were met by a levy, a church rate.

The accounts of all of these officers were adopted and signed either by the jury or by the vestry. Set out as they are in meticulous detail, they are evidence of the extent of the organization of voluntary administration before the growth of population and other considerations led, more and more, to the centralization of local government and the substitution of the stipendiary for the voluntary officer. But in the self-contained open-field parish, in which the landless members were a very small minority of the community and almost every one was concerned in the administration of affairs in one way or another, the voluntary system worked with a rough and ready efficiency suited to the times and to the people that it served, while it was more truly democratic, perhaps, than any that this country has ever known.

A description of farming and administration at Laxton would not be complete without some account of the nature and incidence of tithe before the passing of the Tithe Commutation Act, in 1836. Without going into its origin, it may be stated that long before this date, tithe had become a legal charge upon the land; the church, or a lay impropriator, had a right to one-tenth of the yearly produce of the land. The rectorial or great tithes consisted mainly of the produce of the corn lands, while the vicarial or small tithes were levied on the livestock and minor crops. At Laxton the rectory had been bestowed upon Jesus College, at Rotherham, by Archbishop Rotherham when he held the manor; after the Dissolution of the monasteries it passed to the Crown and ultimately to the family of Pierrepont, as lay impropriators. The first statement of the vicarial tithes occurs in the year 1240, upon the presentment of one Richard de Nottingham to the vicarage, and translated it runs as follows:

> . . . which vicarage consists in the underwritten articles, viz., in the whole Altarage of the same Church with the Farm and Croft, . . . and in the herbage of the whole Churchyard, and in all the Tithes of Corn and Hay of the Men of Morhus . . . and in the Tithes of Corn and Hay of all the Men of Lexington of the Places which are called Plogstalls, and in the Tithes of Corn of the whole Demesne of the Church aforesaid of Orchards also and of Mills of the Townships aforesaid. . . .[1]

A transcript from the Vicar's Easter Book for 1714 shows the nature of the vicarial tithe and the manner of its payment:

> Memorandum. For House duties every Man pays three half pence Duty for his House Offerings two pence for every person that is above sixteen Years of Age. A new Milch'd Cow three half pence, for every old Milch'd Cow or Stropper One halfpenny. For every Dole in the Meadow one halfpenny. Mainport three half pence each. Each Oxgang four pence. Bees each Swarm one penny. For every young Foal one penny. For every Sheep Skin that dies between Candlemas and Clipping time one halfpenny. Each servant five pence per pound for the Wages. Plaister one shilling for every Ten Tuns if taken in kind the fifth part. The Windmill to pay two shillings. If any Sheep be bought into the Parish before clipping time to pay four pence per Score per Month. If any Sheep be sold between Candlemas and Clipping Day to pay one penny for each Sheep. If they be Couples [i.e. ewes and lambs] to pay one penny half penny each couple. Tythe Eggs for every Cock three Eggs and for every Hen two Eggs—if the Hen sits she is payable. Herbage for depastured Cattle.

[1] Registry of the Consistory Court of York.

Moorhouse

For every new Milch'd Cow two pence—and for every Stropper one penny. Eggs two for each Hen and none for the Cock. House Duty three half pence. Offerings for every person above sixteen Years' Old two pence. Every Foal one penny. Bees for every Swarm one penny, John Herring a Main port three half pence Richd Hardy Do. three half pence. Herbage for depastured Cattle. The Tythe of Sheep is here the very same in every particular as at Laxton. But in this Liberty and precinct of Moorhouse The Vicar hath all the Tythes both great and small. As to the manner of tything Pigs and Lambs both at Laxton and Moorhouse it is thus Viz. if the Owner hath but five Pigs or five Lambs he pays the Vicar but half of one, if above five he pays a whole one, if hath ten he pays no more. The Vicar pays the Owner a halfpenny each for so many as falls short of ten, if the owner hath fifteen Pigs or Lambs he pays the Vicar one and a half, if above fifteen he pays him two if Twenty no more, but then the Vicar pays the owner an half penny a piece for so many as there is wanting of Twenty. And the Vicar hath Tythe of all the Orchards and Dovecotes both of Laxton and Moorhouse, and also Tythe in kind of all the Wool growing in both places. The manner of Tything Chickens, Geese, Ducks, Turkeys, and Pidgeons is the same as the manner of Tything Pigs and Lambs as above described, and other Vicarial Tythes both at Laxton and Moorhouse, is that of Hops and Rape, but of these the Vicar hath no more than the Fifteenth part in kind.

The payments for milch cows, stroppers, and foals were moduses, arranged at some much earlier date as a way of rendering a tithe which could not be taken in kind on these small farms. The elaborate arrangement for tithing lambs and pigs described in the Easter Book shows how necessary some form of commutation must have been for larger animals, the progeny of which were not enough in any one year to yield a tenth part for delivery to the vicar. Payments of half a lamb or half a pig were made, presumably, in carcass form. Mainports were small tributes, commonly loaves of bread, which the parishioners in some places paid to the incumbents of their churches.

In 1743 the houses and other property paying tithe to the vicar were recorded in the Easter Book as follows:

In Laxton & Laxton Moorhouse are Eighty two Houses which pay three half pence each, Sixty two Orchards, Twenty seven Dove Cotes, Seventy one Crofts that pay Tythe to the Vicar, which contain Sixty seven Acres, one Rood and nineteen Perches of Ground. In the long Meadow are three Hundred and forty nine Doles. In East Kirking Meadow are an Hundred and thirty five Doles. In the South Meadow are Seventy two Doles. In Shitterpool Meadow are Ninety five Doles, that pay tythe to the Vicar. The Church yard is one Acre two Roods and nineteen Perches. The Vicarage Yard & Croft is one Acre two Roods, & sixteen Perches. Moorhouse Chappel Yard is two Roods & twenty four Perches. There is a Tythe here paid which is called Mainports & Oxgangs.'

The following is a typical example of one man's tithe payment, as recorded in the Vicar's Easter Book of 1814:

Pinder, Samuel

	£	s.	d.
Modus for 4 cows			6
„ 1 foal			1
Agistment of young cattle . . .		12	0
Dove Cote		4	0
Wool of 12 Sheep		4	8
12 Lambs		12	0
2 Houses			3
Inhabitants			8
Servants		8	4
Croft		6	0
	£2	8	6

Here is another:

Quibell, William

	£	s.	d.
Modus for 3 cows			$4\frac{1}{2}$
„ 1 stropper . . .			$\frac{1}{2}$
Agistment of young Cattle . .	1	0	0
Croft	1	5	0
Dove Cote		8	0
1 Sow		5	0
Wool of 20 Sheep		8	0
8 Lambs		8	0
2 Houses			3
Inhabitants			8
	£3	15	4

The crofts in these two accounts are the inclosures of meadow-land made and allotted when the dole meadows were inclosed in the eighteenth century.

The total value of the vicarial tithe in this year was £107. 12s. $5\frac{1}{2}d$. at Laxton, and of the vicarial and rectorial tithes at Laxton Moor-house, £70. 1s. 6d.

All tithes at Laxton and Laxton Moorhouse were commuted for rent-charges in 1838, under the provisions of the Tithe Commutation Act, 1836.

XI. RECLAMATION, INCLOSURE, AND REDISTRIBUTION

EVEN a cursory examination of the survey and map of Laxton in 1635 makes it plain that the farming system was a living institution, changing and developing with the needs of the community. The ideal strip in the Open Fields, being one day's work for the plough, still predominated, but there were many larger ones, representing consolidations effected under various circumstances and at various times. The predominant farmers were still the small freeholders and tenants, but their oxgangs or virgates conformed only with a good deal of latitude to the historian's conventional acreages. Already, too, the spread of cultivation outward from the village had set a limit to the practicable extension of the Open Fields, and the later re-clamations from the woodlands and wastes on the parish borders were closes, not furlongs. While we have no documentary evi-dence of what happened on the land at Laxton before 1635, it may safely be assumed that the processes of consolidation and re-allotment of strips, of the combination and subdivision of holdings, and possibly, too, of the creation of closes, were normal incidents in the evolution of the manor from very early times. After 1635, however, there is a wealth of documentary evidence for the continuation of these processes.

Following the purchase of the main manor by the Earl of Kingston, he and his descendants in title pursued a policy of acquiring freeholds in Laxton, large and small, as they came into the market. In the year 1726, upon the succession of Evelyn, second Duke of Kingston, as a minor, a period of great activity in the further development of Laxton was inaugurated by his trustees, Lord Cheyne and others. It began with a great reclama-tion of woodland to increase the area of farm lands. Working eastward from the demesne closes, the greater part of East Park Wood [No. 3022] was cleared, 106 acres in all, leaving only 30 acres still in woodland. The new land was divided into seventeen closes, ranging from 10 acres to 4 acres, just as they are today, all of which were allotted and let to tenants of other lands in Laxton, in 1727. At the same time some 65 acres of Bollombecks [No. 3024], which forms the eastern part of the big woodland below South Field, was cleared, and it was divided into seven closes which were allotted and let in the same year.

In 1727, also, two large pieces of what were probably rough

M

grazings were divided and let. These were Freerfalls [No. 1623], a freehold of 66 acres which had been bought by William Pierre-pont, Esq., in 1664, and Knapneys [No. 3057], being 32 acres of Mr. Augustine Hinde's freehold, which had been bought in 1654. Freerfalls was divided into nine and Knapneys into six closes. Thus, some 270 acres of woodlands and rough grazings were cleared and inclosed at this time, and this was the last intake of land for agricultural use at Laxton.

Another undoubted improvement made at the same time was the inclosure of the common meadowlands, South Lound, Shitter-pool, East Kirk Ing, and Long Meadows. Together they amounted to about 130 acres, and they were held in no fewer than 586 strips, each of one or more doles, which averaged barely one quarter of an acre each. By purchase and exchange the whole had come into the hands of the lord of the manor, and they were now inclosed to form about forty-seven meadows, and re-allotted. The new allotment meant the dispossession of some of the occupiers of doles, but the concurrent reclamation and inclosure of woodland and waste provided for their accommodation elsewhere.

Mention has just been made of exchanges of land made between the lord of the manor and other freeholders, to facilitate inclosure of the meadowland. This process was not confined to the common meadows. During the early part of the eighteenth century, exchanges between the lord and the other freeholders were constantly being made when purchase outright was not possible.[1] The purpose of these exchanges was to consolidate the strips in the lord's ownership in certain parts of the Open Fields so as to enable him to carry through a policy of inclosure in the remoter parts of the manor, upon which he and his advisers were resolved. The extension of the farming area outwards from the village to its farthest limits accentuated one of the handicaps of open-field farming in a large manor, particularly if, as at Laxton, the village were not centrally placed: namely, the loss of time in getting from the homesteads to the remoter furlongs and closes, though this was not so great as sometimes represented.[2] So, following the necessary exchanges, some of these furlongs were inclosed and withdrawn altogether from common farming in the Open Fields, to form holdings for occupation in severalty. Five such holdings were created, as follows:

Westwood Farm, from some of the furlongs on the west of Mill Field and West Field, together with the Westwood closes. In all, it amounted to about 174 acres, of which 144 acres were inclosed land, while the farm still retained about 30 acres in the Open Fields.

1 *Thoresby Deeds*, Series II, pp. 273–484: Manor Court Papers and Exchanges.
2 See p. 139, *ante.*

Brockilow Farm, composed of furlongs inclosed at the south end of Mill Field and South Field, together with Shitterpool meadow and some existing closes. It amounted to about 156 acres, of which 140 acres were inclosed and 16 acres still in the Open Fields.

Knapney Farm, composed of furlongs in the south-east corner of South Field and the adjacent closes. It amounted to some 140 acres, being 120 acres inclosed and 20 acres of Open Field.

Copthorne Farm, consisting of South Lound and South Lound Meadow and the closes below Long Meadow. It amounted to 136 acres, 120 inclosed and 16 acres of Open Field.

Brecks Farm, formed from the various Breck closes of the Laxton demesne, to the east and south of East Park Wood, and amounting to about 135 acres.

Each of these farms was equipped with a house and buildings. Some of them have received various additions from the Open Fields from time to time, and their acreages in 1938 were:

Westwood	.	.	.	286 acres
Brockilow	.	.	.	173 ,,
Knapney	.	.	.	207 ,,
Copthorne	.	.	.	126 ,,
Brecks	.	.	.	96 ,,

The evidence for the above summary of reclamations, exchange, and inclosure is provided by notes and plans added by later hands to Mark Pierce's *Booke of Survaye*. The next records of importance are the Tithe Award of 1838 and a manuscript survey made, at about the same time, for the purpose of rating assessment.

The survey discloses fifty-two owners of land in Laxton and Moorhouse, as follows:

	Acres
Earl Manvers.	2,438 (excluding Commons)
Earl of Scarborough . . .	714
John Evelyn Denison, Esq. . . .	111
Dean and Chapter of Southwell . .	20
The Church of Laxton	17
The Vicar of Laxton	4
34 occupying owners (together) . .	263
12 other freeholders. . . .	108
Total	3,675 (excluding Commons)

This analysis of owners should be compared with that which has been made for the year 1635.[1] The lands of the lord of the manor have increased by some 300 acres, when allowance is made for the commons, most of it bought from Mr. Augustine Hinde and the rest from various smaller freeholders. The Earl of Scarborough, of Rufford, holds Mr. Peter Broughton's freehold nearly

[1] See p. 123, *ante*.

intact; and John Evelyn Denison, Esq., owner of the adjacent property of Ossington, holds the remainder of Mr. Augustine Hinde's lands. For the rest, it is interesting to note the increase in the number of those owning small estates in land and in the total area in their possession. In 1635 there were about twenty-five of them owning about 196 acres. In 1835 there were nearly double this number, and they held about 390 acres. Both Robert Shipton's freehold of 76 acres and the Chantry Lands had been dispersed at various dates, and some small parts of Mr. Augustine Hinde's property had also been sold to little men. The constitution of an open-field farm facilitated its dispersal piecemeal in a way which is quite incompatible with the sale of an inclosed farm. For example, between the years 1639 and 1662 Robert Shipton and his heirs made no fewer than six sales to different people of small parcels of land, parts of his freehold.

Perhaps the most interesting change between 1635 and 1835 is in the size and distribution of the holdings.[1] There had been a steady reduction both in the number of the smaller holdings and in the total acreage they represented, while at the other end of the scale the area occupied in holdings of more than 200 acres had fallen by one-half. Whereas there were 69 men occupying 415 acres in holdings below 20 acres in 1635, their number had fallen to 31 in 1835 and they occupied only 254 acres. The size group 20 to 40 acres remained stationary, both in numbers of farmers and acreage farmed. The land lost both to the smallest and to the largest of the groups went to increase the number of farms between 70 and 200 acres. There were 21 of them in 1635, occupying 1,615 acres, or an average of 77 acres each; 200 years later there were 25, occupying 2,456 acres, an average of 98 acres each. Even more striking than the increase in the number of larger farmers is the increase in the size of their holdings. It would seem that farming for profit was now displacing subsistence farming, and that the commercial farmer was swallowing up his self-sufficient neighbours.

The next event in the history of Laxton lands was the inclosure of Moorhouse Open Fields and Commons. The Moorhouse section of the manor comprised a small hamlet and a chapel, together with about 330 acres of land. So far as our records go, it had always been a separate entity, with a self-contained farming economy and its own parish officers. An attempt by the men of Moorhouse to establish their right to put stock on Laxton Common was successfully resisted by the men of Laxton in the seventeenth century.[2]

---

[1] See Table, p. 167, *post*.　　　　　　　　　[2] *Thoresby Deeds*.

By 1860 all the lands except for one or two small freeholds had passed by purchase and exchange into the hands of Earl Manvers and Mr. Speaker Denison. In 1853 the latter had bought the 20-acre holding which the Chapter of Southwell had held in unbroken descent since Robert de Lexington had bestowed it to found a chantry 600 years before.[1] The Inclosure Award was made in May 1860. The greater part of Moorhouse was already in closes and about 125 acres were affected, described as 'arable pasture, and waste land'.

The inclosures within Laxton itself, round the borders of the Open Fields, were made, all of them, by voluntary agreements following exchanges and purchase. In the first half of the eighteenth century, when much of this work was done, parliamentary inclosure was only just beginning, but apart from the novelty of this procedure it may fairly be assumed that it might have been difficult to get so large a body of freeholders, occupying as they did so much of the manor, to agree to an application for an Act of Parliament. Thus, voluntary inclosure was the only way, and its scope was limited. At Moorhouse, in 1860, on the other hand, nearly all the land was the property of two landowners, both of them anxious to inclose, and there was no difficulty, whatever the attitude of the few small freeholders may have been. So Laxton provides us with examples, not only of the Open Fields, but also of voluntary and of statutory inclosure.

In 1866, following the inclosure of Moorhouse, Lord Manvers took steps further to consolidate his Laxton property, by the acquisition of that which still remained outside his own estate of the old sub-manor which had been created within the main manor 600 years earlier. Exchanges were arranged with Mr. Speaker Denison, the effect of which was to bring all Lord Manvers's land together on the Laxton side of Moorhouse, while Mr. Denison's estate was consolidated, in the same way, on the Ossington side. Straw Hall and Hartshorn Farm, two farms inclosed on the southeastern side of Laxton from portions of Mr. Augustine Hinde's freehold, were not affected by this arrangement, and remained part of the Ossington estate.

In the next year a further important exchange was effected, when Lord Manvers acquired the remainder of what had been Mr. Peter Broughton's freehold, in Laxton, from the Earl of Scarborough's trustee. It extended to 675 acres, and lands in Eakring parish, forming part of the Thoresby estate, were given in exchange. With this transaction the lordship of the manor of Laxton was re-established once more as it had been at the time of the Norman Conquest.

---

[1] From information given by the Ecclesiastical Commissioners.

During the next forty years Laxton experienced no important changes either in the ownership or in the occupation of its lands. In 1904, however, a very important reorganization was under-taken. In discussing the economics of farming in the Open Fields in an earlier chapter, the difficulty imposed by this diffusion of the holdings in very small parcels was minimized. It was pointed out that each strip provided not less than one day's ploughing, and that except for the time involved in dragging the plough from one strip to the next, the system imposed very little handicap upon the farmers. By the end of the nineteenth century, however, economic conditions had changed. Whereas the plough and the harrow were the only aids to manual labour at its beginning, and sowing, reaping, &c., were then performed by hand, the farmers now had all the mechanical inventions of the nineteenth century, and parti-cularly the seed-drill and the reaper, at their disposal. An acre strip was no longer an economic unit for all the operations of corn-production, for it was too small to give scope for the efficient use of these machines. So, in 1904, the fourth Earl Manvers sanc-tioned a consolidation and rearrangement of the strips in the Open Fields.

The first step towards the reorganization was to consolidate the strips by throwing many of them together and then re-allotting the larger blocks so formed amongst the tenants affected in a manner such that every one had approximately the same acreage as before scattered throughout the same fields, but in fewer parcels.

But the amalgamation of small strips was not the only purpose. It would seem that there was a demand for more freedom of crop-ping than was possible in the Open Fields, with their fixed rotation and common grazing-rights. The strips, even as now enlarged, were too small to be fenced, but this difficulty did not apply to the furlongs, and so it was resolved to reduce the area under com-mon arable cultivation by throwing certain of them out of the ancient course of cropping and common grazing, thus leaving the occupiers of the strips within them free to crop as they pleased. It was, in fact, an attempt to secure to the farmers some of the advan-tages of inclosure without incurring its cost.

This reorganization was pretty drastic. The whole of the East or Little Field was thrown out of common cultivation at this time, together with 61 acres in West Field, 85 acres in Mill Field, and 100 acres in South Field. But the land left for farming in common in these three fields, though much reduced, remained very roughly in the same proportions as before (see first Table on next page).

The average size of the new parcels, including, of course, both the closes and the open-field strips, was now about $3\frac{1}{4}$ acres, con-trasted with an average of $\frac{3}{4}$ acre before. The inclosure and en-

PLATE 28

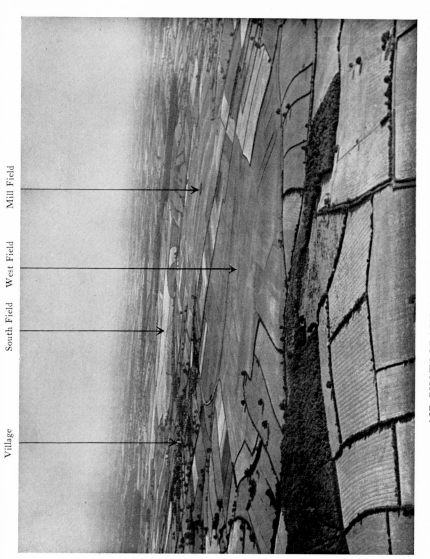

Village   South Field   West Field   Mill Field

AIR PHOTOGRAPH OF LAXTON OPEN FIELDS

grossment of strips was carried out during three consecutive years, upon the fallow field of the year. Thus, there was no interference with the cropping or stocking of the land, but a complete redistribution as between tenant and tenant was involved. It is obvious that such radical changes could have been effected only with confidence and goodwill, and it is a tribute to the lord of the manor and to his agent[1] that the work was carried through without any serious friction. Here and there a complaint might be made

Reorganization of Laxton Open Fields, 1904–6

Field	Before reorganization		After reorganization		
	Acres	No. of Strips	Acres withdrawn	Acres still uninclosed	No. of consolidated strips
East Field .	67	100	67	none	23
West Field .	217	264	61	156	65
	—284	—364	—128		
Mill Field .	294	400	85	209	97
South Field .	269	398	100	169	78
	847	1,162	313	534	263

against some portion of the new allotment on the grounds that it was not so well situated or that the soil was inferior but on balance, it was agreed that the advantages of the new holdings outweighed the disadvantages. The system of farming remained unimpaired, while the holdings in the Open Fields had been adapted by amalgamation of strips into larger blocks, to bring them into line with the demands of modern farming technique.

With the passage of time and the spread of farming for profit instead of for subsistence, the tendency has been to reduce the number and to increase the size of holdings, as the following table shows:

Number and Size of Laxton Holdings in 1635, 1835, and 1929

Size of Holdings (acres)	1635		1835		1929	
	No.	Acreage	No.	Acreage	No.	Acreage
I. 200 and over .	3	928	2	472	2	487
II. 70–200 . .	9	940	18	2,107	20	2,333
III. 40–70 . .	12	675	7	349	9	478
IV. 20–40 . .	13	353	14	355	6	139
V. 9–20 . . .	20	240	13	164	4	54
VI. 5–9 . . .	16	105	10	66	6	42
VII. Under 5 . .	33	70	8	23	12	16
	106	3,311	72	3,536	59	3,549

[1] The late Mr. R. W. Wordsworth was agent at Thoresby at this time. A note in the Court Rolls states that he sent a letter to explain the scheme and that it was unanimously approved.

More than 500 acres is still farmed in common under the three-course rotation. The sikes, commons, and wastes remain, and the common grazing and grass-lettings go on as before. The question is often asked: 'Why have the Open Fields survived at Laxton and nowhere else?' The answer is not easy. Until 1867 there was still a freehold of 675 acres, and when this had passed to Lord Manvers by exchange with Lord Savile, and inclosure might have been more easily arranged, the Golden Age of English farming was passing. Inclosure, with all the expense it would have entailed in fencing, roadmaking, and the construction of new homesteads for the inclosed farms, would not lightly have been undertaken. Moreover, Lord Manvers was engaged upon the building of the great mansion in Thoresby Park, and the long agricultural depression which followed so soon must have made any further large outlay on the estate undesirable. Thus it may have been that Mr. Wordsworth's amalgamation of strips was the obvious compromise.

Since then the only notable alteration in the Open Fields has been the inclosure of about 39 acres at the far end of South Field, and their allotment to the tenant of Brockilow Farm, who put them down to grass. The land was remote from the village and the dung-cart had to travel far to reach it. Moreover, at the time of its withdrawal, wheat prices were very low and plough farming was unattractive.

Otherwise the fields lie as they were allotted in 1907. Until the limits of cultivation were reached, every change, since the addition of new furlongs from the waste had given place to the construction of closes, has tended, first, to the consolidation and enlargement of the strips and, second, to the inclosure of furlongs or blocks of strips. Gradually the area in open-field farming has been reduced, but always the principles which regulated it have survived, and the acres that remain in the three fields present all the characteristics of the system as it has been practised and administered at any time during the long years that have passed since first they were ploughed. So long as corn-growing should continue in this country, the Laxton Open Fields may be expected to survive as a living example, and the only one, of the foundations of English farming.

Since the above was written, in 1938, there have been changes in the ownership and administration of the Laxton Open Fields. The fifth Earl Manvers died in 1940 and was succeeded by his cousin, Gervas Evelyn Pierrepont, M.C., as sixth Earl. On 28 February 1952 he conveyed to the Minister of Agriculture the Laxton estate, containing 1,758 acres in the parishes of Laxton and Kirton. Included in the conveyance was that part of Lord Manvers's property known as the Open Fields and the farms with which they are linked. The manor of Laxton and Laxton Moorhouse was conveyed subsequently by Earl Manvers to the Minister by Deed dated 11 December, 1952. No conditions were laid down in these deeds as to the future of the property, but it is understood that the purchase by the Ministry was effected virtually for the preservation as an historical document of the only surviving example of this ancient farming system.

The Agricultural Land Commission was appointed to manage the property on behalf of the Minister, their local representative becoming a member of the jury of the Manor Court, which continues to function. In the Commission's Fifth Report, it is stated:

The Open Field system at Laxton has survived many centuries of social and economic upheaval, and vast changes in land tenure and the organisation and practice of farming, by adapting itself in some measure to serve the changing needs of the local community. As a system of farming it is not without its critics; as an example of a once common way of regulating the life and work of an English rural community, it is unique. The Commission's task now, remembering the Minister's desire to preserve the Open Fields, is to help their tenants to meet the demands of the future.[1]

[1] *Fifth Report of the Agricultural Land Commission for the year ended 5th March* 1852, (H.M. Stationery Office), p. 7.

EPILOGUE

THE accepted theories of the origins and evolution of the Open Fields have been based, it may be said, upon considerations of the system as a social institution. This implies that it was a scheme of things adopted at some stage in their history by groups of people who had advanced so far from the primitive state that they could decide to survey areas of land, often very large, and to parcel them out in minute strips which they would then proceed to allot amongst each other, actuated only by the desire to secure equality for all.

It has been the purpose of this book to consider the Open Fields as an agricultural institution. Given communities of people whose only way of life was the land, what, in fact, would they do in order that they might get the best living from it? They had evolved so far as to use the plough, but otherwise their technique was simple and there was a common fund of knowledge which led every one to pursue the same system of farming. From these premisses an alternative theory has been advanced in the foregoing pages which suggests that the evolution of the Open Fields was the natural and inevitable consequence of the common experience and the common technique of communities who had settled down to till the soil with the mould-board plough. The common life of the people sent them out to work at the same seasons, upon the same tasks; the first of these was ploughing, and the action of the mould-board plough gave them the strip; working side by side their strips were intermingled one with another as day followed day. The number and the assembly of the strips into the furlongs which made up the fields was determined by the lie of the land, and as the communities grew and plough was added to plough, so furlong was added to furlong until the limit of expansion imposed by practical considerations was reached. So far from there having been a deliberate planning of the fields, and an allotment of strips thereafter to individuals, as runs the accepted theory of the formation of the Open Fields, the suggestion put forward now is that the alternate strips, the furlongs and the fields themselves grew naturally out of the need to live, the common way of life and the practice of plough-farming.

For long years there was little change either in the principle of tenure or in the practice of husbandry. Nothing appears to be known with any certainty about the growth of population in the Middle Ages, but the system of allotment of land by the operation of ploughing was so flexible that it provided almost automatically

for increases in numbers of cultivators. The cultivated area encroached slowly upon the woodlands and wastes, first, by the addition of furlongs to the Open Fields, and later, by the formation
of closes along their borders. The common system of husbandry
which was fundamental to farming in the Open Fields was no
handicap on enterprise during the long time in which the husbandman's art was more or less static. Closes, and the inclosure
of furlongs which had begun by the sixteenth century and continued at varying speeds until the process became general, provided the individualist with sufficient opportunity, until the time
when the great advances in farming technique which were associated from the middle of the eighteenth century, onwards, with
increasing opportunity for commercial agriculture, made the
rigidity of open-field farming irksome to many. For the pace of
progress in the Open Fields was inevitably slow, and so, neither
the demands of the individual, on the one hand, for the opportunity to apply his knowledge and his ability, nor the requirements
of the nation, on the other hand, for the increased supplies of food
which his knowledge and ability would furnish, could be satisfied
under the open-field system. It had served its day and it had to go.

This is the general conclusion of all those who have studied the
history of farming in this country. Whatever their criticism of the
methods sometimes adopted to bring about the change from
champion to severalty, whatever their regret for the extinction of
the yeoman and the peasant, few today would assert that some
change such as this had not been inevitable. But while it is not
the purpose of this study to dispute this generalization as to the
balance of national advantage, the history of Laxton shows very
clearly what the industrialization of agriculture has cost the
English countryside, both in the loss of economic opportunity
for the workers and in the loss of the sense of personal responsibility in the members of the village community for its social
institutions.

The history of the tenants, for the most part, has been one of steady
progress from the smallest beginnings. A Laxton lad would leave
home for employment on one of the big estates of the neighbour-
hood, or on a farm, and he saved a few pounds. A cottage holding
at Laxton became vacant, and he applied for it or it was offered to
him. The landlord, not infrequently, used to help him to take it
by allowing him time for the payment of the ingoing valuation.
At first, he continued to work for wages, cultivating his holding
as a part-time job and hiring the help of his neighbours for horse-
labour. Cultivating a Laxton holding meant growing corn. In
six months he had his first harvest, and with the proceeds he could
buy a few sheep. These he would turn out, as was his right up to the

number of twenty, upon the fallow field of the year, where they would get their living, to be sold in due season for more money than he gave for them, and this increment had cost him nothing.

So he went on, supporting himself by his wages and building up some capital by the profit on his crops and stock. Later, a larger holding fell vacant, and he felt strong enough to apply for it, becoming a full-time farmer and giving up his other employment. He might move again or even more than once, each time into a larger holding, and the most successful of his like might move right away, ultimately, into substantial inclosed farms. Alternatively, they might help their sons to start in small holdings in the Laxton Open Fields.

Examples of the ascent of the agricultural ladder from the bottom rung may be met with commonly enough all over the country, but nowhere else in England will there be found a village community nearly every member of which is at one stage or another in his progress from the bottom to the top. The rate of progress varies, of course, and not every one reaches or expects to reach the top. But the opportunity is there, and it arises solely from the organization of farming in the Open Fields. A man may have no more than an acre or two, but he gets the full extent of them laid out in long 'lands' for ploughing, with no hedgerows to reduce the effective area and to occupy him in unprofitable labour. No sort of inclosure of the same size can be conceived which would give him equivalent facilities. Moreover, he has his common rights which entitle him to graze stock over all the 'lands', and these have a value the equivalent of which in pasture fields would cost far more than he could afford to pay.

Every one knows the value of the work of the county councils in providing stepping-stones towards economic advancement for rural workers by the creation of small-holdings. It is a need that has arisen solely from the inclosure of the Open Fields, and whatever the success of this modern land-settlement policy, it can never be an adequate substitute for the opportunities that the Open Fields afforded. The Laxton people are fully conscious of the strength of their position, and even the larger farmers, including those who now occupy the few inclosed farms which have been created in the parish, are strong in the opinion that the Open Fields have served them well and that inclosure would be contrary to the best interests of their community. This community is in every way healthy and vigorous. The system of farming is traditional with it, and it asks for nothing better than to be left alone to pursue it. On economic and social grounds, therefore, as well as from their unique interest as an historical monument, the maintenance of the Laxton Open Fields is to be desired.

Another strength of the open-field parish comes from its administrative organization. The government of the Open Fields is a pure democracy, for every one, sooner or later, has personal responsibility for it. It is obvious that a farming system under which there is such complete interdependence amongst the occupiers of the land would be possible only under a strong administration, with powers to enforce its decisions against the individual in the interests of the many. Such is the manor court.

It has been shown that the court itself consists of all tenants and freeholders, and that the field juries appointed by it are responsible for the observance of the customs of the manor and for the regulations made, from time to time, by the court. They present persons for breaches of these customs or regulations without fear or favour. The court passes judgement upon the presentments, and the bailiff of the court collects such penalties as may be imposed by it. Another officer of the court, the pinder, is responsible for distraining upon stock straying in the fields, for impounding them, and for collecting the fines authorized by the court upon replevy by their owners. All of these people, the court itself and the juries and officers which it appoints, are freeholders or tenants of the manor, so that every one within it has direct personal responsibility, not only for the decisions of the court but for their enforcement. Thus, both legislative and executive functions are vested in the people themselves.

Until about a hundred years ago, the administrative powers of the village were wider still, for they included the relief of the poor by the overseers, the repair of the highways also, and the keeping of the peace through the parish constable. All of these voluntary services, which every one might have to perform, have now been merged in larger administrative units, but in the personal responsibility for the preservation of the general good, which still devolves, sooner or later, upon every one, Laxton has retained something which has been lost everywhere else in the process of the inclosure of the Open Fields. Its people control their own affairs in the daily incidents of their work, by a scheme of voluntary administration maintained by public opinion without recourse to the law of the land and without the expenditure of a single penny. Encroachments upon the highway and upon the commons, trespass by straying stock, disputes as to boundaries, the cleansing of ditches and watercourses and the cutting of hedges—all of these things, together with the observance of the agreed system of husbandry, are settled here by the community at its own court. In other places recourse must now be had to the law, failing compliance with the instructions of paid officials in whom are now vested the powers once exercised by the community. In place of attendance at the court, of sharing in the responsibility for the regulations made thereat, of serving on a jury charged with the duty of securing the observance of such regulations, the dwellers in other parts of rural England can do no more than cast a vote for the election of some one to represent them on some local administrative body. After holding up his hand at a parish meeting or making a cross on his ballot paper, if, indeed, he do so much, the ordinary man thinks that his responsibility for local administration is fulfilled. Small wonder if his attitude towards it, thereafter, is one of complete detachment or of unconstructive criticism.

Students of the Open Fields today are influenced, inevitably, in their judgement of the system by the views of Arthur Young and of his contemporaries, strongly held and expressed, that it was bad. But so might the enthusiastic pioneers of the first railways have written of the canal system which preceded them. So, indeed, do advocates of motor transport speak today of the electric tramways. 'Time makes ancient good uncouth.' The eighteenth-century writers were intoxicated with the idea that only by inclosure could commercial farming, and the opportunities for profit which it offered, have full scope. But Arthur Young himself came to realise that among the consequences of inclosure might be the impoverishment and degradation of many of the smaller members of the village community. In a paper which he published in 1801, he drew attention to the losses suffered by the poor, particularly in grazing and fuel rights, upon inclosure of commons and wastes. 'By nineteen out of twenty Inclosure Bills' he wrote 'the poor are injured, and some grossly injured. . . .'

This is not a plea for a return to the conditions either of the occupation or of the administration of land which prevailed in the districts in which the Open Fields flourished for so long. The arguments for their inclosure were unanswerable in the changing circumstances of the economic life of the country. But, considering them apart from the national life as a whole, we should not forget what rural England has lost, both in economic opportunities for the people and in their social education, by the destruction of the system of which Laxton, today, is the sole surviving example.

PLATE 29

A PLAT AND DESCRIPTIO OF THE WHOLE MANNOR OR LORDSHIP of Laxton with Laxton Moorhouse in the County of Nottingham and also of the Mannor or Lordship of Kneesall lying adiacent to the prefaid Mannor of Laxton within the said County Which Survey was first taken and two severall Plats thereof made by Francis Mason & William Mason in the year of our Lord 1625 by the appointment of the Right Honorable the Duke of Buckingham then posfesfor of these Mannors And Renewed & feated and this one entire Platt & Booke of Survey made of both the said Manno by Mark Pierce in the yeare 1635 by the appointment of the Right worshipfull Sr William Courten of London Knight Purchafer & pofsefsor thereof In the descriptio of all the every pcell of the Lands there is placed certaine numbers which are in reference to the correspondent numb in the bookes of Survey with showeth the name of every Common Field & of every close & furlong therein with the name of every Tenant & Freehold to whom each pcell belongeth & the mesure thereof And at the end of the particulars of the Lands belonging to the feverall Manno there is placed the Collections or Totall Sumes of Meddow Pasture & Arable houlden by every Tenent & Frehould therein With all the feverall Tenements of Lands lately purchafed by the said Sr William Courten now Lord of these Mannors of Mr Augustine Hind Efq Francis Rosse Esqr within the Manno of Laxton and of Mr Samuell Hartup within the Mannor of Kneesall knowne & distinguished in the Platt by a light yellow colour And at the end of the Totall Sumes of the Lands of all the Tenants & Freeholders there is placed the Totall Sume of each Mannor And after the Sum a Sum and or generall Totall of both the said Mannors are placed Tables of Parcels serving for the more speedy finding out of the Lands belonginge to every perticular Tenement Besides the distinction of colours where by the Demefne & Tenement lands are feverad from the Lands of the Free Tenents which are all left white All which numbers before mentioned both in the Booke of Survey and in this Platt are equally correspondent the one to the other as by comparinge them together plainly appeareth

DESCRIPTION ON MAP OF 1635.

APPENDIX

A NOTE ON THE ORIGIN OF LYNCHETS

No mention has been made of a feature of the hill-sides occurring in many parts of England, and very commonly in some, which is attributed by many writers to the action of the plough and associated by some with the Open Fields, namely, the lynchet terraces. They occur most commonly on the chalk formation in the southern counties, where they may be seen either singly or in numbers along the sides of the Downs anywhere from Cambridgeshire or Kent to Dorset. But they are met with, though less frequently, on other formations; on the Old Red Sandstone, in Somerset; on the Great Oolites, in Gloucestershire; on the Middle Lias which rises above the Vale of the Red Horse, in Warwickshire, and on many of the hill-sides of Wales, of the West and North Ridings of Yorkshire, of Westmorland, and of Cumberland. All these have been observed casually in travel about the country, and a systematic search would surely bring to light many more. They are known locally by various names. In the south of England they seem generally to be called 'lynchets', though sometimes 'banks', while in Yorkshire the terms 'benches' and 'reens' occur.

Recently, the subject has been complicated by the application of the name 'lynchet' to something entirely different from the clearly defined terraces of the hill-sides, namely, to the little banks enclosing the small crofts or cultivation plots which archaeologists associate with a farming system earlier than that of the Open Fields.

It is now almost universally accepted that terraced lynchets were formed by ploughing across the hill-side or slope. The plough cannot turn a furrow-slice uphill and thus, it is said, a 'land' marked out on a hill-side and ploughed by turning the furrow-slices always downhill, the plough running idle one way, would be turned in course of time into a terrace, as the slices were cut out from the upper side and laid up along the lower side. The explanation is old. William Marshall, writing in 1798, quoted it as current in his day, though he himself doubted it, remarking: 'This sort of artificial surface is common in different parts of the Island, and the antiquary might be less profitably employed than in tracing its origin.'[1] Poulett-Scrope, writing in the *Geological Magazine* in 1866, reaffirmed the ploughing theory, and since then it has never been questioned. On the contrary, it has been re-stated frequently, and, in 1931, the Congress of Archaeological Societies published a *Report on Lynchets and Grass Ridges* which associated the formation of lynchets with arable cultivation in the Open Fields. The report says, in fact, that they are 'an adaptation of the strips of the Open Fields to the steep hillside'. The suggestion is that when the furlong spread to the foot of the hill, lands continued to be set out up the hill, which, if steep enough, entailed one-way ploughing downhill, and thus a succession of terraces was formed.

Crawford records an example from Calstone where, he says, the strips of the open fields are carried on to embrace a series of lynchet terraces

[1] Marshall, W., *The Rural Economy of the Southern Counties*, vol. ii (1798), p. 302.

there.[1] This he regards as positive proof of their formation by ploughing. The suggestion we offer is that some, at all events, of these lynchets are much older than the Open Fields, and that they have been made by means other than ploughing. If so, is it not possible that Calstone is nothing other than an example of the opportunism of the early farmers, who found these flat surfaces lying to hand when the furlongs of their open fields had reached the foot of the hill, and who decided, naturally enough, to exploit them? Certainly this is what seems to have happened at Credenton Hill, in Warwickshire, where the lynchet terraces are laid up in one or more high-backed lands like the rest of the country by which the hill is surrounded. And at Bagnor, in Berkshire, a series of terrace lynchets outcrops in a field still in arable cultivation today, which are cultivated and sown with the rest of the field every year in season.

We have no explanation of the formation of lynchets which we can offer in substitution for that which suggests that they are strips of the Open Fields which have assumed this form from the exigencies of ploughing on a hill-side. At the same time, our observations, extended over some years and in many parts of England, have led us to the conclusion that the plough theory is untenable.

In the first place, most writers from Seebohm onwards have been familiar, apparently, only with the terraces of the chalk, which occur usually on fairly sharp slopes. We have found no evidence to show that there has been any systematic study of the great variety of lynchets which even a cursory investigation discloses. Even the terraces of the chalk conform to no uniform pattern. Some are single, outcropping on the side of a combe, beginning nowhere and ending nowhere, and having no apparent purpose. Others form isolated sets of terraces, occurring here or there with nothing whatever to explain their presence in one spot or their absence from another. Nearly all run horizontally, of course, but some may be found which run up and down hill. Some are wide and some are narrow; some are deep and some are shallow. In the Yorkshire Dales and in Westmorland, great systems of well-defined lynchets occur in many places, which may extend, with breaks, over 100 acres or more. As a rule, their faces are not very high and they occur in situations without any pronounced slope, quite unlike the gradients of the chalk and limestone escarpments. There are a few lynchets in the Open Fields at Laxton. It will be obvious, at once, to any one who takes the trouble to study them, that no one explanation of how and why they were made can fit them all.

In the second place, dealing with the terraces of the chalk, about which the generalization of formation by the plough in Anglo-Saxon times as part of the Open Fields has been made, the case against this theory can quickly be stated. The suggestion is that when the strips of ridge and furrow reached the hill-side, the bank above them was then laid out for ploughing in strips, with grass balks between each, but that the ploughmen, ploughing along the hill-side, found that their ploughs would not turn furrows uphill. And so the plough was dragged back idle, to plough a second furrow downhill against the first, and so on until the whole strip had been ploughed in furrows lying along the slope, downhill. Repeated ploughings would build up the soil at

---

[1] Crawford, O. G. S., and Keith, A., *Wessex from the Air* (1928), p. 166.

the bottom of the strip and dig out a bank at the top of it. The objections are as follows:

1. Lynchet terraces occur in many places where the topography makes it very unlikely, if not, indeed, inconceivable, that they could have had any connexion with an open field.

2. On most of the chalk escarpments where terrace lynchets occur there is very little either of soil or of subsoil. Seebohm says: 'Every year's ploughing took a *sod* from the higher edge of the strip and put it on the lower edge', and the Report on Lynchets talks of the *soil* travelling downhill and accumulating 'a very considerable bank at the expense of the *soil* in the upper part of the plot'. Now some of the lynchets in the chalk country measure 20 feet in the vertical, and assuming that half of the bank consists of material superimposed in the formation of the terrace above, it means that the slope of the hill has been dug out by ploughing to a depth of some 10 feet. But on these chalk slopes there is a turf of 2 or 3 inches, about the same depth of soil below it, a few more inches of disintegrated chalk, and then an unmeasured depth of chalk rock. Is it conceivable that the ploughs of the Dark Ages could cut into this chalk rock to a depth of some 9 feet and turn it downhill to form a flat terrace? And if they could, what agricultural purpose would be served by burying a thin layer of turf and subsoil under an immense mass of chalk rubble? It is true that these terraces are covered today with soil and herbage, but if they were made according to the accepted explanation, there would have been a period of waiting far longer than the lifetime of the first plough-man before Nature, by means of earthworms and humus, would have pro-duced a soil on his chalk terrace in which he could have grown his crops.

3. If the terraces were formed by ploughing as part of the Open Fields, what happened when they were finally level? Did the ploughman continue to plough them one way? If so, some of them at least should show a piling up of material at the outer edge, with the surface falling inward to the back of the terrace. But none are like this. If, on the other hand, the ploughman reverted to the ordinary practice when he had got his terrace level, these terraces should show high ridges in the middle, just like the lands in the Open Fields, with the surface falling to either side. The only place where this appearance has been found, Credenton Hill, suggests comparatively modern cultivation on an ancient site.

4. There seems to be no foundation for Seebohm's assertion, repeated in the Report on Lynchets and by several writers, that the terraces 'approximate to the standard English acre, 220 yards by 22 yards, or its fractions'. Many measurements of lynchets have not produced any evidence that they conform to any particular standard.

5. But it is the dependence of the plough theory upon the provision of a balk of unploughed land between each ploughed strip which finally disposes of it. As shown above, no convincing evidence has been found, either on the ground, or in documents, or in maps, for such balks. If there were no balks between the strips, there could have been nothing upon which to pile up the materials brought down the slope as the result of ploughing downhill. Ploughing along the contours of the hill-sides *without* intervening balks between the lands may be seen in a thousand fields, and the effect of this movement of the soil and the action of rain and frost is to cause a gentle

slipping of the surface. In time, a bank, Dr. Curwen's 'positive' lynchet, is accumulated at the bottom of the field, and a 'negative' lynchet is cut out at the top. But the contour of the field is unchanged, and there is no suggestion of terracing.

To sum up, then, we suggest that terrace lynchets have no connexion whatever with the system of farming attributed to the Saxons, because it is difficult to conceive of a land-hunger in those days which would have driven people to cultivate such unprofitable sites; because it is difficult to believe that their ploughs could cut deep into chalk and limestone rock to make the terraces; because terraces thus produced would be useless for cultivation for many years; and because the whole theory of their construction by the plough depends upon a balk of unploughed land left between each man's strip, and there were no such balks in the layout of the Open Fields.

These conclusions are confirmed by the results of an excavation of the magnificent terrace lynchets ranged along the north-western slope of Blew-burton Hill, in the parish of Blewbury, in Berkshire. The hill is an outlier from the great range of the chalk Downs sweeping up from Dorset, along which many fine examples of hillside terraces are displayed. Blewburton is surmounted by an Iron Age hill-fort, and the four great lynchets, 36, 28, 36, and 24 feet wide, respectively, descend steeply into the Thames valley from it, the top one having been made by filling in the Iron Age ditch and cutting back the rampart scarp.

The excavation of Blewburton hill-fort was begun in 1949, by the Berkshire Archaeological Society and the Reading Museum, in association, the work being under the direction of Mr. A. E. P. Collins, now Inspector in the Northern Ireland Archaeological Survey, Belfast. The cutting of a deep trench, 200 feet long, transversely through the terraces down to the undisturbed chalk, was the last operation.

Turning to the final phase at Blewburton, that of the lynchet-making, it is dis-appointing that Cutting F shed so little light. That the lynchets are post Iron Age is established beyond doubt. The filling in of the Iron Age ditch and the cutting back of the rampart scarp, on the one hand, and the complete removal of all Iron Age pottery or other debris, on the other, alike demonstrate this. Yet no date can be given to their construction, since they yielded no small finds at all. On their method of manufacture and function, the section raised more problems than it solved. The solid nature of the chalk into which they had been cut makes it difficult to credit the theory that terracing on chalk hillsides is an unintentional by-product of the cultivation of strip-fields. It is my own view that the terraces can only have been formed by the intentional levelling with pick and shovel of each terrace. . . .

In support of this view that the terraces were formed intentionally and at one time is the apparent lack of humus in the accumulation forming each positive lynchet. If this were the result of ploughing, one would expect it to be comparable in colour and texture with the plough soil in the upper levels within the rampart. Against this view is the finely divided nature of the deposit; this suggests a gradual accumulation during which frost and cultivation broke down all the larger lumps of chalk. Samples of this deposit were taken for analysis by a soil scientist, but his report is unfortunately not yet available. That this finely divided yellowish material needs investigation is shown also by its occurrence in the positive part of 'Celtic' lynchets on Streatley Warren sectioned by Miss Alison Mills in 1948–9.

The absence of any soil between the modern turf and the solid chalk on the inner (negative) half of each lynchet seems to show that the cultivation of, say, corn would have been impossible on that half. Against this, of course, it could be argued that weather removed such soil as had been there before the modern turf had established itself. If the purpose of such terraces was still agricultural, what crop, if any, would have been suited to them? Local tradition says that vines were grown there; but this seems to ignore the fact that the bulk of the terraces, at least as they survive at present, face north-west, whereas, if vines are to succeed in the English climate a southerly aspect would seem imperative. No trace of planting-holes for such a crop was noted. Nor was any light shed on the vexed question of uncultivated baulks or other barriers between the terraced strips. Yet the steep angle of the scarps between the terraces seems to point to some kind of barrier to retain soil on each terrace.

If the Blewburton terraces were made to provide additional level ground for ordinary cultivation, why was this vast labour expended on such poor soil? All around the foot of the hill stretch fertile and level, well-drained fields on the Upper Greensand. One would hesitate to see in the terraces the utilization of marginal lands under population pressure. It seems best, therefore, to leave the purpose of the terraces as an open question.[1]

No doubt these terraces are man-made, but when, how, and for what purpose are matters that still have to be determined. Marshall's doubts, expressed 140 years ago, have never been resolved.

[1] A. E. P. Collins, 'Excavations on Blewburton Hill, 1948 and 1949'. The *Berkshire Archaeological Journal*, vol. liii (1952–3), pp. 57–58.

BIBLIOGRAPHY

I. *Original Documents*

(a) *In Public Custody*

Laxton and Moorhouse Tithe Award and Map, 1838. Ministry of Agriculture and Fisheries.

Laxton Moorhouse Inclosure Award and Map, 1860. Ministry of Agriculture and Fisheries.

Inquisitions *post mortem* of Lords of the Manor and of the sub-manor of Laxton. P.R.O.

Survey of Laxton and Kneesal, 1635. Map and Terrier. Bodleian Library.

Laxton Court Rolls, Suit Rolls, and Juries' Presentments, 1651–1820, British Museum (the later rolls, 1821 seq. are deposited in the Steward's Office at Newark-on-Trent).

Thoresby Deeds. Mostly Series II, from 1600. Nottingham University.

Map of Laxton (undated), *c.* 1790. Nottingham University.

(b) *In Laxton Vicarage*

Laxton Parish Accounts, 1725–37. 2 vols., viz. Constable's, Churchwardens', Overseers of the Poor and the Highways.

Constable's Accounts, 1790–1826.

Churchwardens' Accounts, 1785–1856.

Overseers of the Poor Accounts, 1786–1834.

Overseers of the Highways Accounts, 1786–1830.

Transcripts of the Laxton Parish Registers.

Particulars and Valuation of the Parish of Laxton in the County of Nottingham made for the purpose of equalizing the Parochial Assessments (undated), *c.* 1835.

Easter Books of the Vicar of Laxton, 1714, 1743, 1814.

Materials for the History of Laxton. Compiled by the Rev. C. B. Collinson, M.A., 3 vols.

Miscellaneous Papers.

II. *Published Works*

Agriculture Land Commission, *Fifth Report for year ended 5th March 1952.*

AITKEN, ROBERT and BARBARA. *The Castilian Plough: A Preliminary Study.* Anales del Museo del Pueblo Español. Madrid, 1935.

Baron Court Book of Urie, 1604–1747. Ed. Barron, D. G., Scottish History Society. 1892.

Battle Abbey Custumals. Camden Society. 1887.

BENNETT, H. S. *Life on the English Manor: A Study of Peasant Conditions, 1150–1400.* 1937.

BLOCH, MARC. *Les Caractères Originaux de l'histoire rurale française.* 1931.

CHAMBERS, J. D. *Nottinghamshire in the Eighteenth Century*. 1932.
CHAPMAN, VERA, *Open Fields in West Cheshire*, Transactions of the Historic Society of Lancashire and Cheshire, 1953.
Chartulary of Winchester Cathedral. Ed. in English, Goodman, A. W., 1927.
CLARK, G. N. *Open Fields and Inclosure at Marston, near Oxford*. 1924.
COLLINGWOOD, R. G. *Roman Britain*. 1934.
——and MYRES, J. N. L. *Roman Britain and the English Settlements*. (Oxford History of England.) 1936.
COLLINS, A. E. P. 'Excavations on Blewburton Hill, 1948 and 1949', the *Berkshire Archaeological Journal*, vol. liii. 1952–3.
COULTON, G. G. *The Medieval Village*. 1925.
CRAWFORD, O. G. S. *Air Survey and Archaeology*. 1929.
——and KEILLER, A. *Wessex from the Air*. 1928.
CURWEN, E. C. 'Prehistoric Agriculture in Britain', *Antiquity*, vol. i, no. 3, 1927.
——'The Plough and the Origin of Strip Lynchets', *Antiquity*, vol. xiii, no. 49, 1939.
DEFOE, DANIEL. *A Tour through the whole Island of Great Britain*. 1724.
DAVENPORT, F. E. *The Economic Development of a Norfolk Manor, 1086–1565*. 1906.
DES MARÈZ, G. *Le Problème de la Colonisation franque et du Régime agraire en Belgique*. Mémoires de l'Académie Royale de Belgique, IIᵐᵉ Série, tome ix. 1926.
ERNLE, LORD. *English Farming Past and Present*. Ed. Sir A. D. Hall. 1936.
FIENNES, CELIA. *Through England on a Side Saddle in the time of William and Mary*. Ed. Griffiths, Emily W. 1888.
FINBERG, H. P. R. 'The Open Fields in Devonshire', *Antiquity*, no. 92, December 1949.
FITZHERBERT. *The Book of Husbandry*, 1534. Ed. Skeat, W. 1882.
——*Surveyinge*. 1539.
FOSTER, C. W. *Aisthorpe and Thorpe le Fallows*. 1935.
FOWLER, G. HERBERT. *Quarto Memoirs of the Bedfordshire Historical Records Society*, vol. ii. 1928–36.
GOMME, G. L. *The Village Community*. 1890.
GONNER, E. C. K. *Common Land and Inclosure*. 1912.
GOW, A. S. F. 'The Ancient Plough', *Journal of Hellenic Studies*, vol. xxxiv. 1914.
GRAS, N. S. B. and E. C. *The Economic and Social History of an English Village*. (Crawley, Hampshire.) 1930.
GRAY, H. L. *English Field Systems*. 1915.
HAMMOND, J. L. and BARBARA, *The Village Labourer*. 1911.
HATT, GUDMUND. 'Prehistoric Fields in Jylland', *Acta Archaeologica*, vol. ii, fasc. 2. 1931.
HOLLEYMAN, G. A. 'The Celtic Field-System in South Britain', *Antiquity*, vol. ix, no. 36, 1935.
HOSKINS, W. G. and FINBERG, H. P. R. *Devonshire Studies*, 1952.
LEADAM, I. S. *The Domesday of Inclosures, 1517–1518*. 1897.

LIPSON, E. *Economic History of England*, vol. i. 1929.

Robert Loder's Farm Accounts. Camden Society, Third Series, vol. liii. 1936.

LODGE, ELEANOR C. *The Account Book of a Kentish Estate, 1616–1704.* 1927.

MAITLAND, F. W. *Domesday Book and Beyond.* 1897.

PAGE, FRANCES M. *The Estates of Crowland Abbey.* Cambridge Studies in Economic History. 1934.

PASSMORE, J. B. *The English Plough.* 1930.

POLLOCK, Sir F., and MAITLAND, F. W. *History of English Law.*

Records of the Baron Court of Stitchill, 1655–1807. Trs. Gunn. G.; ed. Gunn, C. B. Scottish History Society, 1905.

Reports on Lynchets and Grass Ridges. Congress of Archaeological Societies. 1932.

Reports to the Board of Agriculture and Internal Improvement, 1793–5 (quarto); *1795–1815* (octavo).

ROUND, J. H. *Feudal England.* 1895.

ROWSE, A. L. *Tudor Cornwall,* 1941.

RUSTON, A. D., and WHITNEY, DENIS. *Hooton Pagnell. The Agricultural Evolution of a Yorkshire Village.* 1934.

SCRUTTON, T. E. *Commons and Common Fields.* 1887.

SEEBOHM, F. *The English Village Community.* 1883.

——*Customary Acres and their Historical Importance.* 1914.

SEEBOHM, M. E. *The Evolution of the English Farm.* 1927.

SLATER, G. *The English Peasantry and the Enclosure of Common Fields.* 1907.

SMITH, TOULMIN. *The Parish. Its Powers and Obligations at Law, its Officers and Committees: and the Responsibility of every Parishioner.* 2nd ed. 1857.

STENTON, F. M. *English Feudalism, 1066–1166.* 1932.

——*Types of Manorial Structure in the Northern Danelaw.* Oxford Historical Studies, II. 1910.

STUBBS, W. *Constitutional History of England.* 4th ed. 1883.

Studies in Leicestershire Agrarian History, ed. W. G. Hoskins. 1949.

Survey of the Manor of Wye. Ed. H. E. Muhlfeld. 1933.

SYLVESTER, DOROTHY, *Rural Settlement in Cheshire.* Transactions of the Historic Society of Lancashire and Cheshire, 1949.

TATE, W. E. *Parliamentary Land Enclosures in the County of Nottingham (1743–1868).* 1935.

TAWNEY, R. H. and POWER, EILEEN. *Tudor Economic Documents.* 1924.

——*The Agrarian Revolution in the Sixteenth Century.* 1912.

VENN, J. A. *Foundations of Agricultural Economics.* 2nd ed. 1933.

VINOGRADOFF, P. *The Growth of the Manor.* 1905.

——*Villeinage in England.* 1892.

WALTER OF HENLEY. *Husbandry.* Ed. Lamond, E. 1890.

WARDE FOWLER, W. *Kingham Old and New.* 1913.

GLOSSARY

(The following definitions are taken from the *O.E.D.*)

Assart. A piece of forest land converted into arable by grubbing up the trees and brushwood; a clearing in a forest.

Balk, baulk. A strip of ground left unploughed as a boundary line between two ploughed portions.

Bovate. An oxgang, or as much land as one ox could plough in a year; one-eighth of a carucate or plough-land; varying in amount from 10 to 18 acres according to the system of tillage, &c. (See *Oxgang.*)

Burleyman, Byrlawman. An officer appointed at a court-leet for various local duties, as the framing and execution of by-laws, looking after nuisances, administration of justice in minor matters, arbitration in agricultural disputes, &c.

Butt. A ridge when short of its full length owing to the irregular shape of the boundary of the field. (See *Gore.*)

Carucate. A measure of land, varying with the nature of the soil, &c., being as much as could be tilled with one plough (with its team of 8 oxen) in a year; a ploughland.

Court-baron. The assembly of the freehold tenants of a manor under the presidency of the lord or his steward. (In modern times lawyers have distinguished between the *court-baron*, which was the court of the freehold tenants, and the *customary court*, which was the court for the copyhold tenants. The early history of this distinction is obscure.)

Court-leet. A court of record held periodically in a hundred, lordship, or manor, before the lord or his steward, and attended by the residents in the district. It had jurisdiction over petty offences, and performed a number of administrative functions.

    1654. Selden, *Table-Talk* (Arb.) 42: 'Court Leet, where they have power to make By-laws, as they call them; as that a man shall put so many Cows, or Sheep in the Common.'

Croft. A piece of inclosed ground, used for tillage or pasture; in most localities a small piece of arable land adjacent to a house.

Dole. A share, a small portion.

Essoin. The allegation of an excuse for non-appearance in court at the appointed time; the excuse itself.

Fallow. Ground that is well ploughed and harrowed, but left uncropped for a whole year or more.

Flat. One of the larger portions into which the common field was divided. (See *Furlong.*)

Frankpledge. The system by which every member of a tithing was answerable for the good conduct of, or the damage done by, any one of the other members. *View of Frankpledge.* A court held periodically for the production of the members of a tithing.

Furlong. 1. Originally, the length of the furrow in the common field, which was theoretically regarded as a square containing 10 acres.

2. An area of land a 'furlong' each way, containing 10 acres.

3. The headline of a common field.

4. An indefinite division of an uninclosed field.

Gate. A right to a run or pasturage for a cow, horse, &c., on a common field, representing a share of the joint ownership of the field; on private ground (let for an annual rent).

Gore. A wedge-shaped strip of land on the side of an irregular field.

Gore acre, gore-butt. A tapering strip of land into which the corners of the field are divided.

Headland. A strip of land in a ploughed field, left for convenience in turning the plough at the end of the furrows, or near the border; in old times used as a boundary.

Homage. A body of persons owning allegiance; the body of tenants attending a manorial court.

Ing. A common name in the north of England, and in some other parts, for a meadow; esp. one by the side of a river.

Land. One of the strips into which a cornfield, or a pasture field that has been ploughed, is divided by water-furrows.

Mainport. A small tribute (commonly loaves of bread) which in some places the parishioners pay to the rector of their church, in recompense for certain tithes.

Merestone. A boundary; also an object indicating a boundary, a landmark.

Modus. A money payment in lieu of tithe. In full, *modus decimandi.*

Neif. One born in a state of bondage or serfdom.

Oxgang. The eighth part of the carucate or ploughland varying from 10 to 18 acres, or more widely, according to the system of tillage, &c.; a bovate.

Pinder. An officer of the manor, having the duty of impounding stray beasts.

Pinfold. A place for confining stray or distrained cattle, horses, sheep, &c.; a pound.

Ridge, rigg. A raised or rounded strip of arable land, usually one of a series (with intermediate open furrows) into which a field is divided by ploughing in a special manner. (See *Land.*)

Selion. A portion of land of indeterminate area comprising a ridge or narrow strip lying between two furrows formed in dividing an open field.

Shot. A division of land. (See *Furlong.*)

Sike. A gully; a dip or hollow. A stretch of meadow.

Stint. The limited number of cattle, according to kind, allotted to each definite portion into which pasture or common land is divided, or to each person entitled to the right of common pasturage; also, the right of pasturage according to the fixed rate.

Stitch. A strip of ploughed land between two furrows. (See *Land.*)

Stropper, strapper. A cow that yields but little milk. (A dry cow. C. S. O.)

Terrier. A register of landed property, including lists of vassals and tenants, with particulars of their holdings, services, and rents.

Thirdborough. Probably a ME. corruption of *fridborgh.* The petty constable of a township or manor.

Toft. Originally, a homestead, the site of a house and its outbuildings; a house site. Often in the expression *toft and croft*, denoting the whole holding, consisting of the homestead and attached piece of arable land.

Virgate. An early English land-measure, varying greatly in extent, but in many cases averaging 30 acres.

Wong, woung. A piece of meadow land. A portion of uninclosed land under the open-field system.

MAP OF LAXTON 1635

Errors and Omissions

The following discrepancies have been noted between the Terrier and Map:

Map I.

104 in Terrier included with 105 in Map.

106   ,,   numbered 104 in Map.

2990, 2991, 2992, 2994, 2995, 2996 in Terrier not numbered in Map, but can be identified in Middle New Dike.

3011 in Terrier not numbered in Map. Lies S. of 3010.

3032   ,,   numbered in 332 in Map.

3035   ,,   ,,   106   ,,

3036   ,,   ,,   3035   ,,

3040   ,,   ,,   3046   ,,

Map II.

3050 in Terrier not numbered in Map. Lies N. of Westwood Common, 3031.

Map III.

1606 in Terrier not numbered in Map. Lies on extreme W.

1636   ,,   ,,   ,,   Lies N. of 1635.

1721–30, Furlong H in Terrier lettered F in Map.

1935 in Terrier, 3 closes; only middle close numbered in Map.

2305–15 in Terrier not numbered in Map. Lie NE. corner, LL.

2367 in Terrier numbered 2365 in Map.

2403   ,,   Common Ground, part numbered 2903 in Map.

Map IV.

3023 in Terrier not numbered in Map. Lies NE. between 1024 and 3054.

3030 in Terrier numbered 3038 in Map.

3038   ,,   ,,   3035   ,,

3041   ,,   not numbered in Map. Lies extreme NE. next to 3055.

INDEX

administration, community control of, 125, 126, 146, 157, 171, 173, 174; *see also* Manor Court *and* vestry

Agricultural Land Commission, administering Laxton Open Fields, 169

Agriculture, Minister of, Laxton Open Fields conveyed to, 168

Alselin, Geoffrey, 72, 73

arable land: under Mark System, 4, 5; allocation of, in Open Fields, 39–42; cropping of, in Open Fields, 53–56; at Laxton in Domesday Survey, 73, 74; in inquisitions *post mortem*, 80; in *1635*, 96–105; *see also* crops *and* fields

Archaeological Societies, Congress of: on Open Fields, 12–14; on lynchets, 175, 177

assart, 17; at Laxton, 91

Averham Hall, Open Fields at, 45

Axholme, Isle of, Open Fields in, 46

Bacon, James, his closes at Laxton, 108

Bailey and Culley, *General view of the Agriculture of the County of Northumberland*, 50

bailiff of the Manor Court, 127, 173

Bakewell, Robert, 136

balks: Seebohm on, 43, 44; *Piers the Ploughman* on, 44; absence of, between strips, 44–51, 100, 177; as means of access, 47, 48, 99, 126, 141; 'half-balks' or stintins, 99, 100; grazing on, 132, 134, 135

de Bekering, family of, 73; Inquisitions *post mortem* of, 81–85

de Birkin, family of, 73, 75

Bloch, Marc, on Open Fields in France, 9–11, 141; on balks, 45

bovate, *see* oxgang

Boyes, John, on Kent, 68

Braunton Great Field, 50, 51

Broughton, Peter, his freehold at Laxton, 88, 106, 108, 126, 163

burleymen, 128, 138

butts, 36, 103

by-laws, of Manor Court, 129, 133, 136, 137, 138, 146; of *1686*, 147, 148; of *1688*, 148–50; of *1789*, as revised *1821*, 150–3; of *1871*, 153–4

Cardington, by-laws of manor of, 47

caschrom, 30

de Caux, family of, 71–76

Cheshire, Open Field in, 65

churchwardens, 157

closes: at Laxton, *1635*, 92, 93, 94, 110; demesne, 76, 89, 104; reclamations from woodland and waste, 104

co-aration, 5, 9, 38, 41

Collingwood, R. G., on origin of Open Fields, 10–12

Collins, A. E. P., on lynchets, 178

commons: 57; at Laxton, 71; in *1635*, 87, 90, 91, 94, 96, 132; grazing on, 132, 133

constable: appointment of, 127, 128; duties of, 156, 173

Cornwall, Open Field in, 66

Courten, Sir William, 73; purchases Laxton, 86–88; lets demesne lands, 107; his estate policy, 113, 115, 122

Crawford, O. G. S., on lynchets, 175, 176

crops: rotation of, 1, 53–56, 142, 143; in pre-Roman Britain, 21; harvesting of, 145, 146

Cumberland, Open Field in, 65

Curwen, Cecil, on lynchets, 178

demesne: lord's, at Laxton, in *1232*, 74–79; in *1635*, 89; scattered, 76, 107; letting of, 113, 115

Denison, of Ossington, family of, 109, 164, 165

Derbyshire, Open Field in, 66

Devon, Open Field in, 65

ditches, regulations for scouring, 142, 173

doles, 60, 74; at Laxton in *1635*, 90, 104, 144

Domesday Survey, 41, 42, 57; entry for Laxton, 42, 73, 74

Dorset, Open Field in, 67

Drew, E., on balks, 50

Durham, evidence of Open Field in, 66

Eakring: Open Fields in, 46, 71; exchanges of land at, 165

Easter Book, Vicar's, *see* tithe

East Field, Laxton, 71; in *1635*, 87, 89, 90; size of, 96; Hugh Tailer's holding in, 139; withdrawn from common cultivation, 166, 167

Elmstone Hardwicke, Open Fields at, 45, 46

Essex, Open Field in, 67, 68

de Etton, family of, 73, 82; Inquisitions *post mortem* of, 79

de Everingham, family of, 73; Inquisitions *post mortem* of, 79–81, 83; Adam, his scattered demesne, 107